EMPIRICAL CLINICAL PRACTICE

EMPIRICAL CLINICAL PRACTICE

Srinika Jayaratne and Rona L. Levy

Columbia University Press / New York / 1979

Srinika Jayaratne is Assistant Professor of Social Work at the University of Oklahoma
Rona L. Levy is Assistant Professor of Social Work at the University of Washington

Columbia University Press
New York   Guildford, Surrey

Library of Congress Cataloging in Publication Data

Jayaratne, Srinika.
  Empirical clinical practice.

  Bibliography: p. 322
  Includes index.
  1. Social service—Research. I. Levy, Rona L., joint
author. II. Title.
HV11.J38   361'.007'2   78-26695
ISBN 0—231-04188-8

To our parents, Francis, Leila, Shirley, and Ben;
and R.L.L.'s grandmother, Sophie

Contents

Foreword

FROM ITS EARLIEST beginnings the profession of social work has proclaimed that it is committed to a scientific approach. But the actual relationship between social work practice and research has been tentative, uneasy, and at worst antagonistic.

The discomfort that many social workers and other clinicians have felt about research has many sources, only a few of which can be mentioned here. For one thing, science is perceived by some as mechanistic and, for that reason, incompatible with the inherently humanistic character of clinical practice. Moreover, research on practice has, more often than not, generated negative conclusions about the value of interpersonal intervention, a contribution not likely to elicit positive attitudes from practitioners. Few studies have ever identified specific things practitioners could do to immediately improve their practice.

This book addresses another source of the clinician's wariness about research—the concern that research is excessively intrusive and therefore will distort that intervention process beyond recognition. What is presented here is a set of research designs and methodologies that, as the authors illustrate, can be incorporated into the normal routine of practice.

But the research methodologies described in this book amount to much more than a palliative for the apprehensions of clinicians. The development of more effective methods of clinical practice depends directly on the establishment of active, vigorous programs of clinical research addressed primarily to evaluating the effectiveness of alternative practice methods. It has been recognized increasingly that traditional comparison group research designs, while they remain indispensable tools in clinical research, have specific limitations that can be dysfunctional for clinical research, especially in the early stages of research programs. On the one hand, comparison of central tendencies across groups invites the leveling effects of statistical regression, and at the same time, reliance on statistical tests encourages the attribution of significance to trivial differences. Factorial designs are most appropriate where both treatment objectives and treatment methods can be defined clearly and reliably.

At this stage in the development of clinical research, what is needed are robust research designs that can be flexibly and economically applied by practitioners in the normal routine of their practice and that recognize the individualized character of clinical practice. Such designs—virtually unknown in our field only a few years ago—now exist, and this book provides an introduction to their use.

These designs which can be used in ongoing clinical practice, place the capacity to conduct rigorous clinical research within the grasp of any practitioner who will take the trouble to master and use them, and thus create the potential for developing a truly empirically based practice. Much work remains to be done to adapt these designs to the immense variety of practice problems and situations encountered by social workers and others, but there is every reason to believe such adaptations can be made, since these tools are inherently quite flexible.

Some critics of clinical-research designs have complained that these methodologies are linked to behavior therapy and therefore are suitable for use only by "behaviorists"—but that is simply untrue. What the clinical-research methodology and behavior therapy happen to have in common is a requirement that intervention objectives and practice methods be defined and measured empirically. (A primary reason for this requirement in this methodology is that a significant source of their scientific power rests on the feasibility of reliable replications—an impossibility in the absence of unambiguous empirical referents for outcomes and treatments.) As long as this requirement is met, these designs can be used with any intervention approach or theory. And intervention theories that do not lend themselves to empirical specification are of questionable value for a scientific profession.

It is tempting to offer some dramatic predictions about the wonderful things these clinical-research methods will make possible, but it probably is best not to promise too much too soon. It is sufficient, for the present, to say that even if only a small fraction of practitioners make use of the methods described in this book, social work and related fields will have taken a major step in the direction of demonstrating and increasing the effectiveness of their clinical activities. Drs. Jayaratne and Levy are to be commended for their valuable contribution toward that important step.

Scott Briar, Dean
School of Social Work
University of Washington
Seattle, Washington

Preface

EMPIRICAL PRACTICE IS conducted by clinicians who strive to measure and demonstrate the effect of their clinical practice by adapting traditional experimental research techniques to clinical practice. We refer to such practitioners as clinician-researchers. The word "strives" is emphasized because we do not see empirical evaluation as a rigidly defined, fixed process. Empirical evaluation can occur in a variety of ways depending upon the constraints of clinical practice. While there have been a number of fine texts on empirically oriented practice, we feel they do not recognize the problems created by attempting to implement an empirical model within certain settings or theoretical orientations. Rather than have clinicians, students, and instructors who have difficulty applying this model to their own practice reject it, we have addressed some of these difficulties and presented possible solutions. We see this model as more broad-spectrum than the more rigorously defined "single case," "time series," or "single subject," experimental models, described elsewhere. Therefore, we have used the term "clinical-research" to encompass these models, as well as other variations on empirical evaluation.

This text includes a representative sample of current applications of the model to a variety of problems and across different experimental designs. The reason that many of the examples in this book are within the behavioral model of practice is that the majority of empirical studies reported in the literature today are behavioral. We expect that the clinical-research methodology will develop as new practitioners with different interests and needs enter the field and make their own contributions. We look forward to this process.

Our goal for this book is to give readers some basic knowledge about empirical practice and increase their commitment to the concept of the empirical evaluation of practice. We aim to reach practicing and student social workers, psychologists, and psychiatrists who seek to improve their practice by the incorporation of an empirical approach. Some may wonder why the incorporation of an empirical approach is an improvement. Empirical evaluation takes time and effort and immediate benefits of it may not be evident. Our first answer is that many supervisors, funding sources, and others with legitimate rights to such information are insisting on evidence of desirable client outcomes. Information or subjectively derived impressions are now often not considered adequate justification for continued support.

Aside from consideration of the demands of others, we firmly believe that clinical practice that can empirically demonstrate its effect provides the basis for the best service to the client. With the individual client, procedures of empirical evaluation will provide the clinician with pretreatment information on which methods are more effective. After treatment begins, good evidence is available on the client's progress, so that desirable progress can be continued and undesirable outcomes can also be responded to appropriately. Furthermore, for the long run, the clinician is building a solid basis of information across many cases. Information used by trained professionals both within each case and across cases should be based on empirically derived facts, not subjective impressions.

Thus, in addition to the benefits available to the client, the model, when consistently applied, promotes the growth and development of the individual practitioner. Such a practitioner can then assume the title of clinician-researcher.

Acknowledgments

AS WITH MOST projects of this sort, our work could not have been accomplished without the help, guidance, and support of many individuals. We owe a great deal of gratitude to a number of mentors, colleagues, and students, whose teaching, ideas, questions, and comments led us in our present direction. We highly value our clinical and research training at the University of Michigan School of Social Work and Department of Psychology. We want particularly to single out four special and superb educators who were at the University of Michigan: Robert Carter, Richard Stuart, Edwin Thomas, and Tony Tripodi.

We also wish to thank some of our present colleagues in our respective schools, especially Scott Briar, Francis J. Peirce, Geoffrey Loftus, and Cheryl Richey, for their support as well as their commitment to an empirical approach to intervention. We want to thank Lesley Link for her valuable editorial assistance. We would also like to acknowledge the students in many of the University of Washington School of Social Work's "educational units" who, through their learning and practice efforts, have made important contributions to the development of the clinical-research model.

Finally, a personal note of thanks to Toby for her love and support throughout this task.

EMPIRICAL CLINICAL PRACTICE

Chapter One

THE ROLE OF RESEARCH
IN CLINICAL PRACTICE

FOR MANY DECADES, the effectiveness of psychotherapy has been under investigation. Ingenious and creative investigators have focused on developing measures, measurement procedures, and experimental designs to evaluate the effectiveness of intervention. But despite the application of large-scale research programs with diverse orientations, "research findings have barely begun to find meaningful expression in more effective ways of changing patient behavior" (Goldstein et al., 1966, p. 3). Research has raised many questions and answered few. As Eysenck (1952, 1965, 1975) has been arguing for nearly a quarter of a century, traditional research on clinical practice has provided the clinical community with little information on the effects of clinical procedures that has been systematically used.

Most practitioners and student clinicians view research with skepticism as something far removed from the client–worker relationship. One of the authors once accepted a position to conduct research on the mental health workers in a university hospital. During their first meeting, a social worker confessed:

You know, we're all pretty glad that you're here to do your research thing. But everyone feels as I do. Please God, just keep it away from me.

This statement makes it quite apparent that the value of research for clinical practice is often unclear and at best dubious to some on-line workers.

As a result of this discrepancy between clinical practice and research, empiricism has taken a back seat in clinical practice. However, since it is the clinician who must ultimately decide whether or not to apply the various theoretical formulations and clinical strategies, uncontrolled and untested innovation has become prevalent, resulting in some degree of faddism in the clinical community.

1

Where a new method is successful (however success is defined), for a while at least it is advocated vociferously (especially when the mass media get into the act). In time the efficacy of the method is tested by clinicians in the field and is accepted or rejected individually. But the practice and testing of these theoretical formulations and assertions, rather than scientific, are experiential and based on trial and error. This mode of operation does not serve the clinician, the client, the theory in question, or, in the long run, public confidence in the purveyors of mental health. Innovation is necessary if a science is to advance, but the innovative procedures must subscribe to empirical and scientific criteria if they are to be of any value.

This research–practice dichotomy is, however, unnecessary. Clinical research can and must be directly relevant to clinical practice, and practitioners in turn must pay heed to the research findings. In the segments and chapters that follow, we believe we have presented one method whereby the clinician can employ good research procedures and thus enhance the clinical process rather than disrupt it. In essence, we are suggesting that the clinicians employ the scientific method and research process in their daily clinical practice.

1.1 Scientific Method, Research Process, and Clinical Practice

The terms *scientific method* and *research process* are used quite loosely in this discussion since they are highly interrelated parts of the same phenomenon. Although both involve moving from an idea to a conclusion through objective measurement and analysis, one could say that the research process deals with the practicalities of a study, whereas scientific method is more of an intellectual stance. Some readers may find that the criteria employed here are somewhat less rigorous than those used in strict experimental designs. And indeed they are, for in this book we are more concerned with the realities of intervention than with the absolute ideals of science. We have attempted, therefore, to present the scientific method in such a manner that it retains its empirical orientation while being relevant to the practitioner. This method is not a specific entity that can be generalized across all cases, for the actual tactics may vary, depending on the particular circumstances and goals of each case. We have outlined a model that we believe is not dependent on any particular theoretical or practical orientation. It is a serial method of solving problems, an indispensable way of thinking, and one that every clinical inquiry should employ. To the clinician this would consist of measuring change, relating this change to a particular aspect of intervention, and basing future clinical actions on these observations.

The research process consists of a series of highly interdependent activities. It involves a method of moving from observation to conclusion via what Runkel and McGrath (1972) call a "series of choice points": (1) formulating the problem, (2) designing the study, (3) putting the plan into operation, (4) collecting the data, (5) analyzing the data, (6) drawing conclusions, and (7) presenting the results. Ideally, these steps would follow in a methodical and invariant fashion, although, practically speaking, many of them are highly integrated. Each choice point presents the researcher with multiple paths, and it is up to the researcher to choose the method best suited to the problem. The decision to pursue a particular path dictates the procedures to be employed until the next choice point is reached. Then another set of alternatives is available to the researcher until another choice point is reached, and so on. The decisions made at each point are of critical importance to the research process; earlier steps determine later ones, and hence it is necessary to anticipate later points at earlier stages. Although the nature of the questions asked may vary from point to point (in terms of the decisions to be made), the purpose of the research should be to "discover answers to questions through the application of scientific procedures" (Selltiz et al., 1959, p. 2).

The stepwise research process described here is analogous to the application of most intervention programs. Both subscribe to a logical progression from the definition of a problem to the analysis and presentation of results (even if in a case record). This overall discussion has been conceived within the confines of a research perspective, but its parallel clinical application is relatively straightforward.

Consider for example a client who feels her life is in chaos and is constantly depressed. The clinician in his or her intervention program may then go through the stepwise process as follows:

Step 1: *Formulating the problem*
General activity:
Identifying the presenting problem and specifying the goals of intervention.
In this case:
Conduct an initial interview with the client and specify the characteristics of the problem(s). The client complains of an alcoholic husband, minimal contact with the family (her mother, it is learned with further specification), and continuous indebtedness. She wants her husband to stop drinking, to see her mother at least once a week, and to be able to pay the rent and food bills without borrowing money.

Step 2: *Designing the study*
General activity:
Determining the intervention strategy and ways to measure the effect of intervention.
In this case:
The clinician and client initially decide to try working on the alcoholism problem. They both feel that eliminating this problem may have an effect on the frequency of the mother's visiting, the availability of funds, and the client's mood. After meeting with the husband and obtaining his agreement to cooperate, the clinician decides to use the husband and wife's monitoring of the husband's drinking and the wife's monitoring of her budget and the frequency of visits from her mother as measures of effective intervention. The clinician also plans to obtain information on the wife's mood. The intervention strategy is to work with the husband and wife on the husband's drinking problem.

Step 3: *Putting the plan into operation*
General activity:
Implementing the intervention strategy according to plan and facilitating its effect.

In this case:
The clinician meets with the husband and wife for three sessions, the main topic being the husband's drinking. The husband finally recognizes that he needs outside help and agrees to enter a 1-month treatment program in a nearby hospital. He and his wife also continue to meet with the clinician on a weekly basis.

Steps 4 and 5: *Collecting and analyzing the data*
General activity:
Collecting and tabulating or graphing the incidents of target problem or goal.
In this case:
The clinician examines the husband's and wife's information on the drinking behavior and the wife's information on her mother's visits and their budget. The clinician also periodically asks the wife how she is feeling and how she might rate her mood on a 10-point scale. The information gathered before, during, and after intervention is compared.

Step 6: *Drawing conclusions*
General activity:
On the basis of the obtained data, determining if the intervention had any effect. Depending on the results, the intervention program can be continued, changed, or terminated.
In this case:
The clinician sees that both the husband and wife report the drinking is eliminated. The wife's budget shows that no further debts are being incurred, and her information indicates that the mother has begun visiting them again. Finally, the wife is consistently reporting moods of 7 or above, where before the elimination of the drinking, she always said she was so depressed that her mood "must be zero."
On the basis of this empirical information, the clinician and client conclude that the intervention has been successful.

Step 7: *Presenting the results*
General activity:
Displaying the results in a manner that communicates the impact of intervention to self and other interested parties. For the most part,

this is a private process, whereby the clinician examines the data for his or her personal edification and clinical growth.
In this case:
The clinician draws graphs and tables for the client on the drinking decline, budget management, increase of mother's visits, and the client's moods. In this manner, the client can actually see the progress that has occurred over time.

This discussion should demonstrate to the reader the feasibility and desirability of the research process during intervention.

The particular forms of research with which we are concerned are experimental and quasi-experimental. Quasi-experimental research differs from experimental research in that the designs of the former provide less proof that the independent variable in fact was the cause of the observed change in the dependent variable (Campbell and Stanley, 1963). Nevertheless, the establishment of cause—effect relations is still the focus of interest. In both experimental and quasi-experimental research the investigator manipulates something (the independent variable) to determine its effect on something else (the dependent variable)—that is, the study of cause and effect.

Selltiz et al. (1959) cite three types of evidence that allow for the establishment of causal relations between two events X and Y. The first type of evidence is "concomitant variation" or "covariation"— that is, the evidence that, whenever X changes, Y also changes. The second type of evidence is "temporal order," referring to the evidence that the presumed cause X always occurred before the presumed effect Y. Finally, the third type of evidence "eliminates alternate explanations," suggesting that X is in fact the presumed cause that brought about change in Y, and not some other factor. Experimental designs usually focus on this last type of evidence, for it offers the highest degree of causal power.

Experimental designs are structured in such a way as to allow the investigator to conclude that the change produced in the dependent variable was in fact caused by the independent variable and not by some other factor. For example, consider a situation in which a group of individuals are measured on some characteristic Y before and after some treatment X. If a change is observed in Y after treatment, there is certainly *some* evidence that X caused this change; that is, Y changed only after the introduction of X. But there is a good deal of room for alternate explanations. For example, it could be argued that, through a simple maturational process and the passage of time, every individual in the group would have changed on Y, regardless of exposure to X. A much stronger case for causal attribution can be made by the inclusion of a control group, that is, a group of individuals who are not exposed to X but are measured for changes in Y. If the individuals in the control group show no change or little change on Y compared to those individuals who received the treatment X, we have far more evidence in support of causal attribution.

The purpose of research-based intervention is to establish cause–effect relationships between the intervention strategy (the independent variable) and the problem(s) of the client system (the dependent variable). As with experimental and quasi-experimental designs, the degree of causal attribution that can be attained by the clinical research designs depends, among other factors, on the specific design selected for use. Continuous applications of the clinical research approach should result in replications and refinements of the therapeutic procedures and thus enhance the clinical excellence of the individual therapist. The particular advantages and disadvantages of the different designs are discussed in more detail in the individual design chapters.

In general then, the application of scientific procedures to the process of intervention allows the clinician to demonstrate, reproduce, and communicate with some degree of assurance. Consider, for example, step 2 (designing the study). The clinician would first be interested in using an intervention strategy that has been successful in the past. As all research builds on previous findings, so too should all clinical practice. When established techniques are available, they should be used, but they should be based on objective evaluation rather than subjective feeling.

Unfortunately, this scenario of interdependence of practice and research rarely occurs, as indicated earlier. Instead, most clinical research has been conducted by clincally oriented academicians. As Bordin (1966) points out, "the predominant feeling today is that practicing clinicians do no research and the active research psychologists have little practical experience" (p. 116). In this book, to reemphasize a point, we are adamant in our belief that this dichotomy is a barrier against effective practice—a barrier that must be overcome. We believe that the clinical research model presented here is one step in this direction.

1.2 The Clinician-Researcher

In recent years the model of clinician-researcher has been promoted in various forms by numerous writers (for example, Bloom and Block, 1977; Briar, 1973; Browning and Stover, 1971; Hersen and Barlow, 1976; Leitenberg, 1973; Howe, 1974; Kazdin, 1975; Thoresen, 1972). Its basic thesis centers around the notion of an empirical, objective, and systematic approach to the implementation and evaluation of intervention. Intervention has been defined by Webster as "to come in or between in order to stop, settle, or modify." An "interventionist"— whether clinician, counselor, psychiatrist, psychologist, psychotherapist, or social worker—becomes then an individual who imposes his or her life space into the life space of an other or group of others to bring temporary or permanent change in the other's life space. (The term *group* is used very loosely here; it could mean an individual who in conjunction with the therapist forms a dyad, or it could mean a family, a class or a group formed for treatment or other purpose.)

This change, whether it is identified as behavioral, attitudinal, or emotional, is of central importance to the clinician. The activity and behavior of the clinician presumably potentiate action among the other participants. It is the clinician who provides the guidance and parameters for action by the group members. To the extent that the clinician is aware of his or her own actions and their probable impact on others, they may be modified to facilitate the development of goal behavior within the group. Similarly, if the clinician is aware of how the actions of each group member affect the actions of other members, he or she would be in a position to systematize these factors in such a manner as to bring about the desired goals in the group as a whole.

As indicated earlier, we are discussing a mode of intervention that clarifies its processes and objectives as it attempts to establish cause–effect relations. The clinician is viewed, not as an artist, but as an individual artfully applying empirically derived scientific concepts. The intervention plan prescribed here rejects vague procedures and unmeasurable outcomes. Its essential component is the systematic and objective determination of specified changes and change procedures.

Terminology such as *identify, specify,* and *cause–effect* moves us into the arena of empiricism. The clinician is asked to examine the process of intervention, to dissect its components, and to evaluate the particulars of these components. It is in this context that Browning and Stover (1971) argue that the "clinician should be capable of objectively evaluating his treatment procedures, and consequently, his understanding of the patient" (p. 1).

The definition of clinician-researcher proposed here encompasses these various facets of the interventionist and thereby brings the clinician into the arena of the scientific method and generates a synthesis of empiricism and clinical integrity. The clinician-researcher, then, is defined as one who has (a) a clear idea of the independent variable, (b) a thorough working knowledge of the client system and its environment, (c) an empirical and objective orientation toward the process of intervention, (d) an ability to put research designs and measurement procedures into operation, (e) an ability to functionally use empirical feedback that is obtained during intervention, and (f) an ability to evaluate, incorporate, and use the research of others.

(a) The clinician-researcher must have a thorough understanding of the treatment methods being employed. Here the clinician-researcher asks the questions: What particular method would be best in this situation? How familiar am I with this method and its applications? What alternate methods are available? Can I explain exactly what it is that I am doing? How clearly can I define the parameters of intervention?

If research is ever going to help clinicians make informed decisions among alternate methods they must move away from conceptualizing their practice as an "unspecifiable experience" (Hollis, 1968). As Bordin (1974) points out, "although the pressure of human suffering requires whatever our crude and mistaken understanding dictates, our commitment to improving our methods and insuring their effectiveness demands a balancing concern with research" (p. 3).

In the clinical research model, a description of clinical practice is not adequate when the description can mean different things to different people and there can be ambiguity about whether the activity described actually occurred. The clinician-researcher must be able to clearly state and specify the nature of the intervention method(s) being implemented (that is, the independent variable). Although a high degree of specificity is often difficult to attain, it determines the degree of accuracy that may be obtained in measurement and communication.

(b) The clinician-researcher must have a thorough knowledge of the client system and its environment. This is, of course, one of the basic axioms of any clinical intervention procedure, and it is a prerequisite for the formulation of evaluative indices. Here the clinician-researcher asks the questions: How well do I know the client and his or her environment? Who in the environment could serve as resource personnel? What major environmental characteristics affect the problem in question? What are the desired goal behaviors, and how can I best facilitate their attainment?

Methods that can be used to obtain a knowledge of the client system are discussed in a later chapter. A thorough knowledge of the system is one of the basic tenets of any assessment procedure and crucial to effective intervention. The identification of target problems, specification of treatment goals, and selection of intervention techniques is highly dependent on this knowledge.

(c) The clinician-researcher must have an empirical and objective orientation toward the process of intervention. Empiricism and objectivity are key words in scientific method. Here the clinician asks the questions: What measures and measurement procedures would provide the most accurate data? What aspects of my intervention are bringing about change? Am I objective in my evaluation of treatment effect? How can I maximize reliability in my measures?

However target problems and goals are defined, it is imperative that they be specified in such a manner that they can be measured. Whereas quantified measurement is preferable for ease of interpretation, it is not absolutely necessary. The essence of effectiveness is that others in the client's environment perceive a change in the client's actions and attitudes and that they be able to assess this in an objective manner. Simple "feeling" statements should be sustained by objectively determined criteria on performance. Obviously, this assessment requirement necessitates a thorough understanding of the client system and its environment.

In this context it is not a matter of ideology, politics, or even theory. What is required is an objective examination of the entire process. Not surprisingly, perhaps, science and practice appear to have gone their separate ways in this regard. Science maintains that, for "true" evaluation to take place, there must be specifically defined criteria that are tangible enough to be objectively measured. Furthermore, the components of intervention and the effects of nonintervention factors must be examined. This is necessary to determine the degree of confidence one has in saying that it was the intervention rather than some unknown factor that produced change. Science wants to know what caused change. In contrast, practice often appears to be dominated by a global orientation based on the assumption that human action and behavior are far too complex to be measured by discrete criteria.

This divergence in orientation between science and practice is indeed unfortunate, for it is the clinician who ultimately decides on the success or failure and the efficacy of a given technology. But when the decision is made on the basis of haphazard application and nonscientific evaluation, one cannot help but argue that the techniques have not been given their due. Herein lies perhaps one answer to the viability of a technique: systematic application of a technique and objective and critical evaluation. This is the mode of operation that is demanded of the clinician-researcher.

(d) The clinician-researcher must have the ability to put research designs into operation. Competence in this arena would enhance the effectiveness and the efficiency of intervention. Here the clinician asks the questions: How familiar am I with the various research designs? Can I implement them? Which design should I choose given the present circumstances? The most important factor here is familiarity with the various research designs, their relative strengths and weaknesses, and their possible applications within given environments. In most instances the situational context determines the applicability of a given design.

The notion of efficiency plays a central role in the practice arena. Efficiency may be defined as achieving the greatest amount of success with the least amount of cost, where cost may be considered as therapist, agency, and client time. It is by now redundant to note that the average clinician in a human service agency is overloaded. The obvious question is, would not the allocation of time and energy into the application of the research method aggravate the problem even further? While it may be true that these methods take time and energy, the long-run benefits of demonstrable effect far surpass the short-run problems. But even in the short run, this charge about extensive costs would be somewhat tenuous. The clinician may render the same unsuccessful treatments, or forego a partially successful one, simply because he or she does not have the data to analyze the effectiveness of the interventive components. If the clinician had used empirical techniques and systematic data collection procedures, he or she would be in a better position to use different modes of intervention. This, in turn, would reduce wasted time and effort. In the long run, efficiency would be much more predictable, as would treatment effect. Where the practitioner employs the scientific method, data are available to evaluate the effectiveness of given strategies with given clients. By determining similarities in client systems and situations, the clinician is able to use tested techniques and thus reduce the time wasted in trial-and-error strategies. Such procedures would facilitate the development of individual and agency accountability.

(e) The clinician-researcher must have the ability to functionally use empirical feedback that is obtained during intervention. Here the clinician-researcher asks the questions: Am I collecting therapeutically valuable data? Am I using the information that I am gathering for interventive purposes? What other data should I collect? How effective has the technique been?

In this situation the clinician-researcher attempts to be as objective as possible. Data are available for scrutiny, and what the clinician-researcher does with them is entirely dependent on his or her orientation. This is where the previously mentioned "objective orientation toward the process of intervention" comes into play. If the clinician-researcher collects data but does not systematically and continuously analyze them for clinical decisions, they may as well not be collected. Not all clinical decisions need be made on the examination of these data alone, but the data should be given at least as much value as the clinician's own intuitive notions and feelings.

(f) The clinician-researcher must have an ability to evaluate, incorporate, and use the research of others. Clinicians select intervention strategies based on personal experience and reports in the literature or other forms of communication. Here the clinician-researcher asks the questions: Am I familiar with the literature in this area? What are the reported positive and negative effects of this approach? How does the literature say I can best implement these strategies? How much confidence do I have in the reported results?

A professional should not have to keep inventing the wheel but should build his or her actions on cumulative information. The information used should be evaluated on the same scientific criteria that the clinician-researcher employs in judging his or her own work—namely, empirical rigor and attention to the requirements of adequate design procedures. This means that the clinician-researcher must be well acquainted with the literature and research procedures that may not be personally used in his or her own practice.

1.3 The Clinical Research Designs

Much of the research on intervention per se and on the effectiveness of intervention has been conducted across cases with client groups. In such cases large numbers of subjects with randomly varying characteristics have been lumped together for purposes of statistical analyses and the determination of statistically significant success. While this is indeed a time-tested mode of determining the applicability of a technology, it has some interpretive problems (Bergin, 1971; Kiesler, 1966). Most importantly, this procedure minimizes the clinically important characteristic of idiosyncrasy. Whereas a technology may be communicated from one clinician to another, its efficacy of application depends on the uniqueness of the case, the clinician-researcher, and the situation. Thus, it is quite apparent that the traditional approach to clinical evaluation is burdened with a variety of problems.

The clinical research approach, with its focus on case-by-case analysis, serves, on the other hand, a more critical and pragmatic function for the clinician-researcher. The ideal clinical research designs, in terms of establishing causal inference, are those termed "time series," "single case" or "single subject" designs. These designs provide an objective series of measures or data points over time (rather than just one measurement point before and one measurement point after treatment) and thus allow the clinician-researcher to better meet the "validity threats" addressed in chapter 4. That is, the single subject designs would give the clinician-researcher greater assurance that the outcome was in fact caused by treatment rather than some artifact. We have, however, allowed for some measurement procedures and design alterations that, if used, would be inconsistent with the ideal model just described. It is in view of these changes and the expected role performance by the therapists that we have opted for the term *clinical research design.*

Any client system that is in treatment—an individual, a family, or a treatment group, that is, either a unitary client or an entire client group, is an acceptable target for the clinical research model.

Finally, we are not demeaning nor minimizing the importance of information that some group design research can and has produced for the clinician. The clinician-researcher must be familiar with and be able to evaluate the research of others. This certainly includes non-single-subject research. In this book we present a framework for the clinician to develop research procedures with his or her own practice methods using a clinical research approach. However, to become a "complete" clinician-researcher who possesses the ability to evaluate other research, a knowledge of group design procedures is necessary. There are several excellent texts on this topic. See, for example, Campbell and Stanley (1963), Selltiz et al. (1959), and Simon (1969).

1.4 Conclusion

Regardless of theoretical differences, it is clear that psychotherapy, as practiced today, is often an individualistic process (London, 1964) based on untested assertions and formulations. The clinician-researcher, as presented here, represents the interventionist who is striving to impute some degree of objectivity, replicability, and accountability into the clinical process.

The terms *specificity, objectivity,* and *empiricism* are often used to identify a scientific or research approach. Terms such as *spontaneity, creativity,* and *sensitivity* are cited as belonging to the artistic or clinical realm. The two approaches are often presented as occupying irreconcilable positions.

A scientific approach to intervention has been viewed, incorrectly, as an attempt to define and constrain the spontaneity between the clinician and the client. Hollis (1968, p. 7) takes such a position:

Is casework just a coldly intellectual process? Heaven forbid! Casework is in essence an experience between two people—a totality that rests upon the feelings of both and upon delicate nuances of interaction that can only be described as art rather than science.

We propose a truce between these orientations, so that research might give to clinical practice something it sorely needs—the demonstration of effect in addition to possessing good clinical attributes. While there may be minimal need for the researcher to be sensitive and spontaneous, the contrary does not hold. The clinician must be specific, objective, and empirical. The product of this truce is the clinician-researcher who "attempts to specify the conditions under which a particular set of therapeutic interventions leads to a given result, and he tries to determine which characteristics of the patient and therapist, which qualities of their interaction, and what environmental circumstances bring about the result" (Strupp 1971, p. 17). In essence, then, the clinician-researcher attempts to bring about a desired outcome while simultaneously attempting to discover cause–effect relationships.

In the pages that follow, we present the clinical research process in five substantive stages. The first stage (chapter 2) suggests procedures and methods of preliminary assessment. It is here that the diagnostic skills of the individual clinician-researcher are employed, defining, refining, and finally stating the goals of intervention. The second stage (chapter 3) offers the reader the issues and concepts related to the measurement of clinical effectiveness. Having defined the goals of intervention, the clinician-researcher should now be in a position to measure its impact. The third stage (chapter 4) discusses the implementation of the measurement plan. Having decided on a method of measurement, the clinician-researcher is now ready to put it into operation. The fourth stage (chapters 5–9) offers the reader several specific research methods or designs to be employed in the clinical research process. Examples from the literature have been used to illustrate the practical utility of the design alternatives. The fifth stage (chapter 10) offers the reader some practical procedures to help interpret the data that have been gathered.

Chapter Two

THE FIRST STAGE: DEFINING PROBLEMS AND GOALS DURING PRELIMINARY ASSESSMENT

THUS FAR THE reader has been introduced to the broad notions of empirical intervention and the distinguishing features of the clinical research model. In this section we present the concepts and methods that form the framework for practice within this model, a framework formed by the clinician-researcher's systematic application of assessment procedures.

Assessment refers to all those activities involved in the selection of information (data) for clinical practice, the actual data collection process, and the interpretation of these data. In the early stages of intervention, assessment is the procedure by which the clinician-researcher identifies and empirically characterizes the presenting problems, with their related situational and social-psychological factors, and the goals of intervention. Its aim is to help the client and clinician-researcher determine the target problems for intervention and delineate intervention goals.

Assessment has received much less attention in the past than treatment techniques themselves have (Goldfried and Pomeranz, 1968; Kanfer and Saslow, 1969; Mischel, 1968; Peterson, 1968). In addition, there has been little empiricism in the operationalization of these procedures when they did occur.* The essential goal of assessment is to gather information about the client system and related problem situations and to interpret these data in a way that enables the clinician-researcher to understand and act on the situation he or she is encountering. In practical terms the clinician-researcher must

---

*Recent books by Hersen and Bellack (1976), Mash and Terdal (1976), Cone and Hawkins (1977), Ciminero, et al (1977), and Keefe et al (1978), as well as a new journal devoted to assessment only, sponsored by the Association for the Advancement of Behavior Therapy, have made significant contributions to this field. We recommend them to the interested reader.

17

begin by *identifying a target problem* and its situational context and *specifying a related goal* for intervention. This is in keeping with Whittaker's (1974, p. 120) notion that a "statement of the client's problem should not be viewed as an end to itself, but as a means of producing concrete change goals and a plan of intervention."

Once the clinician-researcher follows the procedures for correctly identifying problems and goals, a firm foundation for research-based intervention exists. Without this foundation, the effect of treatment cannot be measured. Once this basis has been established, auxiliary steps based on the clinical research method should be added.

In this chapter we begin by describing the concepts and appropriate procedures necessary in the identification of problems and goals. We cannot overemphasize that every potential clinician-researcher should strive to establish these activities as the basis of his or her practice, for they are appropriate, regardless of theory base or practice orientation, and are central to the clinical research method.

The presentation may sound to the reader as representing a clinical situation involving a single verbal and cooperative client. For example, we frequently ask clinicians to specify and select problems and goals with their "clients." By "clients" we are, however, referring to the appropriate information and/or action sources with each case. (These may be an individual or group.) Thus, the clinician-researcher may decide to specify these problems and goals by talking with significant others (hospital attendants, parents, teachers, etc.) in a referred child's environment. We do not attempt to resolve the question of who is the client (e.g., the child, parents, both, etc.) (see Pincus and Minahan, 1973, for extended discussion). We are mentioning this merely to point out that the clinical research model as presented here is applicable across all treatment contexts and clinical situations.

2.1 Identification of Target Problems

Intervention, by definition, requires the presence of something to be altered—something generally referred to as the target problem—the specific symptom, behavior, or personal characteristic to be changed.

In the clinical arena the clinician-researcher must be able to identify the specific nature of the problem within its larger situational and
structural context. But the mere identification of the problem can only
be a beginning. To proceed in practice, the clinician-researcher
needs to specify all of the other elements related to the problem. The
clinician-researcher must be aware of the *who, what, when,* and
where of the target problem for the specification to be complete and
eventually lead to the identification of goals. Information and accuracy about the effect of the intervention will be reduced unless there
is knowledge and understanding of the situational context surrounding the problem. The clinician-researcher must not only know *what*
the problem is but also find out *who* defines it as a problem and
when and *where* it is visible and perceived as a problem.

Some comment is necessary with regard to what are often called
immediate, intermediate, and ultimate goals. In our perception a
goal is directly related to the target problem. Therefore, that target
problem, along with its related goal, which is intervened with first,
becomes by necessity the immediate goal. The importance, then,
lies in determining the priority problem for intervention. As a general
rule, we suggest the criteria offered by Sundel and Sundel (1975).
When the clinician-researcher is in the position (along with his/her
client) of selecting a priority problem for intervention:

1. Select the problem that is the immediate concern of the client or signifi-
    cant others.
2. Select the problem that has the most aversive consequences, to the indi-
    vidual, significant others, or society. That is, minimize the pain that
    may be inflicted on self or others by the external situation.
3. Select the problem that can be corrected most quickly. Such a selection
    would give the client a successful experience in therapy, resulting in
    increased motivation and trust in the clinician-researcher and the clinical
    process.
4. Select the problem that must be dealt with before any other problem can
    be resolved.

In using these criteria, it is the clinician-researcher, with active
participation by the client (where possible), who must select the
target problem for immediate intervention.

Target problems should be defined in such a way as to make them as concrete and observable as possible. Webster defines concrete as "characterized by or belonging to immediate experience of actual things or events." It should be apparent then that we are talking not about global intrapsychic concepts but actual events. For example, to say someone is depressed is not a concrete statement. It indicates a psychological state of being, an existential state, but it does not describe the situational and contextual referents. On the other hand, if we were to say that a person is depressed (as defined by self or others), because that person sees friends very infrequently, does not leave home in the evenings, thinks thoughts such as "I am horrible," and cries frequently, we have provided a series of referents that are indicators of the state of being depressed. This perception translates the abstract concept of depression into observable and/or reportable phenomena. (Note that we are not implying or asserting any causal notion here. We are merely indexing the behaviors that led an observer to label one as being depressed.)

In this sense we see that concreteness is directly related to observability, in that concrete events can be readily observed. Furthermore, when we make any abstract concept such as depression concrete and observable, we have made it potentially measurable. For example, the frequency of visiting with friends and the crying behavior can be readily observed and measured. Similarly, the individual's isolation behavior can be therapeutically translated into the lack of activities with friends in the evening. As will be seen later, this type of specification also makes the determination of goals somewhat tangible and easier to attain.

The specification of target problems (and of goals) introduces an issue that will come up again in this book: there are more and less desirable ways to approximate the clinical research model. We present what we perceive to be the model's ideal form. However, we also recognize that many clinician-researchers who want to be empirical may not consistently practice in this form. This may be due to circumstance or individual choice. Therefore, we encourage all attempts toward greater empirical practice that approximate the clinical research model.

In the best possible (clinical) world, targets and goals would be highly concrete and could be observed (and therefore potentially measured) by more than one person. This would produce data in which the clinician-researcher could have a high degree of confidence. (Here we are dealing with questions of reliability and validity that are discussed in the next chapter.) In contrast, if the problem is simply specified as the occurrence of self-deprecatory thoughts, we are dealing with something that can be observed only by the thinker. Sometimes this is the best level of measurement that the clinician-researcher can achieve.

Although we feel that referents at (at least) this level of observability are usually available, we do recognize that clinician-researchers may decide that with some problems they are simply not interested in specificity even to this extent. In such (we hope exceedingly rare) cases where more specificity is not achieved, the clinician-researcher can still strive for an empirical approach by producing some data. For example, a clinician-researcher who specifies a problem only to the extent of saying that the client complains of low "self-worth" may be able to develop a scale or employ an already existing scale to measure this problem. This procedure has minimal value, however, and we hope it will be improved by the clinician-researcher.

Several examples of tools that could help in the early assessment process are presented here as illustrative examples. Figure 2.1 is a checklist of a child's problems in various home situations, developed by Wahler and Cormier (1970), that serves several practical purposes. First it exemplifies the degrees of specificity that the clinician-researcher desires from the client. Second, it cues the client onto behaviors that may have otherwise been overlooked. Finally, while this type of predetermined checklist delimits the client's responses in some ways, it also makes the process somewhat more efficient in that it focuses on the specific issues under consideration. This does not mean, of course, that the client and the clinician-researcher cannot refer to alternate problem behaviors, nor does it preclude the relating of other situational contexts. Similarly, Figure 2.2 presents a method of determining the relative value or importance attached to a given problem by the parents. This procedure followed by some type of ranking (for example, use of the Goal Checklist in Figure 2.7) should result in effective focusing on the

The following checklist allows you to describe your child's problems in various home situations. The situations are listed in the column at left and common problem behaviors are listed in the row at the top. Examine *each* situation in the column and decide if one or more of the problem behaviors in the row fits your child. Check those that fit the best—if any.

	Always has to be told	Doesn't pay aten.	Forgets	Dawdles	Refuses	Argues	Complains	Demands	Fights	Selfish	Destroys toys or property	Steals	Lies	Cries	Whines	Hangs on or stays close to adult	Acts silly	Mopes around	Stays alone	Has to keep things in order	Sexual play
Morning:																					
Awakening																					
Dressing																					
Breakfast																					
Bathroom																					
Leave for school																					
Play in house																					
Chores																					
Television																					
Afternoon:																					
Lunch																					
Bathroom																					
Play in house																					
Chores and homework																					
Television																					
When company comes																					
Evenings:																					
Father comes home																					
Dinner																					
Bathroom																					
Play in house																					
Chores and homework																					
Television																					
Undressing																					
When company comes																					
Bedtime																					

From Robert G. Wahler and William H. Cormier (1970). Used by permission of Pergamon Press.

Figure 2.1 Checklist of a child's problems in various home situations.

The following behaviors are often problems with adolescents. Which would you classify as inappropriate and which as unacceptable in your family?

	Mother		Father	
	Inappro.	Unaccept.	Inappro.	Unaccept.
1. Being late to dinner	I	U	I	U
2. Talking back to the teacher	I	U	I	U
3. Not hanging up his/her clothes	I	U	I	U
4. Fighting at school	I	U	I	U
5. Staying out all night	I	U	I	U
6. Playing music loud	I	U	I	U
7. Smoking marijuana	I	U	I	U
8. Spending his/her allowance on clothes you don't like	I	U	I	U
9. Wearing sneakers to church	I	U	I	U
10. Skipping school	I	U	I	U
11. Swearing at home	I	U	I	U
12. Smoking cigarettes	I	U	I	U
13. Failing math	I	U	I	U
14. Wearing hair long	I	U	I	U
15. Selling drugs to other kids at school	I	U	I	U
16. Putting his feet on the table	I	U	I	U
17. Failing gym	I	U	I	U

From Richard B. Stuart and Tony Tripodi (1972).

Figure 2.2 Checklist for determining relative importance attached to a problem by parents. Used by permission of Richard B. Stuart.

target problems. Both these forms delimit client responses. A similar end can be achieved by obtaining a list of the problems and their situational contexts and then having the client attribute ranks, values, and importance, to each of them. The Sundel–Lawrence Problem Checklist (Figure 2.3) (1974) used in a family service agency illustrates such a procedure. These forms present a general format that is easily modifiable.

The specification of a target problem is perceived as part of the evaluation (assessment) process, in that the ultimate goal of therapy is its elimination. By employing such procedures, we have emphasized the tangibility of the target problems and thus allowed them to be measured. We have now achieved a degree of concreteness and specificity that is desirable in identifying target problems in the clini-

Check which of the following relationships are dissatisfying to you or present problems for you. Use a *double check* for those that *most* concern you.

__Parents   __Co-workers
__Brothers and sisters   __Subordinates at work
__Husband or wife   __Friends of the same sex
__Children   __Friends of the opposite sex
__Other relatives   __Neighbors
__Work supervisor or employer   __Myself

For each of the relationships you *double checked,* what are one or two problems you are having with that person or persons that *most* concern you.

Examples:

Person or persons   *Problems*

1. Wife   We are constantly quarreling. She usually sleeps in the children's room
                     instead of with me.
2. Oldest son   When I ask him to do his chores, he doesn't obey me. He often fights
                     with and beats his younger sister.
3. Girls and work   I do not participate in the conversation with the girls during lunch or cof-
                     fee breaks.

Problems of major concern to me
Person or persons   *Problems*

From Paul Glasser, Rosemary Sarri, and Robert Vinter, eds. 1974.

Figure 2.3 Sundel-Lawrence problem checklist.

cal research model. This allows us to proceed to the next step of goal determination.

2.2 Identification of Goals

In discussing interview procedures with parents, Holland (1970, p. 127) notes that "it is surprising how often parents voice complaints about their children without being able to state clearly what they want the child to do" even in a general way. This then, is the dilemma of goal specification facing the clinician-researcher, for what is true of the parent is apropos of the clinical context in general. The goals, just as the target problems, need to be concrete and observable while being set within its situational context.

For obvious reasons, target problems and intervention goals are highly related, in that the latter are the desirable replacement of the former. The form of the relationship is, however, decided on the basis of clinical choices. For example, a problem may be defined as the high frequency of occurrence of some behavior, and the goal may simply be a reduction of this problem behavior. In this type of relationship the problem and goal are defined on the same continuum. The clinician-researcher may not, however, want to focus attention on the problem by having it measured, and so he/she may choose to measure some other desirable behavior whose occurrence is incompatible with that of the problem behavior. If this alternate behavior is selected appropriately, an increase in its frequency would mean a decrease in the frequency of the undesirable one. In this case the problem and goal are defined on different continua.

Since the definition of an "appropriate" goal is critical in any intervention situation, we have focused in on the "reduce undesirable–increase desirable" example. Consider Figure 2.4. Along the abscissa, some measure of time is plotted. A frequency count is graphed along the ordinate. Figure 2.4 focuses in on the problem behavior "staying home frequently" and charts the number of days the person stayed home in evenings per week. In contrast, Figure 2.5 charts the number of days the person "went out in the evenings" and

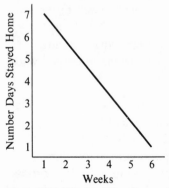

Figure 2.4 Graph of frequency of undesirable behavior.

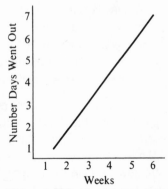

Figure 2.5 Graph of frequency of desirable behavior.

thus provides a more positive orientation. While both graphs signify and illustrate the same phenomenon, they dramatically point out the close relationship between goal behavior and target problem. The choice of whether the goal or problem (or perhaps both) needs to be emphasized is a clinical decision. But again, the opportunity for the clinician-researcher to determine whether the target problem has been eliminated and/or the goal has been achieved is maximized if the targets and goals have been specified and stated in concrete and observable terms.

Consider, for example, this goal-focused intervention strategy. Working with two groups of elementary school children, one social work student was interested in increasing the amount of positive statements and replies that the children made to peers. She also wanted to increase the rate at which they complied with requests. Before any measurement or intervention could begin, it was necessary to define these goals in operational terms, as follows:

1. Making positive statements, attention getting in a nondisruptive manner, was to include
   –complimentary statements to others,
   –statements expressing approval to others,
   –offers of help or advice to others,
   –addressing specific people.
2. Replying when spoken to by peers was defined as
   –answering questions addressed to them by name by a peer,
   –any verbal acknowledgement of statements addressed to them by name by a peer.
3. Complying with directions or requests from others would include
   –performing a behavior requested by a peer or the researcher when asked to do so only once.

In this instance the student preferred to employ a goal-focused measurement strategy. She purposely looked only at operationally defined and observable, desirable behaviors.

While the target problems are identified and verbalized during the interview, the written format accentuates the end results. This procedure has its theoretical advantage in that it focuses on the positive aspects of intervention, emphasizing what could be in the future, and thus minimizes scapegoating and a spiraling of negative discussion (i.e., discussion of how bad someone is rather than what can be done about it) that may take place when problems alone are discussed. Figures 2.6 and 2.7 illustrate two goal determination forms.

1. List five things you would like your child to do (desirable behavior).

Mother   Father
1.   1.
2.   2.
3.   3.
4.   4.
5.   5.

Do you agree on what the rules are for your child?

2. List three reinforcers or rewards for which your child would obey rules.

Mother   Father
1.   1.
2.   2.
3.   3.

3. List three instances in the past week when you gave your child attention (praise, compliments, affection) for doing something you liked.

Mother   Father
1.   1.
2.   2.
3.   3.

From Richard B. Stuart and Tony Tripodi (1972).

Figure 2.6 Goal determination checklist.

These goal checklists could easily be used in conjunction with the problem checklists presented earlier. Together, they provide a high degree of specificity, concreteness, and directiveness to the therapeutic regimen. Another device often used is the Goal Attainment Scale (Kiresuk, 1973; Kiresuk and Sherman, 1968). The reader is referred to the original sources for clarification of procedure. This method not only leads to goal specification but also forces the clinician-researcher to specify expected outcomes.

The reader is again reminded that these are merely illustrative examples. The actual forms and processes employed by the individual clinician-researcher should reflect the specific problems and needs faced by the worker in question. On the other hand, an instrument such as the Goal Checklist (Figure 2.7) could be widely used in

NAME OF CLIENT: _____ CLINICIAN-RESEARCHER: _____ DATE: _____

Which of your child's behaviors do you like and wish to maintain?	What % of time does it occur?	Three items to work on first	What could you do to facilitate this behavior?	What could you do to reward this behavior?
1.		1.		
2.				
3.		2.		
4.				

What would you like him/her to start doing or do more often?	What % of time do you want it to occur?			
		3.		
1.				
2.				
3.				
4.				

From Richard B. Stuart and Tony Tripodi (1972).

Figure 2.7 Client's goal checklist. Used by permission of Richard B. Stuart.

parent/child situations, and the Goal Attainment Scale (Figure 2.8), in virtually any situation. While idiosyncrasy is uniquely important, one should also remember that it is far better to use "existing measures that have proven themselves with respect to criteria discussed" than to "construct measures ad hoc for particular investigations" (Nunnaly 1975, p. 111). Such a procedure would allow for the accumulation of evidence in support of various treatment techniques and problem situations. And most importantly, these procedures are critical to the development of the individual clinician-researcher, and it is also the essence of the clinical research model of intervention.

Some authors tend to dichotomize goals into process and outcome. Hackney and Nye (1973), for example, indicate that "process goals are related to the establishment of therapeutic conditions necessary for client change" (p. 41). Kiesler (1971), on the other hand, argues that this distinction is an unfortunate misconception and that, in fact, to some extent they are indiscernible. We agree with this latter perspective in the sense that, if you cannot develop rapport, empathy, and unconditional regard with your client system, the likelihood of your being able to identify the target problem and work toward the desired goal is somewhat limited. Thus the clinician-researcher, like any other clinician, tries to understand his or her client system and its ecology, to see things from the client's perspective, and to clarify and accurately perceive the client and stated problems. The specification of the target problems and goals is seen as an additional task facing the clinician-researcher, something that can be done only after the establishment of an adequate client–worker relationship. We do not present the procedures deemed valuable in the establishment of this relationship, since these techniques have been widely discussed elsewhere (Benjamin, 1974; Carkhuff, 1969; Kadushin, 1972). As is evident, our central concern is with specification to a degree where it is easily observable and measurable.

Note that these are preliminary assessment techniques. The data provided by these techniques only *identify* the target problems and goals. How data can be collected in a manner that shows clinical progress is discussed in the next two chapters.

Figure 2.8 Sample clinical guide: crisis intervention center, program evaluation project. Used by permission of Dr. Thomas Kiresuk.

Level at intake: ✔
Level at followup: *

Check whether or not the scale has been mutually negotiated between patient and CIC interviewer	*Yes_X_ No____*	*Yes____ No_X_*
Scale Attainment Levels	*Scale 1: Education*	*Scale 2: Suicide*
a. most unfavorable treatment outcome thought likely (−2)	Patient has made no attempt to enroll in high school ✔	Patient has committed suicide
b. less than expected success with treatment (−1)	Patient has enrolled in high school but at time of followup has dropped out	Patient has acted on at least one suicidal impulse since her first contact with the CIC but has not succeeded ✔
c. expected level of treatment success (0)	Patient has enrolled in school at followup but is attending class sporadically (misses more than ⅓ classes/week)	Patient reports she has had at least four suicidal impulses since her first contact with CIC but has not acted on any of them
d. more than expected success with treatment (+1)	Patient has enrolled in school at followup and is attending classes but has no voc. goals *	*
e. best anticipated success with treatment (+2)	Patient has enrolled in school at followup, attends classes, has some voc. goals	Patient reports she has had no suicidal impulses since her first contact with CIC

Yes____ No _X_	Yes _X_ No____	Yes _X_ No____
Scale 3: Manipulation	*Scale 4: Drug abuse*	*Scale 5: Dependency on CIC*
Patient makes round of community service agencies demanding medication and refuses other forms of treatment ✔	Patient reports addiction to ''hard narcotics'' (heroin, morphine)	Patient has contacted CIC by telephone at least seven times since his first visit
Patient no longer visits CIC with demands for medication but continues with other community agencies and still refuses other forms of treatment	Patient has used ''hard narcotics'' but is not addicted and/or uses hallucinogens (LSD, Pot) more than four times a month ✔	Patient has contacted CIC 5–6 times since intake ✔
Patient no longer attempts to manipulate for drugs at community service agencies but will not accept another form of treatment	Patient has not used ''hard narcotics'' during followup period and used hallucinogens between 1–4 times a month *	Patient has contacted CIC 3–4 times since intake
Patient accepts nonmedication treatment at some community agency *	Patient uses hallucinogens less than once a month	
Patient accepts nonmedication treatment and by own report shows signs of improvement	At time of followup patient is not using any illegal drugs	Patient has not contacted CIC since intake *

2.3 A Framework for Action

Stuart (1974, p. 403) views assessment "as a plan for clinical action, and therefore, limited to those observations which can be readily translated into clinical maneuvers." This statement perhaps best illustrates the clinical assessment procedures developed and further elaborated by Gambrill (Gambrill et al., 1971; Gambrill, 1977) for practice in open settings. Although these procedures were articulated within the confines of a behavioral model, we believe that the basic paradigm detailed provides a useful preliminary assessment context, regardless of the theoretical orientation or the treatment modality. We have adapted these procedures for the clinical research model, because they lay the groundwork for its practical application.

These guidelines are not empirical in the strict sense of the word, but they emphasize specificity, objectivity, and measurement as core characteristics—all of which are necessary empirical elements. In essence they guide the clinician-researcher toward a systematic analysis of the client system and its environment. The stepwise procedures do not imply specific interviews; that is, step 1 is not necessarily the first interview, although it may be; step 2 is not necessarily the second interview, although it may be; and so on. Furthermore, these steps are neither invariant nor unique. Steps may be used in conjunction with each other, and repertoires within steps may overlap in many instances. Furthermore, it may be necessary to backtrack on procedural steps, when a given intervention proves unsuccessful.

Step 1: Inventory of problem areas

(*Assessment*)

Objective:

To obtain the spectrum of presenting problems as seen by the client and clinician-researcher.

Rationale:

To provide the client and clinician-researcher with an early profile of the problem areas so that each can discern priorities and arrive at some basis for deciding which problems to address first.

Operation:
The clinician-researcher obtains the client's descriptions of the presenting problems. At this time, there is little attempt to specify detail or form of the problems or their situational context or history. The focus is on getting an idea of the spectrum of the problem areas. The clinician-researcher keeps track of this information so that it can be considered in detail at a later point.

Example:
Family referred by public school system because of truancy and acting-out behavior by 14-year-old teenager. Preliminary assessment reveals that the father is a heavy drinker and mother works in the evenings. There is little supervision of the child at home, and only cursory attention is paid to the child's school performance.

This step can be used as a platform for "ventilation." While the clinician-researcher guides the client through the problem areas, the client should be given ample opportunity to elaborate on the affective factors as they emerge. By the time this step is completed, the clinician-researcher should have a reasonably good idea of the nature of the problems he or she is faced with, as well as of the range of situations in which intervention would have to take place. As the experienced interventionist is well aware, the presenting problems are not necessarily the targets of intervention. Furthermore, as Pincus and Minahan (1973) have pointed out, the client system is not necessarily the target system for change. The availability of an overall picture allows for a thorough analysis of the person–situation configuration, as well as the development of the potential "action system [those with whom the interventionist deals] in his/her efforts to accomplish the tasks and achieve the goals of the change effort" (Pincus and Minahan, 1973, p. 61).

Note that this first step in the assessment framework is extremely global. Information and data collected are generally subjective and qualitative. Little if any quantified or empirical information has been gathered. Step 1, then, occurs during the very early stages of intervention and is more in line with the traditional trust building, rapport development type of interview sessions. The emphasis is on the client's feeling state, and minimal direction is being offered toward problem specification beyond client-initiated global statements.

Step 2: *Problem selection*

Objective:

To identify and select the one area of primary concern to the client.

Rationale:

Through a mutual focusing on one problem area at a time, it is possible to maximize the efficiency and speed with which assessment is carried out and change efforts initiated.

Operation:

The client is asked to select the area of major concern to him or her. In general this should be a mutual agreement between the worker and client. It may, however, be necessary at times to negotiate this selection, depending on the clinician-researcher's knowledge base and purview and the demands made by significant others and society.

Example:

Because of the school's concern with truancy and acting-out behavior, these were selected as the preliminary targets of intervention. This selection is also supported by the family and worker, since the issues of drinking and supervision may be more sensitive and difficult to work with at this time.

The selection of a problem area for intervention at this time may be purely a function of how much effect it has on the client's daily life. As we said earlier, it may be more desirable to work on the most irritating problem at first, or it may be therapeutically wiser to intercede with a simpler problem (Reid and Epstein, 1972). This decision, of course, is an issue for discussion and determination by the client and clinician-researcher.

This step is only a little more specific than step 1. All it does is to narrow the focus of attention onto a given problem area, such that mutual effort is not dissipated across a variety of issues. It is important to note that, even at this point, the information available to the clinician-researcher is of a global nature requiring a high degree of specification prior to intervention planning and goal determination.

Step 3:   *Specification of target problems*

Objective:

To identify the specific concerns of the client and relevant others associated with him or her that constitute the essential elements of the selected problem area.

Rationale:

An effort is made to determine the exact referents of the labels used by the client and others in describing the problem, as well as to discover desirable alternatives. Client labels are not regarded as adequate in and of themselves, since the same label can have different referents from person to person. Hence, it is necessary to go beyond the superficial label and specify what is controlling the use of these labels (e.g., the observable behaviors) and under what situations.

Operation:

Samples of the observable problems and their situational contexts are sought. Thus, examples are collected in the interview, reports of others, and where possible, observation by the clinician-researcher as it occurs in the natural environment.

Example:

The teachers and counselors at school are interviewed in an attempt to gather some general information about the teen's acting-out and truant behavior. Attendance records show an absence rate of 38 percent. Acting-out is specifically defined in conjunction with the school personnel so that its occurrence can be noted. Three teachers and a counselor are recruited for monitoring.

Whenever possible, the target problems must be defined in such a manner that independent observers would be able to identify them when they occur. To restate a point made earlier, it should be apparent to the reader that we are emphasizing specific observable problems, not global phenomena. Where the problem is expressed in subjective nonspecific terms, the clinician-researcher should translate this into concrete terms. This translation, we believe, would enhance the therapeutic procedure by facilitating problem definition, as well as the measurement of goal attainment.

Step 4:   *Goal selection and contract*
Objective:
To reach a written agreement with client concerning the target
goals of intervention.
Rationale:
Such an agreement between worker and client increases the likelihood of early client involvement and cooperation in the treatment
effort.
Operation:
In general, the selection of the goal, like the selection of the target
problem, should be a mutual effort. Whereas the objective as
stated is to reach a written agreement, this may not be feasible
under certain conditions. In such instances, the best that may be
achieved may be an explicit statement of the target problem and
goal of intervention, followed by verbal agreement.
Example:
Given the parents' minimal involvement with the teen's school activities, it is decided to work purely within the school system to
change behavior. The worker obtains a written agreement between
the teen and the teachers individually, explicating classroom behavioral expectations and related academic performance.

In goal specification, as in problem specification, pragmatics play
a critical role. We agree with Reid and Epstein (1972) that, quite
frequently, a goal is desirable that is easier to achieve in a short
period of time but that simultaneously provides a sense of movement
toward some ultimate goal. Just as it may be necessary to work with
a simpler problem before tackling the more irritating ones, it may
also be more important to achieve a lesser goal before reaching the
ultimate goal. These procedures would reinforce the client by providing him or her with a sense of accomplishment, would positively
reinforce the client's perception of the clinician-researcher as a com-
petent interventionist, and would improve the likelihood of cooperation in dealing with the more difficult problems at a later date.

A subgoal should be as concrete and observable as any ultimate
goal. Consider an underachiever in school. Preliminary assessment

may reveal that underachievement is caused by inattentiveness in class. A treatment subgoal, then, would be to instill attentive behavior in the child (e.g., move to a different seat). Attentiveness could be measured by eye contact with teacher, quality of work, and so forth. The ultimate but related goal would be better academic performance as measured by superior grades in school. In essence, if a distinction is made between subgoals and ultimate goals, it should be explicitly stated, and its achievement should be measured systematically.

The contract as employed here should preferably be written. Data indicate that written commitment is likely to elicit greater cooperation and compliance (Levy, 1977, 1979; Levy and Carter, 1976). The contract should ideally contain the target problems, a specification of the goals of intervention, a specification of the intervention strategies, and a clarification of the roles of the participants (Maluccio and Marlow, 1974). Under some circumstances, however, a contract this detailed may not be feasible at this point in time and could be better put into operation in a later stage (step 5). Instead, a preliminary contract or work agreement is suggested. Such an agreement enunciates the general nature of the treatment relationship and the expected behaviors of the participants. Figure 2.9 presents an example of a family treatment contract, and Figure 2.10, a marital treatment contract. The specifics and format would, of course differ, depending on the agency, situation, problem, and the theoretical orientation of the practitioner.

Step 5: *Commitment to cooperate*

Objective:

To obtain client's agreement to cooperate fully in the activities associated with assessment and intervention.

Rationale:

Commitment to full cooperation tends to enhance the likelihood of compliance with the regimen of assessment and treatment. Compliance is regarded as necessary (although not sufficient) for successful intervention. Accessibility to clients is necessary to achieve change, and in open-service settings, where the clients come vol-

We, the undersigned, agree to work together on the goals specified in the behavioral contract. Each of these goals has been agreed upon by each member of the _____ family and has been approved by the clinician-researcher. The members of the _____ family and the clinician-researcher agree that they will make a sincere and strong effort to achieve these goals. Each person signing this contract will have certain individual responsibilities, and each person understands that treatment may have to be ended if he or she fails to meet these responsibilities.

General Guidelines

1. Although this contract will run for a maximum of _____ days, less time may be needed to achieve the family goals.
2. Each regularly scheduled meeting of the family and the clinician-researcher will follow this general pattern:
   a. review of data gathered during the previous week;
   b. plotting of the data on graphs so that each person may note the progress made during the week;
   c. discussion of goals not yet worked on;
   d. clinician-researcher's evaluation of family's current progress.

Responsibilities of the Clinician-Researcher

1. The clinician-researcher will work with the family and school to help achieve the family goals.
2. The clinician-researcher will help the family work out formal rules or contracts covering the behavior of family members.
3. If necessary, the clinician-researcher will assist the family in getting along better with each other.
4. The clinician-researcher will not discuss anything about the family with any outside agency or person without specific permission from the family.
5. The clinician-researcher will be available to the family for up to 3 hours a week for _____ days for both formal treatment interviews and phone consultation. The clinician-researcher's phone number is _____. In case of emergency only, the clinician-researcher can be reached at _____.

Responsibilities of the Family

1. It is understood that the following members of the family,

   _____ ,

   will attend and take part in all sessions.
2. Each member of the family agrees to keep the records that are assigned to him or her during treatment sessions.
3. Any member of the family may ask questions or make comments about anything that is unclear to him or her.
4. Each member of the family agrees to keep outside distractions (TV, phone conversations, etc.) to a minimum during treatment sessions.
5. Information about progress made will be requested by the project at periodic intervals after the end of treatment. It is agreed that the family members will cooperate in providing this followup information.

Sanctions

Both the family and the clinician-researcher understand that if the conditions of this contract are not carried out to the best of everyone's ability, treatment may have to be suspended or stopped entirely.

_____   _____

    Date   _____

                        _____

                        _____

From Richard B. Stuart and Tony Tripodi (1972). Used by permission of Richard B. Stuart.

Figure 2.9 Family treatment contract.

Mr. _____ and Mrs. _____ have requested counseling to help with the improvement of their relationship. They agree to participate in _____ joint counseling sessions, which will be held at intervals of _____ days. It is understood that any written, telephoned, or spoken messages to the counselor by either spouse will be assumed to be common knowledge. This assumption is necessary to ensure both spouses of the impartial help of the counselor. Finally, both spouses agree to complete every behavioral assignment to which he or she agrees, whether this assignment requires the completion of written forms, the graphing of changes in behavior, or changes in actions toward the other.

The counselor agrees to help both spouses equally toward the attainment of those goals to which all three parties agree. The counselor also agrees to explain to both spouses the logic of all therapeutic procedures, to evaluate the effectiveness of each of these procedures, and to ask spouses to perform only those tasks that are believed essential to the attainment of their goals. Finally, the counselor agrees to be available by telephone between sessions solely to help with the avoidance of conflict.

_____   _____

    Date   _____

                        _____

From Richard B. Stuart (1972). Used by permission of the author.

Figure 2.10 Marital treatment contract.

untarily, commitment to cooperate with the regimen must include an agreement to have regular appointments with the clinician-researcher.

Operation:

The remaining steps of the intervention program are briefly previewed for the client, with emphasis on the importance of obtaining full, accurate information during assessment; of the client's cooperating with what may be requested of him/her during the intervention program; and of maintaining regular contacts at appointed times.

Example:

During the teacher–teen meetings, considerable effort is put into the explanation of the intervention program. Given the worker's belief that the teen has low self-esteem and poor parent–child relations, two scales in these areas are administered to obtain a pre-treatment measurement.

In many ways, this step provides the "go–no go" signals. Where the client refuses to cooperate with the basic requisites of treatment, the probability of achieving success is very low. Under these circumstances, the clinician-researcher may be well advised to terminate contact. However, the clinician-researcher can maximize the likelihood of cooperation by adequately explaining what the therapeutic procedures are, what the client is likely to be asked to do, who is to be involved in treatment, and how long the treatment is to last. Considerable time and effort should be spent in this explanation, since this would be critical in determining and obtaining the cooperation of the participants in one's action system. In addition the clinician-researcher should be sufficiently versed in agency policies and guidelines and other community resources, so that client inquiries can be answered in depth and with accuracy. This is particularly important in using a clinical research model, since this may be a totally novel experience to the client in question.

The active nature of client participation should be stressed. Adequate explanations should be provided regarding the need for diverse measurement strategies, the employment of significant others in the intervention and evaluation process, and the need for systematic monitoring. In this manner the client should be sensitized to the value of accurate and comprehensive data collection as part of the therapeutic format.

It may be apparent to the reader that step 5 is perhaps a more appropriate juncture for formulating a contract. Only in this step is the client fully informed of his or her responsibilities and what can be expected from therapy. Realistically, therefore, the clinician-researcher may amalgamate steps 4 and 5 into a single unit. What is important is to retain the essence of the contract, namely, to facilitate *cooperation and commitment to the process and goals of assessment and treatment.*

Step 6:   *Assessment of environmental resources*
Objective:
To determine what environmental resources may be used in assessment and treatment.
Rationale:
Without access to significant others in the client's environment, the clinician-researcher will not be able to affect changes that would eliminate the problem or accelerate desirable alternatives.
Operation:
It is not infrequent at this point that the requisite information is known to the clinician-researcher, and no additional inquiry is necessary. By virtue of belonging to an agency, the related resources are available to the clinician-researcher. If there is some doubt about the desirability of the available resources, then potential mediators in the environment should be interviewed and usefully employed in the treatment process.
Example:
The teachers and counselor, in addition to being actively involved in the treatment program, are also used as evaluators of change. Additional information is also being gathered by the school system as part of the attendance records. Thus a series of measures are being employed to assess the impact of the intervention program.

This step, as elaborated by Gambrill et al. (1971) is purely a clinical evaluation of resource alternatives. We perceive resource assessment to be somewhat broader for the clinician-researcher, in that both clinical and evaluative advantages can accrue. For example, the resources employed in working with a delinquent child may include the family, school, and police. Chosen members in all of these systems could act as objective evaluators of the success of treatment, as well as be participants in the process of treatment. Although it might be beneficial for the clinician-researcher to observe the problem first hand, the opportunity to do so may be rather limited.

Although the use of outside agents in the therapeutic process may cause problems from the perspective of confidentiality, we believe that it may augment the entire treatment program and can be in the best interests of the client. It not only allows for objective evaluation of intervention but also enables the client to recognize previously untapped bases of support. The mere willingness of a significant other to participate in treatment may indicate to the client that others are interested in his or her welfare. It provides the client with a tangible source of moral support. Since they are important, outside agents should be selected with great care. Their role in the treatment program and the enormity of their responsibility should be thoroughly reviewed with them.

2.4 Additional Considerations

Once a clear determination of problems and goals has occurred, other preliminary assessment activities will be necessary for the clinician-researcher to proceed. These activities will depend on the theoretical and practical orientation of the clinician-researcher.

The reader may have already perceived similarities between the activities described here and those delineated by clinicians with different frames of reference (Rogers and Dymond, 1954; Perlman, 1957; Hollis, 1972). Needless to say, these authors did not prescribe identical procedures. However, preliminary assessment activities in general appear to fall into a system of relatively uniform procedures.

For example, in formulating the problem-focused model of intervention, Perlman elaborated on "focusing and partializing the problem," where focusing was problem identification and partializing was a component analysis. This perspective also included the notion of goal behaviors, those behaviors that were desired end products of intervention. The difference lies, however, in the rationale behind these activities and resulting procedures. For Perlman (1957, p. 148), "the reason for this need to partialize lies in the ego's functioning." The stress is on internal psychological characteristics of the client. To determine the client's goals, there is reliance on reflective and projective operations (Werner, 1974). This mode of practice delimits the application of observable quantitative methods, owing simply to the lack of specificity and tangibility both in the interventive procedures and the treatment goals. This is not to imply that these procedures are ineffective; rather, their operation is less open to objective and systematic analysis.

In contrast, for the clinician-researcher, the value of specification lies in its potential empiricism. A tangible and focal orientation to the problem allows the clinician-researcher to intervene with specific techniques. This procedure enables the clinician-researcher to measure change somewhat more objectively, rather than depend on the client's statements of "felt effectiveness."

Also consider client-centered therapy. It has been portrayed as a "process of reflective therapy in which the clinician's responses are consistently targeted on the internal frame of reference and experiences of the client" (Barrett-Lennard 1974, p. 188).

The similarity of assessment goals in client-centered therapy and the present formulation is strikingly apparent in the following statement by Barrett-Lennard (1974, p. 155); "Human beings act on and respond to reality as they individually experience and perceive it to be; that man is continually relating to his phenomenal field or environment, of which part of the core is his own self-perceived identity. An individual's perceptions are influenced by a variety of factors, including his experience, needs, the behavior of others and non-personal events."

Whereas Rogers and his followers have attempted to evaluate the effectiveness of their intervention processes, observable performance took a backseat in their evaluations. In fact, Rogers and Dymond (1954, p. 433) concluded their psychotherapy to be effective on the basis "that changes in self-perception of the client, in his personality organization and in his daily behavior" occur as a function of intervention. It is quite apparent that the indices were rather global, the intervention was relatively nonspecific, and the primary outcome criteria were therapist/client evaluations of internal psychological states. Furthermore, few data were collected for ongoing therapeutic purposes. In contrast, we believe that the clinician-researcher should employ objective evaluative criteria, as well as additional measures, in conjunction with specifically defined intervantion procedures to bring about change in target procedures.

It should be evident to the reader by now that, whereas there is some degree of overlap in the goals of assessment being promulgated by the different theoretical frameworks, the preliminary assessment activities in the present text are particularly suited to the clinical research model. This formulation not only emphasizes specification and objectivity but also, most importantly, stresses the development of measurement procedures. Another distinguishing characteristic is the rationale for the initial assessment of problems and goals. Simple verbal evaluation should, therefore, be substantiated by quantifiable observation where possible.

Depending on the theoretical bend of the clinician-researcher, the intrapsychic factors (e.g., self-esteem, impulsivity) may play an important role. The clinical research model does not preclude these items, and it lends itself to multiple measurement strategies (discussed in the next chapter). The point to keep in mind is that, the more abstract the concept becomes, the harder it is to measure.

2.5 Conclusion

This chapter has presented the reader with the desired characteristics of problem specification and goal determination. In addition, it has presented the reader with the stepwise procedure by which the empiricism required of the clinical research model can be achieved. Up to this point, however, the clinician-researcher has only the information that will allow him or her to decide on a general course of intervention. The preliminary assessment has provided the focus but not the data for intervention. In essence, this first stage provides the heuristic tools for the sequencing of clinical activities in later stages.

Assessment is a continuous process. As such, the preliminary assessment process is not an end in itself, nor does it provide the totality of problems and goals that need to be worked on. It is merely the beginning. As new problems arise, or treatment strategies fail, it may be necessary to return to the first stage—defining problems and goals.

Chapter Three

THE SECOND STAGE: EVALUATING AND SELECTING BASIC ASSESSMENT METHODS

3.1 Measurement Factors

IN THIS CHAPTER and the next, we focus on assessment activities that occur after target problems, goals, and resources have been identified. During the second stage the clinician-researcher selects measurement methods that he/she will begin to use during the third stage to measure where the client is in relation to the goal. The data one should obtain from these methods are qualitatively different from the type of data gathered in the first stage. According to the clinical research model, data must be collected throughout intervention to demonstrate the effect of the intervention and to gather clinically relevant data.

Just as problem specification is related to goal specification, so too are goal specification and the selection of a strategy to measure the effect of intervention. In fact the ultimate form of the goal statement should actually reflect the measurement method. For example, if the problem is stated as a low score on a self-esteem scale, the single ultimate goal may be simply viewed as a rise in the score on that scale. In this specific instance the scale can be the only measurement method needed by the clinician-researcher. In most cases, however, goals are usually not initially stated with the measurement method "built in" in such a manner, and further refinement of the goals, to the point where the measurement strategy is part of the goal statement, is necessary. Whereas this chapter focuses on the issues in the selection and application of measurement procedures, the reader should keep in mind the interactive relationship between goal specification and measurement selection; that is, the degree to which specificity has been attained in the goal statement determines the extent to which a specific measure can be employed.

The measurement of treatment effect plays a central role in the clinical research model. As a concept, measurement can be vague or meticulous, arbitrary or logical, systematic or unsystematic. The fact remains, however, that, once the target problem has been identified and the goal determined, the clinician-researcher must consider ways and means of measuring the effectiveness of intervention. In essence, the clinician-researcher must consider four questions: *What* does one measure; *when* does one measure; *who* does the measuring; and *with what* does one measure? All these questions are relevant and important to the therapy evaluation process, and the answers to each are interrelated, for all the other salient aspects of measurement and intervention must be incorporated in the decision process. Furthermore, the answer to each is also related to the problem and goal specification. However, for the sake of clarity, each issue is dealt with separately.

What The question of what needs to be measured is perhaps the first issue facing the clinician-researcher. Watson (1952, p. 32) notes that "at present we are in the unhappy state of not knowing what are the criteria of effectiveness of psychotherapy." Strupp and Bergin (1972, p. 51) add: "In our opinion, it is not possible at the present time to draw any strong conclusions concerning the relative value of outcome criteria."

Assuming the goals of intervention have been determined and the procedures of intervention formalized, the clinician-researcher presumably has some notions about the parameters to be studied. As Gordon et al. (1954) and Strupp (1971) argue, all clinicians have their own criteria based on their value systems, theoretical orientation, clinical training, and the conceptualization of goals. We recommend that these criteria depend on the purposes of treatment. Measures of effectiveness should be employed primarily because of their demonstrated clinical importance, and not for their theoretical importance alone (Risley, 1969). For example, if the intervention concerns working with a juvenile delinquent, then the relevant measurement parameters could be school behavior, home behavior, behavior in the community, and attitude toward school (Stuart et al., 1972). In this situation, behavioral measures and attitudinal indices have been suggested in an attempt to tap the differential effects of treatment.

Within the clinical research model, the answer to what should be measured is: whenever possible, more than one thing. Fiske et al. (1970, p. 731) state one reason for this: "There should be more than one measure of outcome, and preferably several diverse measures, since outcome measures tend to have low correlations." Thus, these authors, along with Bergin (1971), Kiesler (1966), Paul (1969), Kazdin and Wilson (1978), and Jayaratne et al. (1974), attest to the use of multifactorial measures of outcome. Since the clinician-researcher is interested in determining the effect of the intervention, he/she should recognize that it would be presumptuous to expect a single outcome measure to tap all different areas of change, particularly where the intervention concerns multiple target problems. Hence, each area should be measured specifically.

A second reason for multifactorial measurement emerges from a design perspective, as explained by Edwards and Cronbach (1952, p. 56): "to take advantage of experimental design the experimenter must have a clear idea in advance of the investigation as to what effects he expects to find." Obviously, this statement is apropos of the clinician-researcher as well. Every evaluative situation has some degree of error built into it. By using multifactorial measurement strategies, the clinician-researcher has come a long way in eliminating some of this error. As Webb et al. (1972, p. 3) point out, "the most persuasive evidence comes through the triangulation of measurement processes. If a proposition can survive the onslaught of a series of imperfect measures, with all their irrelevant error, confidence should be placed in it."

A third argument for multifactorial measurement comes from the systems theory perspective. Client change in one dimension of functioning will more than likely effect changes in other dimensions as well. For example, increasing a child's school attending behavior may result in better grades. If the clinician-researcher bent on increasing school attendance (target problem) measures only attendance, he or she will miss related changes in grades, for example. The measurement of grade performance becomes important because it may be a desired but serendipitous change, and/or failure to achieve better grades may indicate a related problem that needs intervention. In essence, emphasis on multifactorial measurement forces the clinician-researcher to consider the ecology of the clinical situation, so that all aspects of client performance and interaction are considered in the planning and evaluation of intervention.

The concept of multifactorial measurement as discussed here may refer to one (or all three) of the following procedures:

(A) Problems x, y, and z being measured by three separate instruments P, Q, and R respectively. This strategy may be particularly desirable when the problems are related and/or when the measurement opportunities are limited during some phases of intervention. For example, let us assume that you have a client who is trying to reduce smoking (x) and your theoretical model argues that, to reduce smoking, one must reduce anxiety (y) in the individual. You administer the "Taylor Manifest Anxiety Scale" (1953) (P) before treatment, with the intent of readministering the scale after treatment. The clinician-researcher may also choose to measure the frequency of smoking behavior (Q). It might be, however, that agency procedure delimits the clinician-researcher's ability to conduct any extended pretreatment measures since a quick treatment beginning is required. Yet, once treatment begins, it is possible to monitor smoking. Frequency of smoking could then be measured during treatment, even though comparative pretreatment measures are unavailable. This measurement is advocated, since the client's statement of higher pretreatment smoking levels, a purely subjective statement, coupled with the pretreatment–posttreatment comparative measures of anxiety, would provide useful clinical information. In this instance, the monitoring of smoking would produce clinical and evaluative data that would help the clinician-researcher in his/her attempt to evaluate the impact of anxiety in the client. These behavioral measures could, moreover, easily be extended into the followup period (since you have met with agency requirements for rendering service without delay) and thus provide the clinician-researcher with comparative data (between the treatment period and followup period). When these behavioral measures (Q) are employed in conjunction with the anxiety scale (*P*), a much stronger case for effectiveness can be made than by using either one alone, in the event that *x* (smoking) and *y* (anxiety) are related.

(*B*) Problem *x* being measured by multiple instruments *M, N,* and *O.* (*A*) is an intervention situation where multiple problems are being measured with unitary instruments, that is, problem *x* being measured by *P,* problem *y* being measured by *Q,* etc. In (*B*), the unitary problem is being measured by more than one instrument. For example, if problem *x* referred to low self-esteem, the clinician-researcher may employ three different scales of self-esteem and thus increase the accuracy of the findings. We have included both possibilities under the general rubric of multifactorial measurement. Another aspect of multifactorial measurement that needs to be addressed (and is discussed at length under *"who* does the measuring") concerns the use of different individuals in the measurement process.

(*C*) Problem *x* may be evaluated by persons *P1, P2,* and *P3* on instrument *Q.* Although it might be beneficial for the clinician-researcher to observe the target problem first hand, the opportunity to do so may be rather limited. Although the use of outside agents in the therapeutic process may cause problems from the perspective of confidentiality, we believe that it may augment the entire treatment program and can be in the interest of the client. In addition to allowing for objective evaluation of intervention, it also has some clinical advantage. The involvement of outside persons enables the client to recognize previously untapped bases of support. This aspect of multifactorial measurement is elaborated later in this chapter.

In conclusion, (*A*) is the minimal requirement in the clinical research model. If one is intervening with two problems simultaneously, no single measure will usually register success or failure of both characteristics. Thus, two separate measures will be necessary if some semblance of "true" performance is to be established; (*B*) and (*C*), on the other hand, are highly desirable multifactorial measurement strategies but are often impractical. At the same time, the reader should be aware that failure to employ either (*B*) or (*C*) may result in questionable measurement of outcome, for reasons noted earlier (Figure 3.1).

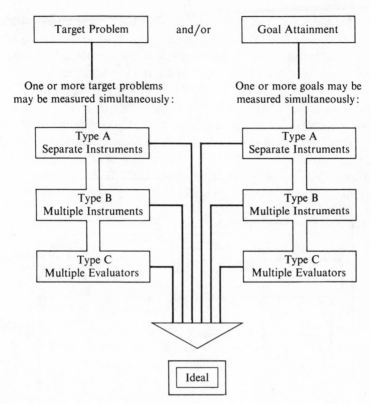

Figure 3.1 What needs to be measured?

When Once intervention procedures have been formulated, the design issues (to be presented later) have been conceptualized, and the measurement strategy has been decided on, the clinician-researcher must decide when to measure. There are two major parameters to this issue. The first is *when* should measurement take place—before, during, or after treatment? In general, the designs discussed in this book call for measurement at least before treatment and after treatment has begun. This is the minimal requirement for determining the effects of intervention (although these designs allow only a limited sense of causal attribution). The premeasurement establishes the current level of functioning of the individual before treatment, and postmeasurement indicates the client's functioning after treatment has been terminated. A simple comparison of these pre–post recordings (of intensity, duration, scores, etc.) would allow for some judgment to be made regarding the impact of intervention. Some visual feedback (such as graphs, to be discussed later) would provide trend and absolute information about whether or not the identified problem improved or worsened (Figure 3.2).

Whereas pre–post measurement is considered a must in the determination of treatment effect, most authors have stressed a third point of measurement (followup) sometime after the end of treatment to "maximize transfer effects" (Baer et al., 1968; Goldstein et al., 1966; McNamara and MacDonough, 1972), establish generalizability, and

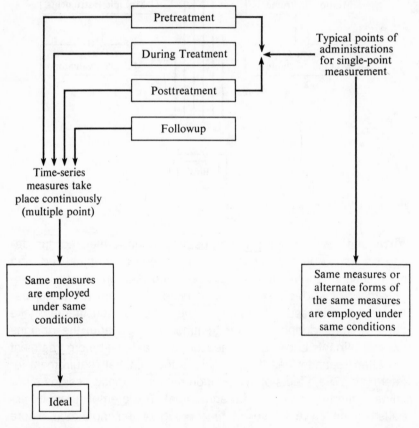

Figure 3.2 When should measurement take place?

detect the emergence of other problems (Gelfand and Hartmann, 1968). Furthermore, although a significant change may be evident at the end of active treatment, the practical value of the effect and hence the intervention will be limited unless the change is maintained posttherapy. Similarly, there may be a delayed effect that will become evident only if measured at followup (Goldstein et al., 1966). McNamara and MacDonough (1972) argue that, for followup to be useful, it must be done systematically, if possible according to a reasonably ordered continuum; the problems assessed at followup should be the same problems studied during treatment; and the methods used to assess the problems should be the same in all phases of the intervention period. Finally, the duration of the followup period should be at least as long as the pretreatment (baseline) measurement and, where possible, much longer. Where easily administered instruments are used, lengthy periods of followup should be considered. In contrast, extended followup with some methods (such as multiple point observation, discussed later) is somewhat improbable, given the time, effort, and expense necessary.

Now that we have established the need for pre–post measurement, the second major *when* question may be addressed: within each phase, that is, within each pre, post, and followup periods, should the measurement be made only once (single point) or a number of times (multiple point)? Once again, it is necessary to recognize an ideal versus a less-than-ideal-but-better-than-nothing polarity in clinical research practice. The ideal of the clinical research model requires a series of measures over time (time series) within each phase. Indeed, the single-subject designs discussed later in this book, and within which clinical research practice should operate, were developed as "time-series" designs. The essence of time-series measurement is the "presence of a periodic measurement process" (Campbell and Stanley, 1963, p. 37). In the framework of the pre–post measurement strategy, this means that a *series* of measures must be taken before intervention and the same series of measures must be taken after intervention. By the same series we mean that the same units that were observed before intervention must be reevaluated after intervention within the same physical and time framework. For example, if a series of Friday absences were used as a record of truancy in a given case before treatment, a series of Friday absences must also be used as the measure after intervention (not Monday through Thursday, because of possible variations).

Multiple-point measurement makes sense clinically as well. One advantage is that, with a series of measurements over time, the clinician-researcher is able to observe trends in the client's progress and make treatment decisions based on these trends. For example, a slow but steady decline in a problem may lead a clinician to choose either to maintain the current treatment with the expectation that a desirable level will eventually be reached or to alter treatment to speed up progress. A problem that is at a currently acceptable level but that shows a worsening trend might indicate a different treatment response on the part of the client. For obvious reasons, such trend data are unavailable with single-point measurement; thus they serve primarily an evaluative function.

Another problem with single-point measurement is concerned with reliability, or "the extent to which the measurements are free from error due to chance fluctuation and biases involved in the collection of data; it refers to consistency in measurement procedures, and to the reproducibility of measurements" (Tripodi et al., 1969, p. 36). Simply put, one measurement taken at one point in time may not be truly representative of the client's performance at another point in time in the same situation. Inaccurate judgments of evaluation and clinical decision making may result. Multiple-point measurement could increase reliability by virtue of numerous time comparisons. If single-point measurement is necessary, one suggestion is to use several different kinds of measures to minimize this error.

A related concern has to do with validity: "the extent of correspondence between the measurement of a variable and the intended meaning of that variable." (Tripodi et al., 1974, p. 40), that is, the extent to which the measure being used actually measures the target problem or goal. For example, the act of repeatedly answering a questionnaire or a scale may influence the answers the client gives (owing to practice) and weaken the validity of the data. Thus, multiple administration of paper-and-pencil tests is somewhat questionable, although they are being used in this manner (Hudson, 1977). In contrast, behavioral measures are much more suited for multiple-point measurement since they are directly measuring the target behavior and, hence, are less susceptible to validity problems.

It appears, then, that problems or goals that are specified in such a way as to place them low on the concrete and observable continuum are also poor candidates for multiple-point measurement. In essence, the ideal clinical research models (single-subject designs) should use either multiple-point measures or a combination of multiple-point and single-point measures. If only single-point measurement is possible, the clinician-researcher should attempt to employ either Type B or C procedures, or both. As indicated earlier, the minimal requirement in this model is single-point pre–post intervention measurement.

Now that we have stated the basic requirements of the clinical research approach, a word of caution is necessary. The most desirable alternatives of the clinical research approach are those termed single-subject designs. As such, multiple point measurement becomes critically important. We therefore strongly urge all clinician-researchers to employ multiple point strategies whenever possible. To reemphasize some points already made:

1. Single-subject designs have minimal empirical value (by definition) unless multiple-point measures are employed.

2. Multiple-point measurement offers continuous feedback for clinical purposes—single-point measurement does not.

3. For single-point measurement to have maximal value, it must have a normative comparison base if paper-and-pencil tests are used.

4. A higher degree of validity can be achieved with multiple-point measurement.

Who The third measurement issue the clinician-researcher is concerned with is the question of who does the measuring (Figure 3.3). In the past the two major evaluators of treatment outcome have been therapists and their clients. These two parties have dominated the outcome scene to such a degree that half of all studies examined by Bergin (1971), in his exhaustive literature review, used therapists and clients as the sole evaluators of outcome. This finding is even

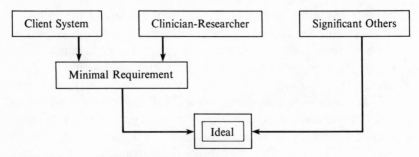

Figure 3.3 Who should do the measuring?

more astounding in the face of such statements as the following: "Therapists are notoriously unobjective observers when the validity of their favorite treatment technique is in question" (Gelfand and Hartmann, 1968, p. 211). "The most dependable means of assuring a favorable evaluation is to use voluntary testimonials from those who have had treatment" (Campbell, 1969b, p. 426). In addition, Breedlove and Krause (1966) note Hathaway's "hello-goodbye effect"— referring to the tendencies of clients to overestimate treatment effect. Therefore, for assessment purposes, many studies use salient members in the community (such as teachers, police, and employers) as additional sources of data. The clinician-researcher, having followed Step 6 in the previous chapter, should have an idea where to look for such members. "Triangulation" procedures incorporating many different sources of data (Types *B* and *C*) would certainly enhance the ability of any clinician-researcher to legitimize the success of intervention.

The availability of multifactorial sources of evaluation and measurement offers a greater opportunity to increase the reliability and validity of the outcome of intervention; that is, having several people agree on the degree of effectiveness of one's intervention program allows one to have a higher level of confidence (Type *C*). In addition, having participants in different geographical and physical locations may allow for the gathering of more accurate information. For example, a client who wants to reduce weight may eat constantly while in his office but not at home. In attempting to determine the extent of this eating behavior, his secretary and colleagues could be employed as part of the action system in the office, and his wife may do the same at home. This type of diversified but situation-specific information regarding an identified behavior provides valuable information.

Clinical considerations may also be important in selecting non-client observers. Pincus and Minahan (1973) argue that an action system should mobilize all available resources in attempting to bring about change in the client system. This action system should involve all individuals (who agree to participate) identified by the client as having a significant impact on his or her life space. Inclusion of these individuals is justified from the clinical perspective in that they provide a broad-base support community for the client, their active interest and participation in treatment may generate greater interest in client well-being than if they were excluded, and they provide an overall positive picture to the client in that he or she sees that others are concerned and interested about his or her well-being. Of course the inherent negative aspect of such a broad-base system would be that of labeling. This negativity can, however, be minimized by careful inclusion of participants by the clinician-researcher and client.

The question of who does the measuring is, of course, also tied to where the definitions of targets and goals fall along the concrete and observable continuums. As we saw in the last chapter, some problems and goals may not lend themselves to measurement by more than one person. And, as Strupp and Bergin (1972) have indicated, while overt behavioral criteria are currently more impressive, they are not necessarily more important. Thus, while it is possible for several people to observe the same behavior (acting out in class) and record its frequency of occurrence, this measures only the specific activity. The combined ratings on some "attitude toward school" scale by teachers and clinician-researcher could tap a related dimension of equal value.

It should be apparent to the reader that a great deal of thought should go into the determination of *who, what,* and *when* of measurement—simply owing to the integrative character of intervention and measurement as feedback. The clinical research model views these decisions as an integral part of the clinical decision process. Failure to elicit adequate resources and material in these areas will undoubtedly result in weak measurement and intervention, since the feedback data will be unreliable and invalid. The clinician-researcher, then, should maximize efforts both in the knowledge of treatment method and in data collection—since the latter provides continuing and central assessment data.

With What This section deals with the fourth major question in the clinical research model—with what do you measure? A plethora of instruments for measuring various psychological constructs is available in the clinical, personality, and general psychotherapeutic literature (Figure 3.4). The range of instruments runs the continuum from projective tests such as the Rorschach and Thematic Apperception Test (TAT) to the sophisticated electronic and mechanical devices measuring physiological characteristics such as pupil dilation and contraction (pupillography) and GSRs (Butterfield, 1974). Many clinician-researchers shun the use of standardized tests on the basis that treatment by definition is idiosyncratic and hence the measures used should reflect specificity within this context. In contrast, some au-

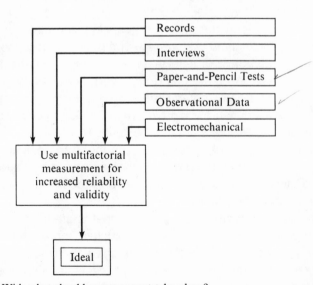

Figure 3.4 With what should measurement take place?

thors argue that "the field sorely needs the development of standard assessment instruments of this type" (Paul, 1969, p. 43). On the one hand, we tend to agree with Paul's viewpoint, in that a collection of individualized instruments, based on subject-specific criteria and clinical biases, could serve no purpose for scientific progress. If a relevant, reliable, and valid measure is available, it would serve no logical purpose for the investigator to devise his or her own. Not only would the use of established measures help in the validation of these measures, but it might also permit cross-study comparisons. On the other hand, a multifactorial approach using some standard measures, as well as some idiosyncratic measures, could both individualize clinical purpose and add to a cumulative body of knowledge. In examining the measurement choices available, it is for the clinician-researcher to decide which procedures to incorporate in the design, and it is at this point that one must weigh the pros and cons of each tactic.

Once the target problems and goals to be measured have been determined, there are several issues that must be addressed in the development and/or selection of appropriate measurement instruments and procedures. First, the clinician-researcher must choose *relevant* measures that will show client progress. The relevance of a measure is determined by the potential areas of change expected as a result of intervention. For example, if a reading program were being evaluated, then two of the primary measures should detect changes in reading ability and comprehension. In addition, it could be argued that a simultaneous change in attitude toward reading may have occurred during the program and was partially responsible for the detected change. Thus, it may be beneficial to add an "attitude toward reading" measure. The clinician-researcher may also believe that the reading program has played such a central role in the child's life space that positive behavior changes may have been recorded in school, and hence he or she may want to use some sort of behavioral measure, perhaps a serendipitous finding. Obviously, this type of extrapolation to relevant factors can get ridiculous at some point, to such a degree that one begins to use totally irrelevant and tangential measures. Thus, while the clinician-researcher attempts to tap all dimensions of change, with regard to the goal, some care must be taken, since the greater the number of measures used, the greater the probability of a chance finding—in essence obscuring a "true" finding (Edwards and Cronbach, 1952). This is particularly true in view of the fact that every measure will have some "irrelevant vehicular component" (Campbell 1969a), and the measured change may be due to one of these irrelevancies. Thus, whereas the clinician-researcher should tap the theoretically expected parameters of change, as well as the defined goals of change, the measures used for this purpose should be carefully selected. The primary emphasis should be on the measurement of goal attainment since they are in fact the explicitly stated items in the intervention program.

The second issue that the clinician-researcher must decide concerns the selection of measures that will show change. *Sensitivity* is the ability to be responsive to external stimuli. In other words, sensitivity in measurement implies an ability to show change. The index in use must be capable of showing change for client purposes. Thus, before the implementation of the baseline procedures, the clinician should thoroughly evaluate the indices he or she is planning to employ.

The implication of thorough evaluation carries with it the time that would have to be spent in it. Like most other activities, practice and research experience would allow for the better application of measurement procedures. Most clinicians are not equipped with the statistical knowledge desired to evaluate the validity and reliability of different measures, nor do they have the time to do so. It is here that such volumes as the *Mental Measurements Yearbook* (Buros, 1972), *Measuring Human Behavior* (Lake et al., 1973), *Measures for Psychological Assessment* (Chun et al., 1975), or the *Measures of Social Psychological Attitudes* (Robinson, 1973) become valuable. These books (and others) offer the clinician-researcher summary descriptions of a large number of indices measuring various psychosocial dimensions. Over time, the clinician-researcher would be able to develop a library of significant measurement tools, which could then be administered when the need arises.

The use of available standardized measures is particularly valuable when one is concerned with the issue of sensitivity. Whereas the use of standardized paper-and-pencil tests would overcome some of these basic concerns, similar problems would be encountered even where the measurement is behavioral. For example, insensitivity would emerge as a problem in an unacceptable but low-frequency behavior. Consider the clinician attempting to change the communication patterns of a marital couple. The presenting problem is one of aggressive behavior exhibited by the husband. On occasion, the husband is physically assaultive, but most of the time he is verbally abusive. The couple agrees that both types of aggressive behaviors are intolerable and need to be changed. In determining the baseline frequency of these qualitatively different behaviors, a problem of sensitivity emerges. While it would be easier to keep track of physical violence (since the definition of verbal abuse may be somewhat complicated), it would be of little practical value because of its low frequency of occurrence. Since the husband's aggressive behavior is literally on a continuum from (low) physical to (high) verbal, minimizing the occurrence of the latter may automatically reduce the incidence of the other. As a baseline criterion, therefore, only verbal aggression would be coded since it would be more sensitive to change in view of its higher frequency of occurrence—hence more room for change.

Consider Figures 3.5 and 3.6. Figure 3.5 illustrates the situation if "physical aggression" were to be recorded, and Figure 3.6, the picture if "verbal aggression" were to be recorded. According to Figure 3.5, there were only two incidents of physical aggression during the pretreatment period. Furthermore, if this is taken with any degree of confidence, this shows an increasing trend. These data may lead the clinician-researcher to err in assessment; for example, given the low

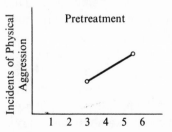

Figure 3.5 Graph of physical aggression.

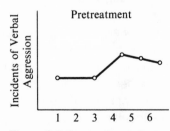

Figure 3.6 Graph of verbal aggression.

incidence, the clinician-researcher may feel that the aggressive notion has been blown out of proportion. Or, given the increasing trend
line, the clinician-researcher may feel the situation is critical because the incidence of physical aggression has increased dramatically. Either decision is, of course, wrong.

In contrast, Figure 3.6, measuring verbal aggression, presents a
relatively stable situation, as well as a relatively frequent activity.
Thus, it should be apparent to the reader that, in situations of this
type, the clinician-researcher has three choices: first, he/she could
increase the period during which measurement occurs while using
the measure of physical aggression. This procedure obviously has
severe ethical and practical limitations. A more likely option is the
second alternative: to choose a different criterion or index of measurement—in this instance, a different index was chosen (verbal
aggression). The final choice involves the selection of a different
method of measurement. For example, the clinician-researcher may
believe that it is undesirable to delay treatment and hence be unable
to gather behavioral pretreatment data. The clinician-researcher decides to administer instead a scale of "aggression" before intervention to both parties in treatment. Given the aforementioned pre–post
measurement criteria, this same index will be readministered posttreatment to determine the impact of intervention as measured by
that specific index. Furthermore, in keeping with the suggestions
made earlier, this latter procedure does not preclude the monitoring
and measurement of aggressive behavior during treatment and followup. Once again then, we are back to the multifactorial measurement notion, which we are repeatedly suggesting as the most desirable model of measurement.

It is obviously a difficult task to determine how sensitive a measure
is before its application in the specific situation. But if the clinician-
researcher were to follow the first stage procedures and obtain the
spectrum of problem areas, and identify the target problems and
goals, and so on, he/she should have some verbal evidence to determine whether or not a particular measure is sufficiently sensitive.
The ease with which such selection can take place will naturally
grow as the clinician-researcher's knowledge base about the various
measures and their potential applicability grows.

A third major issue for the clinician-researcher to decide is whether to use obtrusive or nonobtrusive measures, or both. Quite often, however, there is no choice. In institutions (Allyon and Azrin, 1968) and in classrooms there are assessment reasons for using nonobtrusive data, but in some clinical situations it may be advantageous to use obtrusive measures.

Becker et al. (1967) argue that viable nonobtrusive measurement is a possibility, provided naturally occurring individuals (ward personnel, teachers, etc.) and circumstances are used. In contrast, if outsiders are sent into a system to monitor and/or observe, they seem to stand out, making nonobtrusive measurement virtually impossible (Jayaratne et al., 1974; Patterson, 1971). In essence, this is another argument for the use of significant others in the measurement process.

When measurement is obtrusive, the subject is immediately aware that he/she is the target of an evaluative program, a "guinea pig." The clinician-researcher has thus laid the groundwork for a "reactive arrangement" (Campbell, 1969a; White, 1977). Some recent studies tend, however, to minimize the effect of reactivity in such situations (Johnson and Bolstad, 1975). Given the likelihood that reactivity is a possibility in most instances, however, the clinician-researcher must deal with all the biases resulting from subject awareness such as (1) the "guinea pig effect"—the awareness of being tested may itself affect outcome; (2) role selection—the individual defines an "unnatural" role for him/herself, so that what is seen is not "real"; (3) measurement as change agent—the measurement process itself introduces real changes in what is being measured; (4) response set—tendency of client to agree with certain statements (an example would be the tendency to give socially desirable responses); (5) interviewer effects—variance in responses brought about by the clinician-researcher's personal characteristics.*

As Campbell (1969a, p. 368) points out, "the obvious cure for all these artifacts is the disguised experiment in which the respondents (if not the experimenters) are unaware of participating in an experiment." Unfortunately, however, this is easier said than done—

---

* An excellent discussion of these and other sources of error is found in Webb et al. (1972).

especially in the natural environment where much of clinical work takes place. Under these circumstances several alternatives are available to the clinician-researcher: (1) Goldstein et al. (1966) note that in many situations naturally occurring measures are available— for example, school grades or attendance records. While suscepti- ble to recordkeeping errors, different policies, and so forth, they pro- vide a fairly reasonable source of data if the weaknesses are consid- ered in their interpretation. (2) Cook and Selltiz (1964) point out that social desirability may be controlled for by including irrelevant items in the questionnaire and thereby making the purpose of the question- naire less obvious. (3) To make it unlikely for subjects to give un- desirable answers (or to eliminate socially desirable characteristics and role definition), Cook and Selltiz (1964) suggest that the clini- cian-researcher explain that there is no right or wrong answer and emphasize honesty. (4) For controlling response set, these authors also suggest varying the words of items so that favorable answers reflect both agreement and disagreement, using open-ended ques- tions, and using matched pairs of statements rendering opposing points of view. While it is obvious that these precautionary measures do not totally eliminate these factors as potential sources of error, their advice is worth considerable thought and action.

As we said previously, there may be some clinical advantages to obtrusiveness, at the expense of valid assessment data. For ex- ample, in one study, Patterson and Reid (1970) indicate that the presence of an outside observer (in this case an obtrusive observer) produced changes in the rates of positive and negative conse- quences supplied by family members. Similarly, self-observation (which is obviously obtrusive) may also be clinically advantageous, while also deleterious to good assessment data, since the measure- ment procedure itself may act as a change agent. Change may occur merely as a function of the client's being aware of his or her own behavior (Bernstein, 1969). The positive impact of self-observa- tion has been reported by a number of investigators (Johnson and White, 1971; Mahoney et al., 1973; Thoresen and Mahoney, 1974). While this undoubtedly reduces the validity of the measures as a via- ble base for comparison, it could be considered a strategy of inter- vention. The assessment requirement to determine the effect of this intervention could be addressed by using verbal reports of the client as comparative information—with all the problems inherent in this. Unfortunately, the relationship between obtrusiveness and behavioral change is not always simple and predictable (McNamara and MacDonough, 1972).

The fourth major choice for the clinician-researcher in search of evaluative instruments is to decide on the use of *global* and/or *focal* measures. A global instrument should measure change in a given specific area. A focal instrument measures change in a given dimension within the specific area. Most treatment outcome investigators have attempted to use broad measures of change (Paul, 1969). However, as Battle et al. (1966, p. 187) point out, "global ratings, although useful, are rather uninformative because so many factors contribute to any particular rating and their relative contributions differ in undetermined ways from one to another."

Multifactorial measurement has been emphasized as perhaps the best approach to cover many bases. For example, a wise choice would be a combination of focal and global measures. Since a clinician-researcher is aware of the specific dimensions on which intervention procedures would have an effect (problem area), he/she could most likely devise focal measures that would tap change in these areas (or use already existing instruments of change). As an illustration, let us assume an adolescent is referred to a school social worker for truancy. The school attendance records may serve as a reasonable indicator of change in the truant behavior. At the same time, the clinician-researcher may feel that as a result of increased attendance the adolescent's academic performance should improve, and a direct measure of this is obtained in the school grades. On the other hand, the clinician-researcher may argue that neither of these changes would be possible unless the child's attitude toward school, peers, and family changed in some way. He or she may, therefore, wish to evaluate change in these areas as well. Essentially, the clinician-researcher would end up with several multiple-point measures directly related to the purpose of intervention and a couple of tangential single-point global measures on attitude—a unitary measure could not have tapped all these dimensions.

All the information presented thus far in this chapter is of critical importance in the evaluation of intervention. The discussion around *what, when, who,* and *with what* is central to the operationalization of the clinical research model. The reader should be thoroughly acquainted with these procedural aspects, since they are an integral part of designs to be discussed later.

3.2 Measurement Methods

The discussion that follows, while not concentrating on any specific scales or instruments, deliberates the positives and negatives of five measurement strategies frequently used in clinical evaluation: records, interviews, paper-and-pencil tests (self-report), observational data, and electromechanical (physiological) measures. The general issues discussed earlier in this chapter are addressed in the context of these categories.

Records Treatment evaluation, by and large, has frequently used available data as a basic information source (Bergin, 1971). As Shyne (1967, p. 106) observed, the "use of available data is often a matter of expediency, but it may be dictated by the more fundamental consideration that the nature of the question necessitates recourse to available data."

Some examples of the more commonly used records in treatment evaluation are school performance criteria (attendance, grades, and suspensions); community behavior (court and police contacts, job performance); "other" treatment contacts; institutional recidivism; and case records.

In general, the use of available records requires that the clinician-researcher be familiar with the better known sources of relevant data and perhaps display some ingenuity in discovering lesser known data. The disregard of relevant information may mean the loss of possibly valuable material, particularly where periodically collected information could provide some trend data.

Strengths
1. Records may serve as an unobtrusive source of measuring change on a given target problem. For example, when one is working with adoles-

cents having truancy and academic problems, the school records on attendance and grades may serve a crucial function.

2. They may serve as a supplementary source of information for comparison with other intervention data. For example, school suspension records could substantiate classroom observational data on pupil misbehavior.

3. They could provide information on an inaccessible target problem. For example, where delinquent behavior of an adolescent is a target for change, police contact and juvenile court contacts could provide a wealth of information—information that families may be reluctant or unable to explicate.

4. Where past performance or historical factors are important, records could provide the only detailed and reasonably accurate information available. For example, if one is interested in the number of medical contacts a suspected abusing parent may have had, hospital records may be the only viable indicator given parent denial.

5. Time-cost factors may necessitate the use of available data, since it is undoubtedly cheaper than ongoing data collection. This is particularly true where the available data are just as good. For example, if an achievement test is an indicator in a given situation, the clinician-researcher may save him/herself some time and money by using tests already being employed by the school system.

6. The use of existing records would cause no noticeable disruption in agency procedures, whereas the implementation of new procedures for data collection could create a great deal of disruption. For example, if teachers are asked to keep special records (for treatment evaluation purposes) on attendance and class participation of problem adolescents, it would create an artificial (experimentally created) workload on the teachers. This may lead to resistance and lack of compliance by the teachers.

7. The nature of the problem may dictate the use of records. For example, if a family has had a long history of social service contacts, it may be necessary to find out what avenues of intervention may have been investigated previously, prior to proceeding with intervention again. Under these circumstances, the most accurate information would most likely be found in agency case records. At the very least, these data would provide a subsidiary source of information to any direct information provided by the clients during interviews.

Weaknesses

1. The first possible weakness in using records as data is what Shyne (1967) calls "consistent availability of data." That is, to what extent have the data been compiled over time and recorded with some degree of consistency? Any change in recording style or definition, for example, could interfere with trend data. Jayaratne et al. (1974) point out problems that occurred in a long-term study with predelinquent adolescents owing to administrative changes in school policy regarding grades and attendance, essentially resulting in noncomparable data from year to year.

2. "On rare occasions one has the happy experience of having some evidence of the reliability and validity of the material one is dealing with" (Shyne 1967, p. 113). More often, however, this is usually a matter of educated judgment based on one's knowledge of the possible biases and contingencies (such as selective recording, misrepresentation, and missing data affecting the data collection procedures and the specific agencies. For example, attendance data reported to the school registrar by different teachers may be idiosyncratically biased and thus lead to considerable unreliability. Familiarity with the agency is probably the sine qua non for the recording, of such errors.

3. The data may not be recorded in a categorical and quantifiable form and thus may leave the investigator to categorize and quantify on some presumptive criterion. Such information would have doubtful validity if it is used as an outcome measure by itself, but it could be helpful if used in conjunction with other outcome criteria. On the other hand, if the data are already categorized, the clinician-researcher should not assume that his/her definition of the category is the same.

4. The use of records as a source of data restricts content analysis. That is, only those activities that have been recorded can be functionally analyzed, essentially eliminating characteristics such as "feeling" content or "nonverbal" content in interviews. Furthermore, restricting oneself to such predetermined areas of measurement literally limits the specificity with which a given target problem can be measured.

Recorded data, then, may have inherent errors that makes them a weak comparison base when employed alone. If recorded data are to be employed, the clinician-researcher must determine the degree of consistency attained in the data collection. Once this has been established, then they may be employed either as time-series or single-point measurements, depending on the index under consideration. For example, attendance can be viewed as time-series pre-during-post intervention measure, since such information is collected continuously. In contrast, an achievement test score may be used only in the single-point context. In general, recorded information is typically of Type A (instrument), although in some instances, Type B (multiple evaluators) information may be abstracted. Note, however, that abstraction increases the error even further.

Interviews Most clinician-researchers would agree that the interview process is the primary tool with which much of the information concerning the client's major problems, the client's expectations from treatment, and perhaps even the manner in which treatment should progress is derived. As such, the need for development of rapport with the client system via clinician-researcher honesty, genuineness, openness, and so forth, has been stressed by most authors (for example, Lazarus, 1971; Truax, 1966). Once the initial rapport has been developed, the interview process has been employed as the prime vehicle in assessment and evaluation. For example, Hollis (1966, p. 178) notes that "in diagnosis, the worker attempts to estimate the client's capacity . . . making this estimate in accordance with the answers provided to various questions." However, there still must be serious concern with regard to accuracy of judgment, reliability, and validity. We feel that the interview's potential for generating unbiased measurable data is limited. Its strength lies in its use as a tool for the generation of nonempirical information, such as the initial specification of the problems and goals.

A few researchers have specified within-interview techniques for objectifying the interview process, and strategies for collecting objective data (Thomas, 1973). These attempts have ranged from therapist/client evaluations of the target problem to Lazarus's (1971) "Desert Island Fantasy," which he terms a "structured projective technique that rapidly yields important behavioral data" (p. 66). Other researchers have broken down interviews to representative time samples in an attempt to analyze their content (Carter and Levy,

1972), and these process variables have in turn been employed as another datum of outcome estimation (Stuart et al., 1972). Many of these procedures are, however, relatively sophisticated and time consuming, and thus their pragmatic value to the clinician-researcher is minimized.

The interview, whether conducted with the client and/or with salient others in the action system, is subject to certain biases, and the clinician-researcher should be well acquainted with problem characteristics in using it as a source of data.

Strengths

1. In-depth interviewing can provide information that may have been too subtle to have surfaced in any other form of measurement. Probing techniques could divulge information not accessible to other types of assessment procedures. For example, latent homosexuality may emerge as a central problem in a marital therapy situation where sexual dissatisfaction has been the presenting problem.

2. One interview can possibly accomplish the work of several paper-and-pencil questionnaires. Interviews are flexible, and, depending on the expertise of the interviewer, much valuable data could be obtained in this manner. For example, a questionnaire typically taps only one area of functioning, such as self-esteem. In an interview, not only the lack of self-esteem but also related items such as isolation and anxiety may emerge as clinical indicators.

3. Interviews would permit the collection of accurate and complete data from the illiterate and the less educated. This is a critical point in that illiteracy would virtually eliminate paper-and-pencil tests. For example, a client of less than eighth-grade education may have excellent verbal communication skills but be unable to read the paper-and-pencil test.

4. The clinician-researcher has an opportunity to observe the client and the total situation to which he/she is responding. This could prove to be particularly informative, especially since the context of the interview may range from home to office to institution. Thus, the interview per se becomes of secondary importance to the physical environment. For example, an abusing parent's tangential relations with his/her child during a purely nonthreatening visit may reveal a plethora of behavioral data for initial assessment.

Weaknesses

1. Many of the specific assessment aids, such as the Lazarus (1971) techniques, are somewhat therapist specific and have very little potential wide-range utility. That is, their application may vary from one therapist to another or they may be unique to the style of a given therapist.

2. Various clinician-researcher/interviewer characteristics—such as interviewing skills, personality, and demographic characteristics—could all play a significant role in the assessments' leading to biased results. Thus, the skill of the clinician-researcher may become the critical variable.

3. Subjective interpretations and misinterpretations of client responses by the clinician-researcher could provide a singular important bias in the assessment. Thus, the clinician-researcher may probe certain areas and skip others, depending on perceived importance rather than on objective criteria.

4. Role selection and response set (such as socially desirable responses or compliance) could show up as further sources of error. Interview methods would, however, provide a better opportunity to "cloak" experimentality and fulfill the traditional expectations regarding a therapy situation than that offered by paper-and-pencil tests.

5. As a result of being interviewed, the client may in fact change in the very attribute that is the focus of attention. While a neutral nonadvice-giving method would theoretically minimize bias, this possibility still remains as a plausible artifact and could detract from the objectivity of measurement.

Interviews can generate a broad spectrum of information on problems and desired goals. They can serve as the vehicle to elaborate on measurement and to gather additional information regarding the specific characteristic that was measured by other measurement tools, such as a questionnaire. We do not, however, recommend them as a primary form of empirical data collection, since they are highly subjective and susceptible to numerous errors. We feel that data collection would be enhanced if one institutes additional measures during the intervention rather than relying on this verbal method alone.

✓**Paper-and-Pencil Tests** Questionnaires of one form or another constitute the most widely used evaluative technique. Information derived from various tests of intelligence, behavior checklists, fear schedules, personality inventories, and so on, fall into this general category and quite often are extremely valuable evaluative tools. Many of the measurement devices used in treatment outcome research are nationally standardized measures, such as the Minnesota Multiphasic Personality Inventory (MMPI). Owing to the national standardization procedures, such tests would have a relatively high degree of reliability and validity. Clinician-researchers using standardized instruments should be careful to employ tests that are relevant and that in fact measure the very attribute they consider to be of central importance. The use of standardized measures also necessitates decisions on the focal-global dimension, since many standardized tests provide only global information. Many clinician-researchers use instruments that are "mostly simple, homemade . . . and there is no obvious evidence that one is superior to another" (Strupp and Bergin 1972, p. 58). Some of these so-called homemade instruments appear to be gaining some acceptance among clinician-researchers, such as the Fear Survey Schedule (Wolpe and Lang, 1964) and Cautela and Kastenbaum's (1967) Reinforcement Survey Schedule. Other scale types are being individually modified and widely used. Mash and Terdal (1976) provide a variety of these instruments. Two such scales are presented in Figure 3.7 and 3.8. The most appealing element in these scales is that they refer to relational aspects in a given treatment situation in a quantifiable manner. They are evaluating, not psychological abstracts such as self-concept or self-worth, but rather existing intrafamilial relations. In essence, the clinician-researcher is obtaining basically the same information one would gather in an interview, but the paper-and-pencil procedure allows independence—in that the husband and wife answer the same questions separately and without influencing each other's response. The Likert-Scale (almost always—almost never) allows for minimal quantification; unlike the interview process, clinician-researcher bias will not intrude into the couple's responses.

Paper-and-pencil measures are frequently administered to all the salient members in the action system. Stuart et al. (1972), working

Name of Child: _____ Date: _____

Respondent: _____ Mother _____ Father
1. How often do you and your spouse agree on how to reward your child?
   1 – Almost always agree
   2 – Often agree
   3 – Sometimes agree
   4 – Seldom agree
   5 – Almost never agree
2. How often do you and your spouse agree on how to punish your child?
   1 – Almost always agree
   2 – Often agree
   3 – Sometimes agree
   4 – Seldom agree
   5 – Almost never agree
3. How satisfied are you with your marriage?
   1 – Very satisfied
   2 – Satisfied
   3 – Average
   4 – Dissatisfied
   5 – Very dissatisfied
4. Compared to what you think a marriage should be like, do you believe that your marriage is?
   1 – Much better than you expected
   2 – Better than you expected
   3 – What you expected
   4 – Less than you expected
   5 – Much less than you expected
5. How satisfied are you with the way you and your spouse make decisions?
   1 – Very satisfied
   2 – Satisfied
   3 – Average
   4 – Dissatisfied
   5 – Very dissatisfied

From Richard B. Stuart and Tony Tripodi (1972). Used by permission of Richard B. Stuart.

Figure 3.7 Parent evaluation form (two-parent family).

with adolescents, administered questionnaires to the adolescent client, his or her parents, teachers, and counselors. The client provided a self-report on his or her performance, while the others provided a sort of perceived behavior report. In all cases, however, the evaluations are subjective evaluations of perceived client behavior and attitudes. Thus, it appears that, regardless of who does the eva-

How Often Do Your Parents Do Each of the Following Things?	Almost Always	Often	Sometimes	Seldom	Almost Never
1. Completely ignore you after you've done something wrong	1	2	3	4	5
2. Act as if they don't care about you any more	1	2	3	4	5
3. Listen to your side of the argument	1	2	3	4	5
4. Disagree with each other when it comes to raising you	1	2	3	4	5
5. Actually slap you	1	2	3	4	5
6. Take away your privileges (TV, movies, dates)	1	2	3	4	5
7. Talk over important decisions with you	1	2	3	4	5
8. Blame you or criticize you when you don't deserve it	1	2	3	4	5
9. Threaten to slap you	1	2	3	4	5
10. Yell, shout, or scream at you	1	2	3	4	5
11. Disagree about punishing you	1	2	3	4	5
12. Act fair and reasonable in what they ask of you	1	2	3	4	5
13. Nag at you	1	2	3	4	5

From Richard B. Stuart and Tony Tripodi (1972). Used by permission of Richard B. Stuart.

Figure 3.8 Client evaluation form.

luating, some sources of error are bound to enter the picture in some manner. The essential strength of the paper-and-pencil tests over interviews lies in the uniformity of application and in their quantifiability.

Strengths

1. A number of adequately standardized tests covering a wide range of target problems are available, allowing the clinician-researcher an opportunity to select an appropriate test for his or her specific purpose.

2. Despite the probability of subjective biases, some studies seem to indicate that self-report data are reliable and not significantly affected by prejudicial judgment (Jayaratne et al., 1974; Mischel, 1968). If the clinician-researcher employs multifactorial methods, this would increase the reliability and validity even further.

3. A questionnaire can be constructed so that the data are easily coded, and thus data quantification procedures and analysis can be facilitated.

Since the questionnaires usually provide a score on some scale (such as self-esteem), little data manipulation is necessary on the part of the clinician-researcher. Only the absolute scores need to be compared.

4. Questionnaires are usually less expensive and easier to administer and can be administered to several subjects simultaneously—in direct contrast to interviews. This capability allows for independent, unbiased responses from all participants. Obviously, this would have particular value in families and group situations.

5. The uniformity of administration and standardized instructions makes questionnaire response situations somewhat more uniform than similar data collected by interview. This adds objectivity to the data collection process, and the findings can be viewed as having higher validity.

Weaknesses

1. The respondents may misunderstand questions and answer accordingly—a particularly relevant problem where respondents are illiterate or have little education.

2. Role selection, response set, and reactive effects would play a strong role here, since the administration situation remains static. That is, the clinician-researcher is guided by the institutional and administrative guidelines provided by the standardization. These may be inappropriate in a given situation, but failure to follow the procedure may make the whole test invalid.

3. As a result of being tested, the client may in fact change in the very attribute being measured. Thus the posttest measures not only the effect of intervention but also the effect of the pretest. For example, a husband may realize that he has been paying little attention to his wife after answering a questionnaire on marital happiness, and this realization may change his behavior.

4. Test-retest problems (such as remembering answers to specific questions) may begin to appear unless sufficient time has elapsed between the two test periods. This can, however, be overcome by using "parallel" tests or alternate forms of the same test.

5. If tests of the "homemade" variety are used, then reliability and validity are questionable unless appropriate pretests have been conducted.

We have used the terms *questionnaire* and *paper-and-pencil* tests rather loosely here, implying merely the presence of a written question and response. The questionnaire in this context is comparable to a scale or index measuring a specific behavioral or personality attribute. Such an index usually provides a "score" (a numerical quantity) that can then be compared with another score obtained at a different time or in the event of a standardized instrument, compared to its normative population. The questionnaire is often useful only as a single-point measurement device and should be administered only before and after intervention, and where possible, at followup. As discussed earlier, the validity of some data obtained by tests is weakened with repeated test administration. Unfortunately, as with all single-point measures, the clinician-researcher must be concerned with the representativeness of the information. Care should be taken in interpreting these data. Under these situations, normative comparisons are useful and may be more valuable than a simple comparison of before–after scores—hence, the stress on using standardized measures. Furthermore, when employed only for single-point measures, the questionnaire provides little information for day-to-day questions that may arise during treatment. In this sense it may not provide the feedback advantages of multiple-point measures. Its value is further delimited when a change in a score is questioned by virtue of how much increase is enough to indicate success. (This issue is discussed in a later chapter.)

Observational Data   Observational data, which are primarily directed toward describing and understanding behavior as it occurs, have been widely used in investigations of treatment. Where observation is objective and nonobtrusive, the information obtained is of high value and credibility. As Tharp and Wetzel (1969, p. 66) indicate, "accurate description is the most powerful tool for social problem amelioration."

In discussing observational processes, we must again consider the question of who: (a) participant observer—where the clinician-researcher actively participates in the ongoing program while simultaneously observing and recording what is going on (for example, this could be the clinician-researcher in a family interview situation, recording the nature of the ongoing interaction according to some prescribed format); (b) the "potted plant" observer—where a nonparticipant observer sits in on a given situation (for example, a cothera-pist who sits in on interviews but says nothing). Note that the partici-pant observer and potted plant observer are highly visible, hence obtrusive. That is, while they may be collecting relatively objective data on what is going on, their sheer presence may have actually changed the behaviors being observed (White, 1977). This type of information is, however, more objective than any of the aforemen-tioned information gathered by the previous procedures. There is some evidence, in fact, that the presence of an observer may have little impact (Johnson and Bolstad, 1975).

The following two procedures are relatively unobtrusive: (c) one-way mirror—where activities in a treatment session are observed by the clinician-researcher's collaborators without the clients' aware-ness (this is, however, a unique situation not commonly available and has some ethical implications); the use of videotapes and au-diotapes could be considered within this realm; (d) natural ob-server—although the observer in these situations does not necessar-ily participate, he or she blends into the natural environment in which the observations are being made, so that his/her presence is minimally disruptive (this is perhaps the most potent form of behav-ioral observation); for example, attendants in hospital wards, teachers in classrooms, and family members are minimally notice-able in their respective environments; and finally (e) self-observa-tion—this is perhaps the ultimate in obtrusiveness in that the client is observing his/her own behaviors. Such a procedure can be reactive (that is, the process of measurement may in and of itself bring about change). Furthermore, as a measurement technique, "it is unclear why self-observation alters behavior in some situations but not in others" (Kazdin, 1975, p. 199). Therefore, the use of self-observation as a measurement alternative has drawbacks. However, the process of self-observation itself may be deployed as an agent of change (see Thoresen and Mahoney 1974).

All of these direct observational techniques involve differing de-grees of obtrusiveness. Generally, the less obtrusive the method, the more likely that the data will be valid, provided the observers are well trained. Whereas videotapes and audiotapes have provided an alternate technique for observing and recording, they are less than comprehensive in coverage (for example, audiotapes do not pick up nonverbals) and more liable to interpretation error. Furthermore, these instruments may not be available to the average clinician.

Several types of observational methods are typically used: frequency, duration, magnitude, and interval records being the most common.

1. Frequency is simply a tally of the number of times the target problem and/or goal occurred within a given period of time. For example, in a marital therapy situation, one may ask the two spouses to keep track of the number of times each "put down" the other for a 2-hour period after dinner. Similarly, a simple count of the number of days a child is absent from school per week gives an indication of the frequency of absence. Such a measure would be useful where the object is to increase or decrease the rate of occurrence of the behavior.

2. Duration is the time period during which the target problem and/or goal occurred. Whereas frequency refers to the number of times a given event occurred during a specified period of time, duration refers to the actual time elapsed during the occurrence of this event. Obviously, such a measure would be useful where the goal is to increase or decrease the length of time a given activity is being exhibited. For example, a bright sixth grader may have a tough time attending in class for more than 5 minutes at a time. In this instance, one may devise a plan to increase the attention span gradually to 15 minutes, to 25 minutes, and so on until the desired duration is reached.

3. Magnitude is the size or volume of the target problem and/or goal. Like frequency, this measurement can be a rate and have a time frame attached to it. For example, in working with alcoholics, clinician-researchers may be interested in monitoring the drinking behavior of a client. One way to do this would be to keep track of the amount (volume) of alcohol consumed by the individual during a given period of time. Similarly, one may encounter a family with a teenager, where one of the target problems is the high volume of the music. By keeping track of the number on the volume control dial, the parents can monitor whether or not their teenager is playing the music too loud. In this instance we are concerned with the absolute volume of music, and the time frame is not considered.

4. Interval records refer to the occurrence or nonoccurrence of a target problem and/or goal within a specified period of time. This measurement alternative is different from frequency in the following manner. Consider "interruptive behavior" in a given family treatment session. In a frequency count, the observer may tally the number of times the family members interrupted each other during a 30-minute session. In contrast, in interval recording, the session may be broken into 5-minute blocks of time, and the observer would simply record whether or not interruptive behavior was observed during each of these periods. Even if several interruptions occurred during a given five minute period, it is still recorded as one interruption. Because of this time interval aspect, this is perhaps the easiest method of recording.*

These different procedures can be used in conjunction with each other if necessary. The most simple and commonly used procedures are the measures of interval recording, frequency, and duration. Regardless of the observational method chosen, the critical point is that it must be able to show change.

These observational procedures can be employed in virtually all clinical environments. They can be used in "artificial" situations such as role plays and interviews or in "natural" environments such as homes and institutions. Regardless of the alternative chosen, the clinican-researcher should bear in mind that, if observational data are to be reliable and valid, certain minimal criteria must be met: the target problem and goals must be defined in specific, concrete, unique, and nonoverlapping terms. A goal for data collection procedures is for two separate individuals to be able to identify the occurrence of the problems and goals when they occur, from the description provided, over a period of time. In other words, the clinician-researcher should strive for the data to be highly reliable.†

This, then, leads us to what have been termed "behavioral rating

---

*However, the reader is cautioned that data obtained from interval records will vary, depending on the method of interval recording used. For a further discussion of this, see Powell et al. (1977).

†There are a number of different ways to compute reliability between observers. The interested reader is referred to Kent et al. (1977), Nelson et al. (1978) and a series of invited articles on reliability in the *Journal of Applied Behavior Analysis* (1977): p. 97–150.

scales" and "behavioral codes." These, in essence, are the units of analysis that are fed into the frequency, duration, magnitude, and interval recording procedures. The rating scales and codes can either be highly complex and sophisticated or relatively easy. Several examples are presented here to sensitize the reader to the degree of specificity desired in such operations. Table 3.1 illustrates a behavioral rating scale for fighting developed by Finch et al. (1974). These authors report high reliability (between observers) with these rating scales, and in general, they are easier to administer than the observational codes described in Table 3.2, which presents a subset of a series of classroom behavior codes developed by Cobb and Ray (1976). Table 3.3 illustrates a coding device employed by Linsk et al. (1975) to facilitate verbal interaction in a home for the aged.

Strengths

1. Direct observation allows for the direct assessment of a specific behavior, such as the frequency of occurrence of a target problem. A classroom teacher keeping track of the number of times a given student left his seat without permission is an example of direct observation.

Table 3.1. INDIVIDUALLY TAILORED BEHAVIORAL RATING SCALE FOR "FIGHTING"

Rating	*Content*
1. *Physical aggression:*	Hitting, kicking, spitting on, urinating on, pushing, or biting other people or destroying property. This is the predominant behavior displayed by Juan.
2. *Aggressive threats and gestures:*	Threatening to hit or physically attack somebody; daring others to fight, either verbally or by "staring down"; encouraging other people to fight. There may be some physical aggression, but the threats and gestures must outnumber the physical aggression by approximately 3 to 1.
3. *Aggressive threats and gestures along with some friendly behavior:*	These must occur about equally. Friendly behavior means cooperative play, smiling and laughing with others, pleasant conversation with others, cooperation with staff and peers. There may be no more than two physically aggressive interactions.
4. *Friendly behavior:*	Here friendly behavior outnumbers threats and gestures by approximately 3 to 1. There is no physical aggression.
5. *Initiating friendly behavior:*	Here Juan initiates at least half of the friendly interactions that occur. Again no physical aggression, but some threat gesture (no more than two) is allowed.

From Finch, A., P. Deadorff, and L. Montgomery (1974). Used by permission of Plenum Publishing Corp.

Table 3.2. THE CLASSROOM BEHAVIOR OBSERVATION CODE

NY Noisy.	This category is to be used when the person talks loudly, yells, bangs books, scrapes chairs, or makes any sounds that are likely to be actually or potentially disruptive to others.
NC Noncompliance.	To be coded whenever the person does not do what is requested. This includes teacher giving instructions to entire class and the subject does not comply.
PL Play.	Coded whenever person is playing along or with another person and the classroom rules do not allow playing, e.g., playing tic-tac-toe in class, throwing a ball in classroom.
TT Inappropriate talk with teacher.	Used whenever content of conversation is negative toward teacher by pupil or when classroom rules do not allow interaction with teacher. Examples are, "I'm tired of this lesson," "I won't go to the principal's office."
IP Inappropriate interaction with peer.	Coded whenever peer or pupil interacts with or attempts to interact with each other, and classroom rules are being violated. Examples include behaviors and/or responses such as touching a peer to get his attention, calling peer by name, talking to peer, looking at peer when the student should be working.

From Cobb, J. A., and R. S. Ray (1976).

2. If conducted in an unobtrusive manner, it is susceptible to less subject bias and reactivity due to subject ignorance. For example, in the situation just described, the disruptive student may be completely unaware that the teacher is keeping track of his behavior.

3. Direct contrast of behaviors before, during, and after treatment is simple. Predictions via time-series analysis (to be discussed later) would yield data that pertain directly to the ongoing clinical process.

4. Observational methods are particularly useful when verbal responses are irrelevant, unnecessary, or inappropriate. For example, in observing aggressive behavior, all that may be needed is a simple frequency of occurrence. Similarly observation of infant behavior would be much more profound than infantile verbalizations.

5. Observations are independent of the client's willingness to report. Biases such as role selection are, therefore nullified where the observational method is nonobtrusive.

Table 3.3. CODING DEVICE TO FACILITATE VERBAL INTERACTION

Social Group Worker Behaviors		
Behavior	Recording Symbols	Definition
Questions	G, I	A verbal behavior that demands or suggests a response from one or more group members, indicated by words that suggest a question (i.e., why, how) or a direct request or demand for a response
Statements	G, I	A verbal behavior that gives information and does not call for a response from group members and is not a direct consequence of a previous behavior of individual or group of residents. Includes reading to residents.
Positive comments	G, I	Verbal behavior that followed the behavior of one or more group members and relates to this behavior to encourage similar responses. Suggests recognition, approval, or praise.
Negative comments	G, I	Verbal behavior that followed the behavior of one or more group members and relates to this behavior to discourage similar responses. Suggests disapproval or displeasure.
Listening		Silence on the part of the worker either while a group member verbalizes or while waiting for resident response in the absence of other worker behavior.
Demonstration/participation		Demonstrating equipment or activity or participating in activity.
Attending to		Watching, listening to, or talking to a stimulus outside of the activity.

Note: Questions, statements, and comments were judged in regard to whether the behavior was directed to an individual (*I*) or to the group (*G*).
From N. Linsk et al. (1975).

Weaknesses

1. Observers must be well trained. If more than one observer is used, reliability among them must be established and an effort must be made to maintain this reliability over time.

2. If the observational method is at all obtrusive, reactivity (client responding to the measurement process) may occur, and the validity of the data becomes questionable (Jayaratne et al., 1974; Patterson, 1971).

3. The behavior being observed must occur frequently enough to warrant observation. Otherwise the data may be too limited for analysis, making

trend data uninterpretable, and the time/cost factor for extended observations may become overwhelming.

4. The use of significant others in the observation process is a sensitive proposition. But if they are willing participants with the knowledge of the client, then the clinician-researcher may lose some validity but gain reliability.

5. The usefulness of the data depends on the nature of the category system (behavioral specification) used. Care should be taken in determining the clarity of definitions.

Given the specificity and concreteness required in the definition of observation, these data are undoubtedly more objective and accurate representations than any of the previous systems of data. As such, they could attain a higher degree of reliability and validity. They are amenable to Types A, B, or C multifactorial measurement strategies.

There are, however, many problems with observational data. As Gelfand and Hartmann (1968, p. 211) note, "Extreme care must be taken to assure that truly objective behavior observations and measures are used." Such factors as the "Rosenthal effect" could play a decidedly crucial role. The observations of some evaluators and mediators in the environment may be affected by their changing expectations of improvement as a person progresses through treatment (Rosenthal, 1966). Numerous other studies have pointed to the effects of subject awareness and observer expectations (Campbell and Stanley, 1963; O'Leary and Kent, 1973; and Skindrud, 1973). Reid (1970) found that there appears to be an exaggerated superior performance of observer reliability with the overt measurement conditions, which rapidly deteriorate immediately after measurement. This implies a need for continuous calibration. One way the problems encountered can be minimized is by having a number of different agents in different settings (Type C), with minimal personal contact. Family members, school personnel, employers, colleagues, friends, and neighbors have all been used as effective evaluators. Obviously, the use of multiple observers requires a considerable degree of resourcefulness on the part of the clinician-researcher. Particularly with multiple observers, target problems should be highly specified and stated simply and objectively. Even so, the clinician-researcher must consider the sources of error in the interpretation of the data. By striving for empiricism, however, greater objectivity in evaluative criteria may result, and thus the bias component can be minimized.

Observational data have typically been collected in time-series measures, but it is conceivable that they could be obtained from a single-point measure as well. For example, the totality of the clinician-researcher's preintervention data may come from the observation of a family decision-making exercise conducted during a given interview. The clinician-researcher may have noted that the family does not consider alternatives but merely agrees with the husband. One's intervention strategy may be to teach the family to consider alternatives and democratize the decision-making process. One may intervene by providing the family with decision-making exercises and collecting multiple-point data throughout the treatment process. In this situation observational data provide primary feedback on the day-to-day progress of the client system and thus allow the clinician-researcher to make data-based decisions regarding the intervention process. On the other hand, one has only the data collected in one interview as a comparison base.

Physiological and Electromechanical Measures Physiological measures have had limited use in treatment programs, the major issues being problem specification in physiological terms, the availability of appropriate instruments, the cost factor, and the general rejection of "gadgetry" by the clinical profession. Nonetheless, some creative and productive methods have been developed by clinicians. For example, the SAM system (Signal System for the Assessment of Behavior) of Thomas et al (1970) and Lang's (1969) DAD (Device for Automated Desensitization) are two of the more sophisticated devices—though perhaps impractical in terms of cost—that have been used experimentally in treatment situations. Stuart (1970) effectively incorporated light cues as an assessment aid in interaction analysis in marital treatment.

In general, whereas researchers have been extremely ingenious in their search for more sophisticated measurement devices, the practical utility of such devices has been limited. It is difficult to predict the future of electromechanical and physiological instrumentation in the treatment arena, especially in view of the tremendously complex picture presented by treatment, although there is increasing application of biofeedback instruments. Although these data presumably provide unbiased and objective estimations, the pragmatics of the situation are such that day-to-day feasibility in normal treatment settings is currently impractical.

Strengths
1. Electromechanical indicators are presumably beyond the control of the subject. For example, an individual simply cannot control the dilation and contraction of his pupils in a given situation. Response bias is, therefore, virtually eliminated.
2. Therapist bias is minimized, since the machine is presumably more objective in its judgments. Consider Lang's DAD: The machine detects anxiety via bioelectrical channels in addition to recording the client's responses to automated inquiries by the machine—in essence removing the therapist variability from the picture.
3. Where knowledge exists, electronic tapping of physiological data would provide much more accurate and standardized data in the long run than any of the other approaches discussed.

Weaknesses:
1. Clients may be unwilling and/or fearful of gadgetry—or having electrodes stuck on them or being confronted with obviously experimental devices—devices they do not conceive of as having any relevance to treatment.
2. Instrumentation error via machine malfunction remains a distinct possibility.
3. As already indicated, cost becomes an overriding concern with many of the more sophisticated devices.
4. Generality of a technology dependent on sophisticated instrumentation is a severe handicap. This may require additional training in electronics and computer programming and, failing this, the hiring of a consultant—an added cost burden.
5. Most clients expect personal interaction with their therapist, with little intervening wiring and instrumentation. In other words, the client may

view this as yet another imposition of the computer age, and thus a negative perception of the therapy situation may be created.

By and large, electromechanical measurement is too sophisticated and expensive to be employed in other than experimental situations. While these are perhaps the most objective measurements available, they are also the most impractical. These were presented here to sensitize the reader to the highest order of feasible measurement currently available in the clinical arena.

3.3 Conclusion

In this chapter we have addressed four interrelated issues regarding the choice of a measurement method to determine the effect of intervention: what, when, who, and with what. We have recommended that, whenever possible, the measurements be more, rather than less, concrete and observable. We also recommended that measures be taken at a number of points in time during each treatment phase (including pretreatment). We recognize, however, that both these goals may not always be possible and encourage as much approximation to them as circumstances permit.

We have addressed a number of choices clinician-researchers must make concerning the degree to which their measures will be relevant, sensitive, obtrusive, and global (Figure 3.7). Whereas the answers to these questions must ultimately be a matter of the clinician-researcher's individual choice, we have suggested that a measurement strategy employing a number of measurement methods (multifactorial) would allow the broadest base of information to be obtained along these dimensions. Such a procedure would increase the reliability that can be attributed to causal statements.

Chapter Four

THE THIRD STAGE: BEGINNING MEASURE-
MENTS—ISSUES OF VALIDITY AND
BASELINE PROCEDURES

IN THE FIRST stage the reader was led through the first six steps that together form the preliminary assessment procedures in the clinical research model. The clinician-researcher has now identified the target problems and desired goals. In the second stage the clinician-researcher selected appropriate measures and measurement strategies. In the third stage the emphasis is on putting the selected procedures into operation. Before measurement can begin, however, the clinician-researcher should pay particular attention to the notions of causality and make decisions in a manner that would maximize the probability of establishing causal attribution. To understand the notions of causality discussed earlier, the reader should clearly understand what is meant by "validity" and threats to validity.

The concept of validity, as common as it may be, is difficult to discuss. The major reason for this arises from the different types of validity discussed in the literature—such as face validity, concurrent validity, convergent validity, and others. In this discussion we use the simplest definition that would accomplish our purpose—the discussion of those factors that would interfere with the accurate assessment of treatment effect. As we said in chapter 3:

> Validity refers to the extent of correspondence between the measurement of a variable and the intended meaning of that variable. In other words, a valid measurement device is one which measures what we think it is supposed to measure (Tripodi, 1974, p. 40).

In our discussion of the clinical research model we are particularly concerned with those threats to validity that can be brought about by the specific design being employed and by the nature of the environment of the clinical situation.* While we may in fact have highly valid measures (in that they measure what they are supposed to measure), if they are employed in a manner that interferes with their predictive capability, we have effectively nullified their value. We consider these latter characteristics or phenomena under the general rubric of validity, specifically the topic of "internal validity." (The issues of "external validity" are dealt with in chapter 10.)

4.1 Internal Validity

Campbell and Stanley (1963) argue that internal validity is the bare minimum without which any experimental manipulation becomes uninterpretable. "Did in fact the experimental treatments make a difference in this specific experimental instance" (p. 5). Within the clinical research model the question is whether or not the change produced was caused by treatment. To the extent that alternative explanations can be offered as evidence of possibly contributing to and/or causing change, the internal validity of the study under consideration is weakened.

If change is attributed to a treatment when in fact something else caused the change, an error has occurred. To discuss these errors, we have categorized their sources into three domains or "classes of variables." The domains to be used are *therapist, client,* and *task,* and they have been identified by several methodologists as being the most significant ones (Kiesler, 1966; Paul, 1969; Underwood, 1957).

1. The therapist domain consists of those personal characteristics and activities of the clinician that may cause confounding within themselves and/or with other domains.

2. The client domain consists of those client characteristics and activities that may cause confounding within themselves and/or other domains.

3. The task domain consists of those mechanistic and procedural characteristics and activities that may cause confounding within themselves and/or other domains.

* For an excellent discussion on reliability and validity in behavioral assessment, the interested reader is referred to Cone (1977).

The categorization within each domain is not exhaustive, but an attempt has been made to consider the most significant error components relevant to the clinical research model.

All the variables mentioned within each domain are susceptible to confounding within or between domains. Obviously, no one situation or design is capable of controlling for all the variability, but some situations and designs are more proficient than others. It is up to the individual clinician to minimize the confounding given his or her particular clinical circumstance. In general, every clinician-researcher should be well acquainted with these threats, since as explained earlier, the failure to maximize control over the clinical situations (and hence the errors) will weaken the clinician-researcher's ability to determine the effect of the intervention. Since maximum control is often impossible to achieve, the clinician must be doubly sensitive to the "unknowns" and temper clinical pronunciations accordingly (Jayaratne, 1977).

Much of the discussion that follows is based on the work of Campbell and Stanley (1963), Goldstein et al. (1966), and Carter (1975).

The Therapist Domain

Therapist characteristics. These are the personal chraacteristics of the clinician that may have an impact on the process of treatment. For example, the use of titles such "Dr." or "psychologist" or "social worker" may have an unknown but possibly differential impact. In other situations, appearance and age may make a difference. For example, the "straight," white, middle-class, middle-aged person may have a difficult time getting cooperation from a black ghetto teenager.

Therapist experience. This particular variable may be of greater importance in the more complex design alternatives than in the simpler designs. For example, with multimodal therapies, which may be used in some designs, the ability to implement and partialize them into their respective components may take greater skill—skill that may be acquired by experience. Thus the existence of skill per se, as related to experience, may be a relevant issue in interpreting the impact of intervention.

The Client Domain

Client characteristics. Just as the therapists' personal characteristics may affect the process of intervention, so too can the personal characteristics of the client system. Most of the same differences noted earlier (such as age or race) can become factors here.

Client motivation and commitment. The extent to which the client is willing to participate in the treatment program may in many ways determine the nature of the data collected. This would be particularly true where the data are obtrusive, such as with paper-and-pencil tests, and it may elicit response bias—that is, the client's answering the way he or she thinks the therapist wants the question answered instead of giving a true personal response.

Concurrent history. This poses one of the most serious threats to internal validity, especially in situations of open service, where the client system is constantly in contact with the "natural environment" and influenced, therefore, by activities that occur there. Many things that happen in the natural environment may influence the target problem and thus minimize the possibility of establishing a direct relationship between treatment per se and change. For example, working with a depressed woman, one may find a sudden change in her affect two months after intervention. While this may be partly related to the efforts of the clinician, it may also have been brought about by the fact that she moved out of her mother's house!

Physical changes. Changes can be brought about in treatment purely as a function of physical change or maturational factors within the client—elements that are completely beyond the control of the clinician. For example, a revitalized alcoholic no longer feels tired and rundown since he quit drinking. His reported affect change may have occurred simply as a function of physical changes related to reduced drinking rather than to alcohol counseling.

The Task Domain

Treatment environment. There is evidence suggesting that changes in the treatment environment could result in formative change in measurement and thus act as an intervening variable. Factors such as whether the treatment was conducted at home or office, whether others were involved in treatment, and whether the treatment environments were changed (from home to office, for example) could play a significant role in the interpretation of the results.

Multiple treatment effects. This particular variable becomes important only when multimodal therapies are being used, and the clinician is interested in determining the effectiveness of the components. To the extent that the treatment packages or strategies are interrelated, the more unlikely it is that partialization can take place, thus, creating numerous unidentified interactions.

Assessment variability. The multifactorial measurement strategies often require the use of several evaluators from the client environment. Depending on their commitment to the process of treatment, their feelings about the client, and so on, some degree of variability may enter the picture. For example, a teacher was reported to have rated the academic performance of a child as "poor" because she disliked his classroom behavior. In this instance the assessor's personal biases interfered with objective judgment.

Change produced by measurement. This is the oft-quoted notion that the process of measurement may in and of itself bring about change. For example, as will be noted later, knowledge of being observed may by itself change the behavior. In general, nonobtrusive data collection should minimize its impact—the more obvious the measurement, the greater the possibility of a reactive arrangement.

Instrumentation error. This is a particularly relevant factor in working with paper-and-pencil tests. These tests may contain certain words or other biasing elements that may interfere with the client's (or other assessors') ability and/or willingness to provide accurate information. For example, many self-esteem measures contain items that can be perceived as "self-deprecatory" or "socially undesirable." These clients may then answer these questions "inaccurately" to present themselves to their therapists as "being all right" or "normal."

Change in measurement procedure. This is a highly confounding variable, referring to situations where the clinician-researcher may change the situational context or the actual measurement method during the treatment or prior to treatment. At times, such changes are imposed by uncontrollable factors. Where this occurs, the validity of the entire measurement process is highly questionable.

Instability of data patterns. This is primarily a statistical threat and is discussed later under baseline procedures. It refers to the extent to which the data gathered during baseline or pretreatment show instability (variation in pattern). The greater the variability, the harder it would be to establish the impact of intervention.

Data trend during baseline. Another statistical threat referred to later, this signals the notion that it is important to find out whether or not the baseline data show a distinct directional trend. For example, a decreasing trend leading to a further reduction during the treatment of the same target problem poses some questions as far as determining the impact of treatment. Would the target problem have continued its downward trend whether or not intervention took place?

Regression effects. This is another statistical threat that has major measurement implications. Since most individuals seek help when they are unusually troubled, it is possible that their scores on tests and/or observed behaviors may represent an abnormally high or low level, even for the troubled state. Such a value may be an artifact of the time at which measurement occurred rather than an accurate assessment of individual functioning. Multiple-point measurement would minimize these errors, providing a representative sample of the client's behavior rather than a single extreme example.

If one examines these threats to internal validity, a distinct pattern emerges. The clinician-researcher often has little control over those variables that fall into the therapist and client domains. They are, in a sense, given, and all explanations of treatment effectiveness must consider these factors as possible explanatory variables. In contrast, the variables in the task domain are more under the control of the clinician. The control can be obtained either by the direct action of the clinician-researcher or by selection of an appropriate design. Perhaps the three variables over which the clinician has least control would be assessment variability, change produced by measurement, and instrumentation error. Even here, however, careful preintervention assessment of the client situation and measurement alternatives could minimize these errors. To a great extent then, the implementation of an internally valid clinical research design is very much in the hands of the individual clinician.

By this discussion we have attempted to show that there are many challenges to the drawing of causal inferences (Blalock, 1963;

Craighead et al., 1976). Given the potential errors, we can then ask the question: "Can the effect of clinical practice ever be clearly demonstrated?" The answer is that absolute demonstration is impossible given the currently available methodology. Certain actions do, however, allow for a stronger test of causality than others. Chapters 5 through 9 present a series of design alternatives that offer the reader a number of options for demonstrating effect. We recommend some options more strongly than others, on their strength in allowing for causal inferences. In this manner, we hope to provide the clinicians with the knowledge to make informed decisions within the constraints and preferences of their own clinical practice.

4.2 Putting the Measurement Plan into Operation

Assessment activities that occur before the beginning of intervention are usually called "baseline." Since all single-subject designs have a baseline period and since some pretreatment measurement is of critical importance in the clinical research model, we discuss baseline in this chapter. However, the assessment of client progress toward a goal necessitates continuous measurement during all stages of work with the client. What we say here about baseline assessment activities is, therefore, equally relevant to all activities of this type throughout the treatment program.

Simply stated, a baseline is a point of reference. "The primary purpose of baseline measurement is to have a standard by which the subsequent efficacy of an experimental intervention may be evaluated" (Hersen and Barlow, 1976, p. 74). The term *experimental intervention* merely indicates that we do not know for sure before intervention what the impact of intervention will be, and hence, intervention is always experimental. By the same token then, baseline measurements become critical in evaluating treatment effectiveness. The importance of "good" baseline procedures now become apparent. The empiricism and objectivity that go into baseline measurement then become the standard by which the effects of intervention are judged. The gathering of baseline data, then, becomes Step 7 in our framework for action begun in chapter 2.

Step 7: *Baseline of Target Problems and/or Goals*
Objective:
To obtain a preintervention measure of the specified problems
and/or goals. These should be carefully measured and quantitatively expressed whenever possible.
Rationale
Baseline information provides the clinician-researcher and client
system with a concrete, quantitative basis for judging the severity
of the problem. As a baseline, the data offer one important standard against which the success of the intervention may subsequently be assessed. At a more general level, baseline and the
monitoring of changes that follow intervention provide the clinician-researcher with essential feedback for determining the most
effective intervention techniques for specific problems.
Operation:
Usually, a prebaseline estimate of the problem has already been
obtained. This is generally in the form of a report by the client,
and where possible, by significant others.
The baseline measurement essentially tries to objectify the reported
judgment. The measures and procedures discussed in stage two
become the vehicle. The results of the baseline may disclose that
the identified problem does not merit intervention. If the problem
is found to be sufficiently intense to justify intervention, then subsequent steps are implemented. If it is not, a mutual agreement is
made to identify a different target problem if necessary, and this is
measured during the baseline period.
Example:
Several measures were selected as evaluative indices. To gather
baseline data on school behavior, the Pupil Behavior Inventory
(Vinter et al., 1966) is filled out by the teachers. Attendance data
are being gathered from the school registry. Measures of self-
esteem and parent/child relations are given to the child. All these data
are gathered before the beginning of intervention and will continue to
be collected during the intervention.

4.3 Baseline Issues

What follows is a systematic analysis of some issues and problems facing the clinician-researcher and possible modes of coping with them. Note that no definitive answers or pat decisions are available. The essence of the suggestions is to minimize the error that may otherwise occur.

1. When does one take the baseline measurement? Superficially, this question may appear to be a logical fallacy, in that, by definition, baseline is a measure that one takes *prior* to the implementation of intervention strategies. This poses, however, some practical and ethical questions to the clinician-researcher. In most agency settings the clinician is required to intervene as rapidly as possible, if not by law, certainly by agency policy. Under such situations how best can the clinician-researcher proceed with the task of collecting preintervention data?

For all practical purposes one has to have completed the steps represented by the two previous chapters: problems and goals must be specified and a measurement device and procedure selected. These choices could occur either during the first interview or after a number of interviews, depending on factors such as the ability to move within each client system, the severity of the problem, and the availability of significant others. Therefore, a practical time to begin baseline measurement is the period that elapses between the interview in which the target behavior and goal specification occurred and the time when intervention begins (often the next appointment).

2. For how long does one measure? McNamara and MacDonough (1972, p. 364) posed the following question: "How long is long enough for a baseline?" This question still remains unanswered, despite an excellent critical analysis of baseline variations by Hersen and Barlow (1976). The lack of an obvious answer allows some flexibility—although this should not be viewed as another attempt to move away from empiricism.

The notion being accepted that the most pragmatic period within which baseline could occur is often the time period between the specification of target problems and goals and the next interview, some other related questions emerge. Depending on numerous factors (such as workload or irritability of presenting problem) the duration of time between interviews may be anywhere from 1 week to 1 month or more. This inherent flexibility by virtue of client idiosyncrasy allows the clinician-researcher some empirical leeway.

On the assumption that the usual tendency is for the clinician-researcher to attack a problem as soon as possible, we would recommend that, as a rule of thumb, the clinician-researcher err in the other direction. That is, the time period allotted for the baseline should be maximized (within ethical limitations). While some may consider that the delay of even a few hours is unethical (and we would agree given certain crisis situations), we believe that it may be equally unethical to pursue a course of action on the basis of insufficient information that may lead to an iatrogenic result. The clinical research model of intervention is data based. To proceed with intervention without sufficient preliminary data may be a serious error.

In addition to the requirements of the clinical research model, the gathering of baseline data and the delay of treatment may also have a pragmatic value. Jay Haley, in *The Power Tactics of Jesus Christ* (1969), argues that "there is a consistent finding that between fifty and seventy percent of patients on waiting list control groups not only do not wish treatment after the waiting list period but have really recovered from their emotional problems" (p. 2). If this observation is indeed valid, then the gathering of baseline data and the delay of treatment may not only serve the purpose of treatment but may also make the delivery of services more efficient by virtue of self-elimination of the less problematic cases.

Note also that the time period required between interviews obviously depends on the specific behaviors and problems under consideration and whether multiple-point or single-point measures are being employed. For example, where the target problem is a high-frequency activity, then the baseline period need not last for extended periods (this is discussed further under stability). On the other hand, low-frequency activity may need to be monitored for longer periods, or alternate measures may need to be found. Similarly, single-point measurements obviously requires minimal time compared to multiple-point measures. It should be apparent that the question of duration is really relevant only in the recommended times-series paradigm. The weaker single-point baseline methods are not faced with this issue.

Given the pragmatic barriers created by the agency and the reality of the client situation, what the clinician-researcher must do is find a legitimate compromise between the demands of clinical responsibility and the demands of recommended scientific procedure. A major consideration in this procedure, stability, is discussed in the next question.

3. How stable should the baseline be? The general rule for the length of the data collection period during all phases of treatment suggests that data be collected until stability or a "steady state" is achieved. Howe (1974, p. 6) defines a steady state as "a situation in which the characteristics of the phenomenon under observation do not change over a period of time." Whereas the attainment of a steady state may not always be clinically ethical or reasonable, like observability, it should be recognized as an important goal.

If a baseline is excessively variable, then the effect of intervention is obscured. Furthermore, instability during baseline may lead the clinician-researcher to make inaccurate judgments on the nature of the problem and on the process of intervention. Stability, then, should be achieved as best as possible before the beginning of treatment. Obviously, stability is not an issue when single-point measurement is employed.

The attainment of "absolute" stability is difficult under normal clinical conditions for various reasons. Under many circumstances it is impossible to maintain a baseline period for an extended period of time. Some reliability has, therefore, to be given up. For example, a child's tantrum behavior may be the target problem. In such a situation it may be clinically undesirable to forego intervention for any length of time. This intervention may have to occur with limited information. Another factor that affects stability and may cause judgmental error is cyclicity. Consider the following example: School attendance is a commonly used indicator of performance in studies with adolescents and juveniles. This index is particularly susceptible to instability by virtue of cyclicity. Studies indicate that adolescent attendance decreases as the school term progresses (Stuart and Tripodi, 1973). Typically, attendance is high at the beginning of the semester and relatively low at the end. Thus, if baseline data are collected at the beginning of the semester and then compared with data collected at the end of the semester (the period during which intervention occurred), the effect of intervention will be artificially reduced as measured by this criterion. In fact, the client's attendance may have deteriorated whether or not intervention took place, and because of the cyclical nature of the behavior, the intervention is seen as less powerful. Alternatively, although less reliable owing to possible record-keeping errors, the client's attendance history could have been analyzed and these data employed for baseline purposes. Simple as the answer may seem, it is an easy trap to fall into under the pressures of treatment needs.

Once the clinician-researcher is aware that the target problem is cyclic, certain precautions can be taken to ensure accurate representation during the baseline period. The simplest procedure would be to collect data during all phases of the cycle. Where the clinician-researcher is uncertain about the phases of the cycle but is certain that the behavior is cyclic, data should be collected at random intervals or continuously for some length of time. Where the latter is infeasible owing to the duration of the cycle or other pressures, the clinician-researcher may use available data as baseline information. Under these conditions, however, intervention should be conducted with caution, since the judgments made regarding intervention procedure may be inaccurate. Continuous data collection during the intervention would, however, tend to indicate any further cyclic tendencies. The determination of cyclicity is important, since it may be a primary extraneous factor that would lead the clinician-researcher to draw wrong conclusions.

Another danger to stability emerges from "warm-up" periods. Some activities may take a while before they appear in full force. That is, time itself may be a factor. Thus, if observations are made at regular intervals or only for brief periods of time, the information gathered may be inaccurate and unrepresentative.

An example might be a teacher who has a problem handling the class toward the end of a 40-minute class period. Upon observation, the clinician-researcher may note that the teacher is very positive toward the students at the beginning of the class, but as time passes, he gets more irritable and less rewarding. The students are, therefore, reacting to his unpredictable behavior. If all observations were made at the beginning of a class period (even if they were taken over a number of days), a glowing but inaccurate picture would have followed. Similarly, if the observations were made only toward the end of the class, an inaccurate negative picture would have emerged. A simple solution would be to order the observation periods randomly or sample both time periods systematically. Observations would then be made at different time periods and contexts and thus enhance the likelihood of gathering accurate and representative information.

Stability can best be demonstrated visually. Figure 4.1 presents a "variable baseline"; Figure 4.2, an "increasing baseline"; Figure 4.3, a "decreasing baseline"; Figure 4.4, a "cyclic baseline"; and Figure 4.5, a "stable baseline."

In addition to these trends in baseline data, any combination of decreasing/increasing/variable is possible. Given enough time, or depending on the nature of the time period selected for measurement, one may encounter any specific format. Obviously, one remedy lies in long periods of baseline such that ample opportunity is presented for any type of variation. Alternately, where predictable patterns are known prior to baseline, the clinician-researcher should take these into consideration and attempt to sample relevant points in the measurement period. Regardless of the method used, the goal the clinician-researcher should strive for is stability (Figure 4.5).

Note, however, that the mere achievement of stability within a short period of time does not guarantee that the event being measured is in fact stable. It is, however, the best one can achieve under the situation. (See Hersen and Barlow, 1976, for an excellent discussion of baseline trends.)

In general, however, the question "When is a behavior stable?" is difficult to answer regardless of the criterion used. The utility of the criterion depends, not on the achievement of absolute stability, but on its reliability and validity. That is, can these procedures be repro-

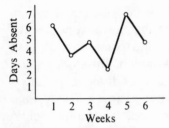

Figure 4.1 Variable baseline.

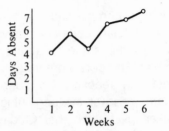

Figure 4.2 Increasing baseline.

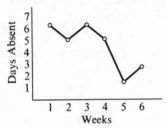

Figure 4.3 Decreasing baseline.

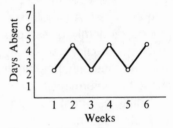

Figure 4.4 Cyclic baseline.

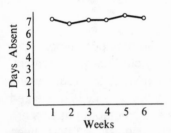

Figure 4.5 Stable baseline.

duced and generalized into similar situations? In general, the accuracy of information gathered in terms of its reliability and validity can be maximized by using multiple measures and multiple evaluators as stated earlier. In the example cited earlier, grades and school behavior as reported by teachers and school counselors would have provided additional relevant information. The reliability of these reports can be increased further by administering an evaluative questionnaire at specified time intervals during the semester. There is no substitute for practice experience, for this knowledge facilitates the use of relevant criteria for change. As Sidman (1960, p. 269) points out, "there must be a considerable amount of experience and intuition involved in the selection of an appropriate criterion."

4. How can you interpret the effect of various factors on your obtained data? In a very real sense, the control available to the clinician-researcher operating in the natural environment is truly limited. The life space of a client system is a complex of activities and behaviors. The only real control the clinician-researcher has over the client's environment is the time during which the client is in an interview. This lack of control effectively inhibits the power of causal statements that can be ascertained by the clinician-researcher— hence the notion of covariance. By thoroughly analyzing the environment in which the target problems occur, however, the clinician-researcher can have some degree of confidence in the measured effects of intervention. The whole procedure can be strengthened further by employing multiple measures (Type B) and/or multiple evaluators (Type C).

Stuart and Tripodi (1973) provide an interesting example. In working with junior high school adolescents, these authors noted that problem adolescents were receiving consistently poor grades. This appeared to be true, even though, to the clinician-researcher, the adolescent seemed to have deserved a better grade that the one received. Upon examining the grading criteria, the clinician-researcher concluded that the teacher was grading the adolescent's academic performance on his classroom behavior and on what the teacher had learned from his colleagues. Thus, as a dependent measure, grades were being influenced by two extraneous factors: teacher expectations and adolescent physical behavior. To maximize the correlation between grades and academic performance, the clinician-researcher and the adolescent met with the teacher in question and obtained from him a "performance program," namely, what does the student have to do to earn the grade A, what does he have to do for a grade B, and so on. In essence, the teacher was "forced" to specify the academic goals for the class, and as a result of this specification, had to make judgments purely on the basis of goal attainment by the adolescent. In this manner the influence of identified outside factors was minimized.

Total control is an impossibility in any treatment context. Under these circumstances the clinician-researcher should identify as many convergent factors as possible and either eliminate them in some manner or measure their effect. In either situation the clinician-researcher should be able to explain the impact of the extraneous factors. Where similar intervention procedures can be implemented across a number of cases, the clinician-researcher may be able to evaluate the effect of the different variables by establishing successive controls in each of the different situations. In short, the clinician-researcher should obtain as much understanding as possible over a complex environment and uncontrollable events, to maximize empiricism and understand the clinical process.

5. In what situations and under what circumstances does baselining occur? Two points should be made here. First, the circumstances and situations in which the data are collected should be indicated (see discussion under observation data, although this applies in all cases). Second, the circumstances and situations in which baseline information is gathered should be (as much as possible) comparable to the plan for data collection after intervention. It often turns out that interventionists take baseline measures in one situation or under one set of circumstances and plan to collect post-treatment data under a different situation or set of circumstances. Some examples will illustrate this:

Error I:
A student had been taking a duration measure of how long it took his son to get dressed. He wanted to test if having the son take this measurement would by itself change the time. This would have been all right, but he was then going to stop taking the measurements himself. He was advised to continue with his measurement, even if he had his son taking it.
Error II:
The same student wanted to obtain duration measures of the dressing behavior when it occurred in the morning, afternoon, and evening. He was cautioned that each separate situation had to be individually baselined and individually measured after baseline. Three separate graphs were suggested for the purpose of simplicity.

In terms of an intervention strategy he was advised to begin on one situation at a time, for example, in the morning. This intervention may affect the other situations owing to their similarity. If not, subsequent intervention should be begun.

Error III:

A student wanted to increase her relaxation state, as measured on a biofeedback instrument. She was going to test out her relaxed state by trying to imagine anxiety-provoking thoughts after intervention. She should have been planning to try to imagine the exact same thoughts during baseline, measure her response, and then measure her response to the same thoughts after baseline.

4.4. Conclusion

Baseline measurement is not a simple process, but neither is it so cumbersome that it has to interfere with the prime goal of intervention. What we have attempted to do thus far in this chapter is to sensitize the reader to the possible pitfalls in baseline that the clinician-researcher may encounter and suggest methods of overcoming these. The adequacy of baseline methodology in fact determines the adequacy of evaluation—since the same method is repeated over time. The clinician-researcher should, therefore, take particular care in the development and administration of the measures, paying particular heed to the issues discussed here and in the previous chapters. We are asking that the clinician-researcher employ a scientific mode of intervention. Tripodi (1974) states that, when new procedures are introduced into practice, the costs may rise rapidly. The costs incurred here are not, however, "primary costs" (money, equipment, supplies), but "secondary costs" (time required for data collection and analysis, recruiting mediators, etc.). We believe that these secondary costs are functional and in the long run create a more demonstrably effective and accountable interventionist.

We have attempted to illustrate the efficacy of these procedures, as well as their inherent weaknesses. We are allowing for some compromises in the clinical situation that fall short of the ideal single-subject or time-series methodology (Campbell and Stanley,

1963; Hersen and Barlow, 1976; Kratochwill, 1978). We recognize these limitations and consider them to be the realities of practice rather than advocacy of sloppy experimentation. We also recognize, however, that, by approaching the ideal, different interventionists will begin on the road to "true" empirical demonstration of treatment effect.

Chapter Five

THE FOURTH STAGE: SELECTING AND IMPLEMENTING RESEARCH DESIGNS

CHAPTERS 5 THROUGH 9 PRESENT several clinical research designs. Their clinical utility is demonstrated by providing examples from the practice arena. The designs have, for the most part, been presented in an order of increasing complexity. The different designs may be applicable in different situations. It is up to the reader to evaluate the nature of his or her practice situations and then to apply the design that would provide the most amount of information.

In the typical experimental situation the researcher usually compares an experimental group that received treatment with a control group that did not. In the clinical research model there is no control group. The standards of comparison (or control) must therefore lie within the client system itself. Thus the logic behind the interpretation of all clinical research designs is simple: The client(s) outcome measure(s) during the time periods (or situations) when treatment is in effect is compared with the client(s) outcome measure(s) during the time periods (or situations) when there is no treatment. The comparison, then, is an internal one, with the individual, family, or group in treatment serving as its own control.

As indicated earlier, the ideal clinical research model proposes the use of multiple-point measurement (time-series measures) to reduce the threats to validity. But a series of measures prior to intervention literally means time—time that is often unavailable! Under these situations most clinicians begin intervention immediately, justifying the noncollection of baseline data on the basis of ethics, problem irritability, and the like. We maintain that such instantaneous intervention is generally unsupportable and unjustifiable (other than in some crisis intervention situations), from the perspective of both clinical process and accountability.

Clinical assessment, by definition, implies evaluation, and evaluation, by definition, incorporates some comparison. It is this comparative basis that the clinical research model attempts to tap. Basically, we maintain that some measurement is better than no measurement, provided that the measurement procedures fall within acceptable scientific criteria. It is on this assumption that we have argued that even a single point of measurement before and after intervention offers a basis of comparison (weak though it may be). Undoubtedly, the strict experimentalist would disagree. But given the requisites of multiple-point measurement (for example, time, measurement methods) and the general multimodal therapies used by most clinicians, single-point measurement often emerges as the only available alternative.

To reiterate a point in our discussions, in view of our acceptance of some variations from single-subject, single-case, or time series models, we have opted to use the term *clinical-research* designs. We have, however, continued to use the traditional symbols and nomenclature associated with these other models, as the clinical-research model is based on them.

5.1 Presenting the Data

An ability to understand and use graphic procedures is central to understanding the material that follows. In this section we will therefore present a thorough exploration of data presentation and interpretation. This discussion has a dual purpose. First, it will allow the reader to better understand the clinical examples in the ensuing chapters. Second, it will allow the reader to better use graphic procedures in his or her own practice.

The most widely used and easily understood methods of data presentation are line graphs and bar graphs. We briefly discuss, therefore, these graphing procedures within the clinical research model. (See Parsonson and Baer, 1978, for an extended discussion.)

As Figure 5.1 illustrates, a line graph within the clinical research model usually has a minimum of two basic components on the horizontal axis (or abscissa): baseline and treatment. Depending on the design being employed, the baseline and treatment periods may occur a number of times or just once. For example, an *ABAB* design

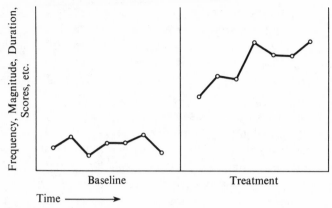

Figure 5.1 Line graphs.

would have two periods of baseline and two periods of treatment represented along the abscissa (Figure 5.2). One other major characteristic of the abscissa within the clinical research model is that it represents the passage of time from left to right. Thus, the units on the abscissa must always signify some measurement of time, such as minutes, hours, days, classroom hours, treatment sessions, and the like.

The vertical axis (or ordinate) represents the dependent measure, that is, the method by which the target problem and/or goal is being measured. It typically represents frequency, magnitude, duration, and the like, of the target problem or goal. Where multiple-point measures are plotted systematically, the line graph provides contin-

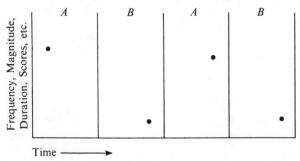

Figure 5.2 Line graph, *ABAB* design.

uous information on the performance of the client across time on the chosen dependent measure. Where single-point measures are used, the graph would have only one point in each phase of treatment (as in Figure 5.2). Here, the day-to-day continuous information is missing. It does not, therefore, possess the explanatory capability seen in the multiple-point graph.

The bar graph is found less often in clinical research literature, because it is typically used in situations where averages of a group of individuals are presented. Since the vast majority of clinical research studies are concerned with one individual or one unit of individuals (families, classes, or groups being treated as single units), the necessity for bar graphs is rather limited. It is, however, a valuable method for presenting group information if such a situation arises. For example, a clinician-researcher working in a school system may want to reduce disruptive behavior in an entire classroom or increase cooperation among a group of teenagers. Such data would be perfectly amenable to a bar graph procedure (Figure 5.3).

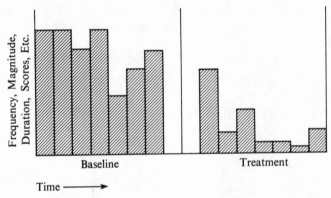

Figure 5.3 Bar graphs.

The same guidelines noted for the line graphs would hold here as well: namely, the abscissa reports the passage of time and must be divided into baseline and treatment segments. The ordinate represents the dependent measures and reflects the movement of the group along some range of frequencies, magnitudes, scores, and so on.

The discussion thus far has been concerned with the plotting of raw data—the absolute scores, the number of occurrences per hour, and so forth. This continuous data collection and graphic representation can then be used both for clinical purposes (by providing feedback to the client) and for scientific purposes (by serving as an exhibit for staffings and transmitting knowledge to other professionals). Presumably, the clinician-researcher is gathering and plotting data only on those dependent variables that are considered to be indicators of clinical success. For example, we may plot the frequency of tantrums by a child. Our plotting is for a purpose—that is, we are attempting to reduce this target behavior to an acceptable level or criterion level, which is the goal of intervention. By plotting the target behavior in this manner, we are obtaining direct indications on the effectiveness of intervention. At this point it may be desirable to enter the goal or the criterion level on the graph, again for clarity of presentation and ease of interpretation.

Figure 5.4 illustrates the insertion of the criterion level into a line graph. By drawing a horizontal line representing the goal performance on the chart, the clinician-researcher has established the mutually agreed upon goal at a visual level. This procedure allows the reader to answer visually the question "Were you successful in your intervention?" The fact that the tantrums were reduced to a level below the criterion level is a visual indicator of the success of treatment with this specific target problem.

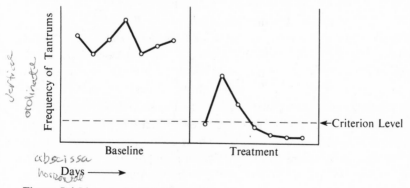

Figure 5.4 Line graph of tantrums.

5.2 Eyeballing

Eyeballing refers to the visual examination of data in graphs. This is one of the most common and simple methods of "evaluation" that the clinician-researcher can employ. Consider Figure 5.4. A visual inspection of the graph provides the clinician-researcher with a substantial amount of information.

1. The number of tantrums occurring during baseline is *fairly high*.
2. The introduction of treatment brought about a *substantial* reduction in the frequency of tantrums.
3. There appears to be a relationship between the introduction of treatment and the reduction in tantrum, in that the tantrums have been reduced to the *desired criterion level*—that is, the mutually agreed upon goal.
4. The reduction in tantrums appears to be *relatively significant*.

In essence, we have concluded that treatment was successful. But note the use of the terms *fairly high, substantial, desired criterion level,* and *relatively significant*—these are not statistical terms. All eyeballing allows us to do is to make an educated (and to some extent arbitrary) judgment about the relationship between intervention and outcome and whether this outcome reached the clinically set criterion. This procedure does not substitute for a statement of statistical significance. Those clinician-researchers so inclined could very easily employ some of the statistical procedures (such as time-series analysis) that are available to determine whether or not the clinically accepted level is also statistically significant. Or they may use one of the rules-of-thumb presented later in this book.

Eyeballing is the one method that is immediately available to the clinician-researcher after the data have been graphed. Regardless of the methods of assessment, what we are concerned with is what Edgar and Billingsley (1974) have called believability of the conclusions. For the independent reader or reviewer of clinical research data to be convinced that there has been in fact a change related to treatment, the data patterns should show a dramatic change and/or the criterion level must be attained and maintained for a period of time. The believability of this relationship is increased when such eyeballing tactics are substantiated by statistical procedures—particularly since it is generally argued that clinical significance is usually higher than statistical significance. This issue will be dealt with later.

In chapter 4 we discussed the various data patterns that may emerge during the collection of baseline data. Briefly, it was pointed out that there was no answer to the question how long is long enough for baseline—the issue of duration. In general, the longer the baseline period, the more likely it is that it represents the true data patterns. As a rule, it was suggested that there be at least three data points during baseline when a multiple-point measurement strategy was being employed. Also concerning the measurement method, we noted that this information is not always visible on a graphic presentation. Hence, it is desirable to find out whether or not the baseline measures and posttreatment measures were conducted on the same procedural format. Were the intervals between the measures the same during the two periods? Were the same measures used? Finally, the issues of data stability, variability, and cyclicity, and their possible impact on the interpretation of the data were discussed.

Thus, five distinct baseline data patterns were identified: increasing, decreasing, stable, cyclic, and variable. The stable baseline is, of course, the data pattern of choice. In general, the cyclic and variable data patterns are undesirable, since neither would allow for clear determination of treatment effect. In contrast, the increasing and decreasing baseline, along with the ideal stable baseline, allow for better assessment of treatment effect.

With these criteria in mind, consider the following series of figures based on an excellent discussion by Jones et al. (1977). Figures 5.5 and 5.6 represent increasing and decreasing baseline situations respectively. A denotes the baseline period and B the treatment period in each instance. If, at posttreatment, the graphic representation looked as in b_2 (in X_1 and X_2), it would appear that the trend during treatment is very much a continuation of what occurred during baseline. Under these circumstances it would be very difficult to establish the effects of treatment or even to say via eyeballing that the treatment had any impact at all. On the other hand, the lines b_1 and b_3 (in X_1 and X_2) suggest that there has been a shift in level. That is, while the rate of occurrence of the target problem has not changed

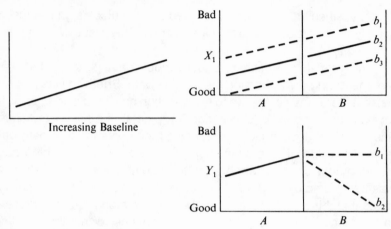

Figure 5.5 Increasing baseline.

(as indicated by the slope of the line), the level at which it is occurring has, but the trend remains the same as before. For example, a couple receiving marital treatment may have had an increasing rate of verbal arguments accompanied by physical aggression during the baseline period. The posttreatment measures may show the same rate of verbal arguments, but with decreased intensity, and the absence of any physical aggression. But since the trend has not changed, the problem gets worse with time, although it may never reach the original level.

If, on the other hand, we consider Y_1 and Y_2 (in Figures 5.5 and 5.6), a different picture emerges. The line b_1 in both instances indicates a leveling off of the target problem or goal at the exact level at which the treatment began. This could mean either that treatment inhibited further deterioration and is maintaining the problem at that level or that treatment was begun at a point where the problem in question would have leveled off in any case (whether or not treatment occurred). While this is a distinct shift in trend from increasing and decreasing slopes to horizontal (or zero trend), whether this was brought about by intervention is hard to say. On the other hand, b_2 (in Y_1 and Y_2) shows a distinct impact of treatment. In both instances we see that intervention essentially produced a reversal in trend. While this may have occurred by sheer chance, this could be verified by such designs as the reversal/withdrawal design.

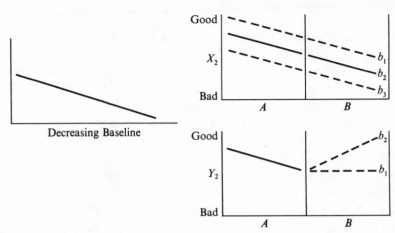

Figure 5.6 Decreasing baseline.

Figure 5.7 presents what Jones et al. (1977) call a "zero-trend line"—it essentially represents the stable baseline situation. In X_3, we see a distinct shift in level, but no shift in trend. In Y_3, on the other hand, we see a distinct shift in trend. Both instances here may signal the relative impact of intervention. The shift in level is of greater significance here than in the increasing and decreasing baseline situations because of the stability of the data patterns.

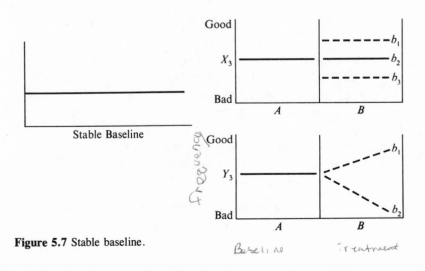

Figure 5.7 Stable baseline.

The data presentation and eyeballing tactics discussed here should help the reader better understand and evaluate the examples that follow. Each literature example presented in chapters 5 through 9 is followed by our *summary* discussion. In these summaries we have tapped those dimensions central to the understanding of the clinical research process. First, the *number of clients* identify the size of the client system with whom intervention is taking place. Second, the *specification of goals* signifies to the reader the specificity and concreteness generally required by the clinical research model. Third, the *measurement strategy* outlines the characteristics of the measurement procedures used by the various authors, pointing out their relative strengths and weaknesses, as well as the options available. Fourth, the *design* dimension specifies the nature of the research method and its implications in the interpretation of data. Fifth, the *data patterns* isolate for the reader those aspects of the graphic presentations that clearly illustrate the impact of intervention. And a final dimension termed *other observations* presents some general comments on the study.

5.3 Clinical research design *AB*

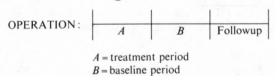

OPERATION:

| A | B | Followup |

A = treatment period
B = baseline period

The *AB* design is the simplest form of the clinical research approach. The clinician-researcher is required to take a baseline measurement of the target problem and/or goal and to administer the same test or measure after intervention has begun. These simple pretreatment–posttreatment administration procedures would be true regardless of whether one were using single-point measures, multiple-point measures, or a combination of the two.

The following points are of importance in understanding this design:

1. *A* signifies the baseline period; no intervention has taken place up to this period.

2. _B_ signifies the intervention period. It is during this period that the clinician-researcher applies a specific intervention strategy to bring about change in the client system.

The intervention _B_ as discussed here is a "package." For example, _B_ can be a contract formulated with a delinquent child and his or her parents, or it can be a combination of a contract, a job training program, and an alcohol treatment program for an unemployed individual. Regardless of its composition, the clinician-researcher should be in a position to elucidate clearly the components of _B_ in a manner that is communicable and reproducible. This implies (1) a clear understanding of the nature of the intervention program, (2) an ability to partialize the program (that is, identify its components), and (3) an ability to communicate and reproduce these elements so that another clinician-researcher may be able to implement them. The partialization is of particular importance, since as the designs get more complicated, the measurement of effectiveness requires greater specification and concreteness that is related to this complexity.

The _AB_ design requires only one alteration in data pattern to demonstrate the effectiveness of intervention. (Figure 5.8 illustrates the ideal pattern of this design). However, while this demonstration is couched in cause-effect terms, all the design is really doing is to

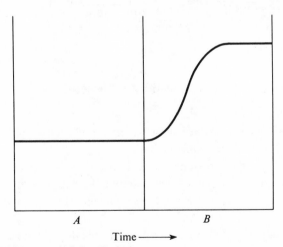

Figure 5.8 Ideal pattern of the _AB_ design.

show that the data pattern changes at the same time the intervention is introduced. Thus the power of the *AB* design to make causal inferences is rather limited. This design may be showing covariation or the fact that the event changed coincidentally at the same time the intervention was applied. For example, an insomniac whose sleeping changed after treatment may now be sleeping because a night train stopped running past the window just when treatment began. Alternately, a single change in data pattern could be attributed to a change to more typical levels of functioning after unusual highs or lows (statistical regression) or unreliability in the measurement procedure where no change has actually occurred.

To reiterate an argument for multiple measurements, the clinician-researcher is in a particularly weak position to analyze whether statistical regression and unreliability are really occurring if single-point measures were to be used. On the other hand, a series of measurements at pretreatment (*A*) and posttreatment (*B*) would strengthen the confidence one has in the measure as representing the actual levels of the target problem or goal.

As weak as this design may appear, it is far more powerful than the typical evaluative procedures that are in general use—where no pretreatment measure is employed and success of treatment is a statement to that effect by the client and/or worker. Without a relatively objective pretreatment measure, there is no comparison base, and therefore, the degree of success achieved is purely speculative and judgmental.

Strengths and Weaknesses of the *AB* Design

Strengths
1. There is a comparison of what happens to the target problem and/or goal, before and after intervention.
2. Compared to the measurement of effect after intervention alone, the design offers a data-based comparison on the impact of intervention.
3. The *AB* design can be used in most treatment situations and settings.
Weaknesses
1. Where multimodal therapies are offered, this design does not allow for discriminative analysis; that is, it would not be possible to isolate more effective parts from the less effective parts of the intervention program.

2. Since there is only one variation in data patterns, there is only minimal evidence to support the contention that therapy in fact produced the recorded changes.

Suggested Design Utility By virtue of its simplicity, the *AB* design has nearly universal applicability. It can be employed with relative ease across almost all environments of intervention and problem situations. As indicated earlier, the *AB* procedure is the minimal requirement in the clinical research model. Given the need for a pretreatment measure, perhaps the only situation in which the clinical research model may not be feasible would be in crisis intervention. Here, the clinician-researcher may be forced to gather data during *B* and use retrospective data for *A* (an extremely weak procedure).

We strongly urge all clinicians to use this approach. While the simple *AB* approach leaves many questions unanswered as far as cause-effect relations are concerned, it adds much to the validity of the intervention process and the measurement of outcome. As will become evident later, the collection of *AB* data may allow for the application of higher order designs (such as *ABAB* and its extensions), by virtue of situational changes or unforeseen circumstances.

Design Extensions The *AB* design assumes that the intervention program employed (*B*) produced positive change. It is, however, possible that the *B* intervention was a failure or that the same results could be obtained by using only part of the original *B* intervention package. In either case a different mode of intervention is suggested. The *AB* design extensions offer a clinical research model for this purpose.

The *ABC* design, presented in Figure 5.9 in its ideal form, illustrates such a design. The periods designated *B* and *C* usually represent two different techniques or packages of intervention.

The reader may find the labelling of treatment phases after *B* somewhat confusing. As no formal rules have been set for labelling, one may come across several systems in the literature. Some writers use *A-B,-B$_2$-B$_3$,* etc. We have chosen to designate separate components with subsequent letters of the alphabet. Thus in chapter 8 we talk of adding to components of a package. Subsequent treatment phases are indicated by *B, (B,C),* etc.

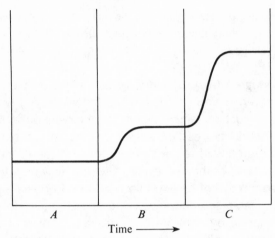

$$A \qquad B \qquad C$$
Time ⟶

Figure 5.9 Ideal pattern of the *ABC* design.

For example, if *B* were a multimodal therapy (relaxation, assertiveness training, and supportive relationship, *C* might consist of only assertiveness training or a series of TA exercises that were not performed before (see section on strip/construction designs). These design extensions can proceed ad infinitum—*ABCDE*. . . . and so on. This possibility leads us to the aforementioned characteristic of all clinical research designs, namely, the ability of the clinician-researcher to describe each treatment period (*BCDE*. . . . etc.) with the same degree of specificity and concreteness. The pragmatic guideline here would be a matter of efficiency. After a point, alterations in procedure would result in increasingly limited success and thus make further alterations unproductive.

Strengths and Weaknesses of the *AB* Design Extensions

Strengths

1. There is a comparison of what happens to the target problem before and after intervention.
2. The extension designs, compared to the *AB* design, offer some opportunity for discriminative analysis, that is, opportunity either to break down (strip) or build-up (construct) multimodal therapies.

3. The extension designs force the clinician-researcher to be sufficiently specific and concrete to discriminate between the various aspects of treatment.
4. These designs can be used in most treatment situations and settings.

Weaknesses

1. This design is not capable of recognizing and isolating multiple treatment effects (validity issues). That is, would B followed by C have produced the same results as C followed by $B?$
2. This design is not capable of discriminating between main effects and interaction effects (see chapter 10). That is, are the results obtained after intervention C a function of C, a function of B residuals, or a function of B and C working in combination (interaction) with each other?
3. Since there is more than one variation in data patterns, there is additional evidence to support the contention that therapy in fact produced change. Given points 1 and 2, however, it is difficult to say which part of the intervention package was the most effective.

These weaknesses are addressed to some extent by the designs described as "reversal/withdrawal designs" (chapter 6). Despite these weaknesses, both the *AB* design and *AB* design extensions have a great deal of pragmatic and heuristic value.

Suggested Design Utility The *AB* design extensions have the same order of applicability as the *AB* designs, the added dimension being the relative flexibility and, in the long run, efficiency in the delivery of services. That is, the clinician-researcher intent on refining services would be able to modify certain aspects of a given intervention package, apply it across the same or similar situations and cases, and obtain some degree of empirical validation on their relative success and failure.

Desensitization as a Self-Control Procedure: A Case Report

HAL ARKOWITZ, Department of Psychology, University of Oregon

The present case report illustrates the successful use of a self-desensitization procedure for a client with interpersonal and sexual anxieties. While several reports of self-desensitization have already appeared (e.g., Kahn and Baker, 1968; Rardin, 1969), the present report illustrates the potential of self-desensitization as a self-control procedure. In this view, desensitization may be utilized as an active process, directed toward the learning of a general anxiety-reducing skill, rather than as a passive desensitization to specific aversive stimuli. This view of desensitization is consistent with Goldfried's (1971) reconceptualization of desensitization as self-control. Training clients in the active skills of desensitization provides them with a long-term means for reducing anxiety without necessarily requiring further therapeutic contact. Follow-up information was obtained over a 2½-year period from the client discussed here.

CASE REPORT

Background Ted was an 18-year-old freshman who sought treatment at the Psychological Services Center on campus. He reported feeling anxious and depressed, with occasional thoughts of suicide. He felt unable to concentrate on his school work and to seek out social relationships on campus. The immediate stress seemed to involve his relationship with his girlfriend who was attending a distant college. She was the first and only girl he had dated, and he found himself preoccupied with thoughts about her, as well as having extremely explosive and jealous reactions to her casual dates with other men. He often made massive and impulsive bids for reassurance from her through highly emotional letters and telephone calls. Ted was also concerned that he

Reprinted from *Psychotherapy: Theory, Research, and Practice*, 2 (Summer 1974): 172–74. Used by permission of *Psychotherapy Today*.

was sexually impotent. He had attempted intercourse with his girlfriend several times, and each attempt had ended unsuccessfully with either premature ejaculation or loss of erection.

Ted was seen by the author for a total of 25 sessions over a 6-month period. The first 14 sessions were primarily directed toward exploration of his feelings about his relationship with his girlfriend, rational decision-making strategies, and roleplaying and homework assignments directed toward increasing his social comfort and participation on campus. At session 14, Ted reported that he had broken up with his girlfriend. At this session he appeared extremely anxious and agitated. He was concerned that his resolve might weaken and that he would return to the relationship despite his preference to end it. Ted also discussed his anxieties about heterosexual relationships and his fears about his sexual performance. At this point the therapist decided to initiate a self-desensitization program to help reduce these anxieties. A self-desensitization program was chosen, in part, to help Ted increase his perceptions of control over his feelings.

Self-desensitization The self-desensitization took place over the course of the last 9 weeks of treatment. During this time Ted designed and executed the program on his own between meetings with the therapist. The meetings with the therapist were primarily concerned with problem solving for difficulties encountered in the self-desensitization program, and a discussion of progress. The therapist's role during this time was structured as one of technical consultant to Ted in his self-directed program.

The first step in the program was having Ted read about the rationale and procedural details of desensitization from a book by Wolpe and Lazarus (1966). The second step was training in muscle relaxation, following the procedure described by Wolpe and Lazarus. The first relaxation session was conducted by the therapist in the office. Subsequent relaxation sessions were conducted by Ted in his room, using a tape recording of the relaxation instructions which the therapist provided to him. After about 4 hours of practice with the tape, Ted was able to relax himself very effectively, and no longer needed the tape to induce relaxation. He found that he was able to relax himself at this point simply by thinking about the relaxation instructions, and without going through the tension release exercises. The third step involved hierarchy construction. Ted generated three hierarchies on his own. The first two were concerned with situations associated with his ex-girlfriend which elicited anxiety and ruminative thoughts. Some sample items from these two hierarchies included "hearing from a friend that Susan (the ex-girlfriend) was dating another guy seriously," "the telephone rings in my room and I think it might be Susan calling." The third hierarchy was concerned with social and sexual contact with other females. This included such items as "starting a conversation with a girl in one of my classes," "a girl invites me into her apartment after a date," as well as higher items reflecting increasing degrees of sexual contact through intercourse.

The fourth step was the actual desensitization, which involved self-directed exposure of the hierarchy scenes with self-administered relaxation. The self-desensitization sessions were conducted by Ted in his room. He typically began each such session with 5 to 10 minutes of relaxation. When he felt sufficiently relaxed, he opened his eyes and read the first hierarchy item from a stack of hierarchy cards on an adjoining table. Next, he closed his eyes and imagined the scene. He reported that this procedure did not disrupt his relaxation. Ted started each new scene with brief exposures and moved on to longer ones if he did not experience anxiety. If, during the exposure of any scene, he did begin to feel anxious, he terminated the scene and relaxed. After two successive repetitions of a scene for about 30 seconds without anxiety, he would move to the next hierarchy item.

For the most part the procedure worked smoothly for Ted. One problem which he reported concerned his anticipation of later scenes in the hierarchy. During one period he reported that he became increasingly tense between scenes, because he began to anticipate the exposure of more anxiety-arousing scenes much later in the hierarchy. The solution he devised for this was to utilize positive thoughts and relaxing images between exposures, so that he would not begin thinking about the later items.

One further problem which Ted experienced was an apparent lack of generalization for some items. That is, even though he had sufficiently passed an item in the imaginal hierarchy, he still often experienced noticeable tension in the real-life situation. For this problem, Ted decided to utilize *in vivo* relaxation procedures. For example, this problem was especially marked for the item "the telephone rings in my room and I think it might be Susan calling." For this item, Ted enlisted the aid of his roommate who telephoned Ted from an adjoining room on a prearranged signal. First, Ted relaxed himself and then signaled for the telephone to ring. Ted let the telephone ring a few times and during this time focused on relaxing himself. He also varied the volume of the telephone bell to gradually approximate the standard one. With two such *in vivo* sessions, Ted reported that he felt quite comfortable about the telephone ringing and that it did not lead him to thoughts about his girl friend. This type of *in vivo* translation was one Ted successfully employed on several occasions for especially troublesome items.

Results Ted reported many changes consistent with his progress through the hierarchies. He was able to confront situations and cues relating to his exgirlfriend without getting anxious and depressed; the frequency of his ruminative thoughts and preoccupation with that relationship markedly decreased; his schoolwork improved; his social participation on campus increased; and he began dating more frequently. In addition, he became less concerned about his sexual performance. He began to date one girl somewhat regularly, and felt quite comfortable with kissing and petting, although they had not attempted intercourse. Finally, he appeared less impulsive and explosive, and was no longer considering the kinds of extreme actions that characterized his earlier behavior.

The MMPI was administered after the first intake meeting with Ted, and again 6 months after the termination of treatment. The second administration may thus reflect more enduring changes after treatment. The pre- and post-treatment MMPI's are presented in Figure 5.10. The two profiles suggest a change from a highly neurotic configuration to one which is comfortably within normal limits. The most marked changes were the decreases in D, Pt, and Sc. These decreases are consistent with the behavioral changes reported above. The increases in the Pd and Ma scales may reflect a concurrent increase in assertiveness and energy level.

The therapist sent Ted open-ended letters for follow-up information at 6 months and 1 year following termination. Also, an unsolicited letter was received from Ted 2½ years after termination. During the year following termination, Ted reported that the changes which were described above were maintained. He reported that he continued to be free of depression and anxieties and his preoccupation with his ex-girlfriend. He was dating frequently and doing well academically. Ted reported that he had utilized the self-densitization during this year for several minor anxiety problems which arose. These concerned test anxiety one quarter and tensions concerning the uncertainty of his long-range career plans. In both these cases, he utilized a combination of imaginal and *in vivo* desensitization as described earlier. Ted reported that in both cases he successfully reduced his anxieties, and felt that

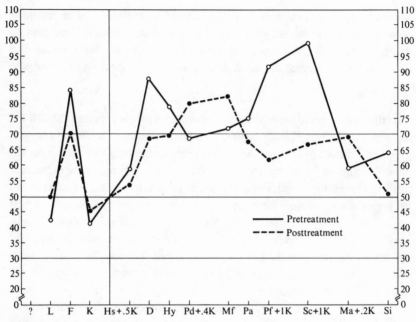

Figure 5.10 Pretreatment and posttreatment MMPI profiles. The posttreatment profile was obtained 6 months following termination of the contact with the therapist.

the use of self-desensitization had helped prevent these from becoming more major problems for him.

In a letter from Ted 2½ years after termination, he reported that he was married. He had been married for almost a year at this point and wrote that "I feel that I can have a lasting and meaningful relationship with a woman without the kind of uncontrollable emotions I experienced before." He reported that their sexual relationship was a good one and that intercourse had not presented any problems for him. At this point he was considering going on to graduate school in psychology after graduation.

References

Goldfried, M. R. 1971. "Systematic Desensitization As Training in Self-Control." *Journal of Consulting and Clinical Psychology* 37:228–34.

Kahn, M. and B. Baker. 1968. "Desensitization with Minimal Therapist Contact." *Journal of Abnormal Psychology*, 3:198–200.

Rardin, M. W. 1969. "Treatment of a Phobia by Partial Self-Desensitization: A Case Study." *Journal of Consulting and Clinical Psychology*, 33:125–26.

Wolpe, J. and A. A. Lazarus 1966. *Behavior Therapy Techniques*. New York: Pergamon Press.

5.4 Summary

Number of Clients In this study the author reports his work with an 18-year-old anxious and depressed client. The intervention period was for 6 months, the client being seen for 25 sessions.

Specification of Goals The goal of intervention was to reduce the anxiety felt by the client when he had social and sexual contacts with females in general and his girl friend in particular. This essentially global goal of anxiety reduction was perceived as the outcome goal, the process goal being defined as the accomplishment of a desensitization program.

From the perspective of the clinical research model, this goal is somewhat nonspecific. Although specific behavioral changes (frequency of ruminative thoughts, better school work, etc.) and highly specific and concrete behaviors (starting a conversation; going into a girl's apartment, etc.) were considered during the process of desensitization, they were not directly measured as end products of intervention.

Measurement Strategy This study exemplifies the minimal requirement in the clinical research approach—a single-point pre–post measurement. Here, the author administered an MMPI after the first contact with the client and again 6 months after termination of intervention. (The results are presented in Figure 5.10) Note that there was a period of 12 months between tests and that the second administration was actually during the period defined as follow-up.

This study dramatically illustrates the "missed opportunities" as far as multiple-point measurement is concerned. The MMPI measures a series of life functions as reported by the client. The author also states that the changes recorded on the MMPI are consistent with the verbal reports of the client on behavioral changes in areas such as school work, social and sexual contacts, and ruminative thoughts. All these related behaviors could and generally should have been measured. In this instance the client himself could have kept a record of the incidence of these activities, which would have provided behavioral substantiation on the other self-reported configurations registered by the MMPI. Such behavioral data would have provided valuable clinical feedback during treatment.

The MMPI is a standardized instrument, and as such, has a relatively high degree of reliability and validity compared to some homemade instrument. As stated earlier, the use of standardized measures is generally more desirable when only paper-and-pencil tests are to be employed.

Design This is the simplest clinical research design that is recommended. It illustrates the single-point *AB* design. The simplicity of the design as observed here greatly enhances its utility.

Note that the information gathered by the MMPI before treatment is of minimal help as far as the day-to-day clinical activities are concerned. It served primarily as a benchmark—baseline information that can be used as a comparison base after intervention. Without this pretest information, the author would have been relying purely on the verbal reports of the client. Here these same verbal reports are used as substantiating evidence rather than primary indicators— a desired shift toward objectivity.

Data Patterns It is difficult to talk about patterns of data when one is faced with single-point measurements, since there are only two points to compare. However, Figure 5.10 does illustrate the changes in MMPI scores on the different scales, presumably as a function of intervention.

The reader should note, however, that the horizontal axis in Figure 5.10 is not time but the different scales of the MMPI. As such, this illustration deviates from the ideal presented in the earlier discussion, where the horizontal axis referred to the passage of time.

Other Observations The second administration of the MMPI occurred 6 months after the termination of treatment. In a sense, then, we are seeing the long-term benefits of treatment (follow-up) rather than its immediate effects (posttreatment). This is indeed valuable and suggests a procedure that should be employed if at all possible. It is, however, a deviation from the traditional pre–post model. This procedure is open to criticism in that it is possible that the change in scores may have occurred as a function of something that happened during the 6 months following termination. This criticism could have been allayed, and additional valuable information could have been gathered, if the MMPI had been administered immediately after treatment as well (but this is precluded by the nature of the MMPI). Here is one example where the value of multifactorial measurement is obvious. If the author had used some of the suggested behavioral measures, a series of related measures could have been evaluated at termination and the data could have been valuable for treatment purposes as well.

A Study Hall Program within
a County Foster Home Setting

JAMES P. MCCULLOUGH AND LARRY D. SOUTHARD,
Georgia Mental Health Institute, Atlanta, Georgia

Psychology currently is expanding its impact through a community model (Sarason et al., 1966). This approach assumes that the learning and maintenance of human behavior is related functionally to controlling stimuli within one's environment. Wahler and Erickson (1969) have demonstrated the effectiveness of the community model through the use of volunteer workers in a community health center. By training nonprofessional workers to apply behavioral theory to living problems, psychologists can increase their influence within the community.

Reprinted from *Journal of Counseling Psychology*, 19 (1972):112–16. Used by permission of the American Psychological Association.

The current project was carried out at the Oak Hill Foster Home in Atlanta, Georgia. Houseparents were trained in behavior modification techniques and then guided in establishing a reinforcement program within their cottages to deal with management problems.

The goals of the project were to demonstrate that selective reinforcement applied individually on a cottage-wide scale following study behavior (target behavior) would decrease the nonstudy behavior rate and to produce an environment in the cottages which would be conducive to academic studying. Such an environment was judged to be a quiet setting with a minimum number of disturbances.

Method

Subjects The Oak Hill Foster Home consisted of 56 adolescents ranging in age from 12 to 18 years. Most of the children came to the home after having lived with one or more sets of foster parents; some had lived in five or more foster homes. The behavioral problems of the children were myriad. Intellectual levels varied from mildly retarded to very bright. The home was racially integrated, and both middle and lower socioeconomic-status children were represented in the total population.

Setting Oak Hill was staffed by late middle-aged female houseparents, an adult male recreation director, and an administrative staff of a director and two assistant directors. The physical plant consisted of four similarly constructed cottages, each housing approximately 15 children, an assistant director's house, a swimming pool, a well-equipped gym, and a large recreation field.

The cottages were divided on the basis of age and sex. Cottage 1 housed the males between the ages of 12 and 15. Females between the ages of 16 and 18 were housed in Cottage 2. Cottage 3 included females between the ages of 12 and 15, while Cottage 4 was made up of males in the 16- to 18-year range. Each cottage was supervised by a full-time houseparent who lived in the cottage and who was intensely involved in the training and management of the children.

Procedure The project was divided into three phases. Phase one consisted of training the houseparents to administer the program, selecting the target behavior, and selecting the reinforcing activities. Phase two included the base-rate period, during which 8 to 13 days' data were obtained on each cottage. Phase three involved 4 weeks of reinforcement application. No extinction phase was included, because of the nature of the target behavior and the fact that the school year terminated at the end of the fourth week of the project.

Houseparent training The houseparents were introduced to the theory of operant conditioning and taught to apply the theoretical principles during the study hall period.

Target behavior selection Study behavior during the night study hall was selected as the target behavior. The study hall was conducted on Sunday through Thursday nights from 7:30 to 8:30 P.M. The children studied in their own rooms. Most of the children stayed in two-man rooms, but each cottage had one dorm room which housed four children. Each child had his own desk. Study behavior was selected for several reasons: the study hall presented each houseparent with a high frequency of disturbing behavior; this aspect of cottage life was easily accessible to behavioral observation and recording; and it was a problem area similar to others in that the houseparents' management techniques were not resulting in improved behavior performance.

Study behavior was divided into four categories as shown in Table 5.1.

The banking system Table 5.1 illustrates the point system constructed to reward study behavior. A maximum of 100 points could be earned nightly and 500 points could be earned per week. Study categories 1 and 2 were reinforced on an all-or-none basis. Categories 3 and 4 were reinforced on a graded basis; that is, the child received his points to the extent that he remained in his room and was quiet. Remaining quiet was defined as a noise level emittance which was below the hearing threshold of the houseparent. Points were administered each night in the form of written checks at the conclusion of the study period. The checks were written and signed by the houseparent. In addition to the check administration each night, a daily point total was posted on the cottage bulletin board for each child.

Table 5.2 illustrates the reinforcing activities provided during 1 of the 4 reinforcement weeks. Similar activities were provided during the other 3 weeks. The children had been requested to submit activity lists several

Table 5.1. STUDY BEHAVIOR CATEGORIES AND THE POINT VALUES OF EACH CATEGORY

Study Behavior Categories	Point Values
In room and prepared to study by 7:30 P.M.	10
Obtained study materials or prepared to study by 7:30 P.M.	10
Remained in room from 7:30 P.M. to 8:30 P.M.	40
(a) left room one time	35
(b) left room two times	30
(c) left room three times	25
(d) left room four times	20
(e) etc.	etc.
Remained quiet while in own room from 7:30 P.M. to 8:30 P.M.	40
(a) one noise disturbance	35
(b) two noise disturbances	30
(c) three noise disturbances	25
(d) four noise disturbances	20
(e) etc.	etc.
	Possible total: 100 per night

Table 5.2. THE REINFORCING ACTIVITIES

Cost (in points)	Week 1	Time
100	Movie: Oak Hill Gym	Friday
100	Movie: Downtown Atlanta	Friday
300	Field Trip: Polaris Room (Atlanta)	Saturday
300	Trip to state park	Saturday
100	Extra dating time	Saturday
100	Recreation: Oak Hill Gym (Sunday evening)	Sunday

weeks before the project began; the lists ranked each individual's five favorite activities. The reinforcing activities were selected from the items most frequently included in the lists.

Activities were assigned cost values depending on their rank when all the lists were compared. The program was designed so that an individual would be able to purchase one activity per day on the weekend if he earned the maximum number of points. A majority of the children earned the maximum number of points possible over the 4 weeks. Many of the activities were obtained from Atlanta merchants who provided their services free of charge.

Activities could be purchased at the conclusion of the Thursday night study period. Points could be carried over from one week to the next on a 1–4 ratio. These were points that were not spent on the previous weekend. The 1–4 ratio was designed to discourage hoarding.

Base rate period The base-rate period was designated phase two for each cottage; base-rate data were obtained regarding the frequency of disturbances during a study hall period. Disturbances were defined as behaviors which were antagonistic to studying and these behaviors were divided into six categories. The categories were as follows: not being in one's room ready to study by 7:30 P.M. (tardy); requesting study materials from the houseparent after 7:30 P.M. (material requests); trips to the bathroom (bathroom trips); trips to the water fountain (fountain trips); trips to the houseparent's room during study hall (visits); and miscellaneous disturbances (miscellaneous). The latter category was defined as cottage crises where the houseparent had to leave her station and attend to the crisis. Such crises included yelling, pillow fights, physical fights, verbal arguments, radio playing, singing, and climbing out of the room to avoid the study period. The miscellaneous category required most of the houseparent's time and energy.

Reinforcement application The children were introduced to the program on Sunday evening of reinforcement week 1. Phase 3 followed immediately at the end of the base-rate period. Reinforcement was applied for 4 weeks, and at the end of the fourth week the program was terminated.

Houseparent observation Houseparents stationed themselves at their observation posts when the study period began at 7:30 P.M. They are able to hear normal conversation within the farthest rooms at the end of the halls when the doors of the rooms were closed. The only times they left their post were to restore order in the cottage. Disturbances were counted by making marks on a clipboard. Competition was not encouraged between houseparents in regard to which unit earned the most points. The writers judged that observer reliability would be higher if each cottage worked as a separate unit. Houseparents were given considerable verbal reinforcement by the authors and the administrative staff for accurate reporting and record keeping.

Results

Figure 5.11 illustrates the total number of disturbances that occurred in each cottage during the base-rate period. The miscellaneous category was the most frequently marked category in all cottages. Two days' data were lost from the Cottage 1 record file, and 5 days' data were lost from the Cottage 2 file. However, the remaining data obtained from these two cottages provided an adequate sample of the behavioral rates.

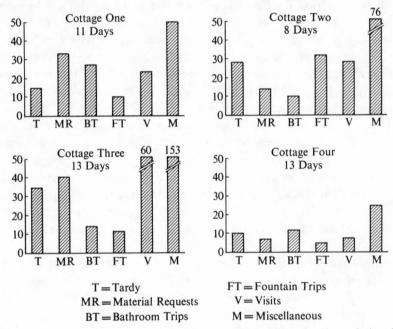

Figure 5.11 The total number of disturbances occuring in each cottage during the base rate period.

Figure 5.12 shows the number of cottage disturbances per study hall hour when the base rate period is compared to the 4 reinforcement weeks. The weekly average was compiled on Thursday night following the termination of the study period. This point signaled the end of a reinforcement week. One week after the program began, the average disturbance rate per hour decreased 57 percent in Cottage 1, 95 percent in Cottage 2, 92 percent in Cottage 3, and 75 percent in Cottage 4. This decrease was maintained

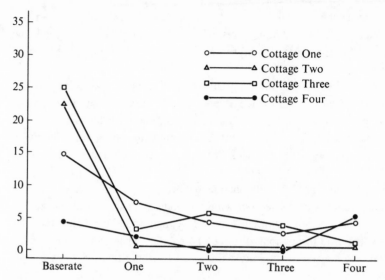

Figure 5.12 The number of cottage disturbances per study hall hour during the base rate period and during the 4 reinforcement weeks.

throughout the remaining three weeks. However, disturbance rates slightly increased in Cottages 1 and 4 the final week. The increases occurred in both cottages the same night. Several boys engaged in a verbal argument with their respective houseparent regarding a disciplinary action which had been taken earlier in the day against one of their friends. The disturbance rate in Cottages 2 and 3 was zero the fourth week.

Discussion

The goals of the project were to demonstrate that selective reinforcement applied individually on a cottage-wide scale following target behavior emittance would decrease nontarget behavior rates and to produce an environment conducive to academic studying. The data support the assumption that both goals were reached. Nontarget behavior rates were reduced in all cottages throughout phase 3 with the exception of week 4, when there was a slight rise in the rates in Cottages 1 and 4. A quieter environment was produced in all four cottages. Thus, the program was effective in modifying the study behavior of adolescents.

The houseparents adapted easily to the new behavioral requirements placed upon them as administrators of the program. They all agreed that "catching children behaving and rewarding them" was a productive way to manage the cottage.

Several implications of the program were apparent following its successful outcome: the project provided a financially practical model to modify behavioral problems in a setting such as Oak Hill, cottage rules were successfully conceptualized as behavioral goals, and the program effectively utilized a variation of the Premack Principle to acquire effective reinforcers for the children (Premack, 1959).

Agencies such as Oak Hill operate on limited budgets, and successful programming must be carried out within a modest financial framework. The current project cost was estimated to be less than $50. This figure includes expenses incurred throughout all three phases. The writers discovered many merchants within the community willing to contribute their services free of charge.

The program also illustrated the effectiveness of conceptualizing rules as behavior goals. Several staff members told the authors during the project that they felt less like policemen and more like teachers. A further consequence of the program was the realization among the staff that positive reinforcement was a more effective teaching variable than punishment.

Lastly, the program effectively utilized a variation of the Premack Principle in obtaining effective reinforcers from the natural environment. The children at Oak Hill communicated to the staff which activities would be most effective reinforcers to be used in the program. They did this through their activity lists. The success of the project was due to the effectiveness of the reinforcers.

The greatest limitation of the design was its lack of reliability measures in regard to houseparent observation. In order to correct for this limitation, the writers worked closely with each houseparent and supervised their record keeping. They also attempted to neutralize competitiveness between houseparents. Since improvement occurred in all cottages, competitiveness should not have been a significant variable affecting the recording procedure. All houseparents were motivated to record correctly, and the data were an accurate representation of their cottage's behavior.

The program was terminated at the end of the fourth week because this signaled the beginning of final examinations and the end of formal class sessions.

References

Premack, D. 1959. "Toward Empirical Behavioral Laws in Positive Reinforcement." *Psychological Review,* 66:219–33.

Sarason, B., M. Levine, I. Goldenberg, D. L. Cherlin, and E. M. Bennett 1966. *Psychology in Community Settings: Clinical, Educational, Vocational Social Aspects.* New York: Wiley.

Wahler, R. G. and M. Erickson 1969. "Child Behavior Therapy: A Community Program in Appalachia," *Behavior Research and Therapy,* 7:71–78.

5.5 Summary

Number of Clients The subjects in this study were 56 adolescents living in four different cottages run by houseparents. The entire cottage population was the subject of intervention.

Specification of Goals The goals of the study were broadly defined as improved study behavior and the production of an environment conducive to academic studying. These goals were decided upon from the perspective that a quiet environment is one that is conducive to study. As such, a series of behaviors were identified that were noted as being disruptive of study behavior, and the intervention was aimed at reducing the incidence of these behaviors.

Measurement Strategy The measurement strategy employed in this study is consistent with a Type B procedure within an interval record method. Here a single observer (the houseparent) served as a relatively nonobtrusive interventionist and evaluator. As indicated, the presence of appropriate study behavior was actually measured by the absence of a series of disruptive behaviors. Thus a number of indices were employed to measure the presence or absence of the latter.

Although the target problems were defined in observable behavioral terms, the authors were unable to obtain a reliability measure across houseparents for reasons they stated. Thus the possibility remains that the different houseparents were measuring similar but not identical behaviors.

A related issue is the essentially indirect method of measurement used in this study. The authors did not measure study behavior per se but, rather, measured the incidence of behaviors judged to be incompatible with study behavior. Whereas such a procedure is indeed theoretically valid, it would also have been beneficial to have obtained a direct measure of at least one study behavior. If this were impossible, one appropriate related measure would have been class grades. This type of measurement procedure would have resulted in both a direct and indirect measurement of goal achievement and thus added credibility to the incompatibility assumption.

Design Figure 5.12 clearly illustrates an *AB* multiple-point design. The baseline measures were taken during periods ranging from 8 to 13 days, and this was followed by 4 weeks of intervention.

Data Patterns It was difficult to discuss data patterns in the first example, where single-point measures alone were employed. In this example we see the distinct value of using multiple-point measures. The apparent impact of intervention is demonstrated by the data patterns across 4 weeks of treatment and all four cottages. This is valuable clinical information. The power of the intervention method is thus demonstrated across essentially similar but situationally different configurations involving different individuals. If the data patterns had indicated ineffectiveness, the treatment program could have been changed.

Other Observations As indicated, the multiple-point approach offers much more feedback for clinical purposes than single-point measurement does. It provides empirical data on which decisions about procedural change can be based.

Chapter Six

REVERSAL / WITHDRAWAL DESIGNS

6.1 Clinical Research Design ABAB

OPERATION:

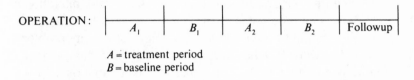

A = treatment period
B = baseline period

ACCORDING TO THIS diagram, the ABAB design basically involves two periods of baseline and two periods of intervention. To state it differently, this is an extension, a "building on" of the AB design presented in the previous chapter. The first $A_1 B_1$ periods are identical to the AB periods in the AB design.

The following points are of central importance in understanding this design:

1. A_1 is the first baseline period; no intervention has taken place during this period.
2. B_1 is the first intervention period. It is during this time that the clinician-researcher has applied specific intervention strategies in a attempt to bring about change in the client system.
3. A_2 is the withdrawal period. Theoretically, the conditions comprising this measurement period should be identical to those comprising the baseline period (A_1). The implication here is that intervention must be withdrawn, and the effects of intervention must somehow be reversed.*

---

* Hersen and Barlow (1976) make an important and useful point regarding the terms *reversal* and *withdrawal*. In the clinical research designs, when we talk about withdrawal, we are referring to the removal of the intervention strategy (the independent variable). When one withdraws the intervention, one has in effect changed the independent variable—in that the situation now is similar to the one that existed before the application of intervention. A reversal design, as compared to a withdrawal design, would actually require the reversal of the intervention strategy. For example, if a behavior is being rewarded during intervention, an incompatible behavior is rewarded during reversal.

4. B_2 is the second intervention period. During this time the identical intervention (as in B_1) is reinstituted (on the assumption, of course, that it produced positive results during the intervention phase B_1). Where B_1 produces undesirable results, obviously the clinician-researcher would be ill advised to reinstate the same intervention program, and under these circumstances, different designs (*ABAB* extension designs) can be employed and are discussed later.

As indicated earlier, the *AB* design requires only one alteration in the data pattern for a demonstration of treatment effect. However, we noted earlier, it could be argued that a number of validity problems are associated with drawing causal inferences from this evidence. The reader is reminded of the apparent relationship that existed with the insomniac client between the halted night train and increased sleeping.

To provide greater confidence in attributing the cause of change to the treatment, the clinician-researcher could withdraw the treatment program. This may produce a graph that looks something like Figure 6.1 in its ideal form. Such a design is called the *ABA* design—or the first three periods of the *ABAB* design.

In this ideal example it should be evident that the design, as illustrated here, has led to a major conclusion, namely, that the application of intervention *B* produced a desired change, and withdrawal of

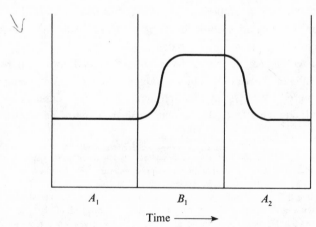

A_1 B_1 A_2

Time ———→

Figure 6.1 The *ABA* design.

B led to a reduction in these desired behaviors. That is, with two changes in data patterns rather than one, this design has enabled us to establish a higher degree of confidence. The reader may question the adroitness of this conclusion, since for example, it is quite possible that some unknown variable(s) may have produced the change both times. But we may reason that this is less likely with the ideal *ABA* pattern than with the ideal *AB* pattern. We may draw this conclusion on the basis of what Carter (1976) has aptly labeled the "principle of unlikely successive coincidences." In other words it is a likely possibility that a data pattern could show change once because of something other than the treatment coincidentally affecting the dependent measure at exactly the point in time that the treatment is introduced or withdrawn. With each successive pattern change, however, it becomes increasingly unlikely that the change can be attributed to such coincidence on the basis of probability.

Since the principle of unlikely successive coincidences is central to the understanding of how the various clinical research designs address the threats to internal validity, we explain its basis in one more way. Think of a single toss with a fair coin. In the first toss the probability of throwing a head is 1/2. On two successive tosses, the probability of getting two successive heads is $1/2 \times 1/2$, or 1/4. On three successive tosses, the probability of getting three heads in a row is reduced to 1/8. Under most situations you would still probably believe that the coin was fair, even after two or three successive heads. But at some point, you would probably say to yourself—"Wait a minute. The chances of this happening with a fair coin are getting small. I wonder whether this *is* a fair coin."

Analogously, if the data pattern changes once when the intervention is introduced (as in an *AB* design), we may be willing to attribute this change to intervention. If on the other hand, the patterns changed twice consecutively in conjunction with changes in intervention (as in getting two heads with two successive tosses), we may be more willing to attribute change to intervention. That is, we are more than likely witnessing change that is in fact being produced by intervention rather than some unknown variable(s). Of course, there can never be 100 percent certainty, and therefore clinical pronouncements must be tempered accordingly.

While the *ABA* design has its use, it is of little practical value to the clinician-researcher in terms of determining cause-effect relations, since the withdrawal of treatment resulting in the original state of functioning is not a desirable end state. The client needs to have the positive effects restored by adding a final *B* phase, creating an *ABAB* design (Figure 6.2).

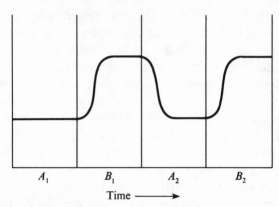

A_1 B_1 A_2 B_2

Time ⟶

Figure 6.2 The *ABAB* design.

Comment The *ABA* or *ABAB* designs are superior to the *AB* design in their ability to justify cause-effect statements. By the same token the introduction of "withdrawal" has produced some major problems. The strengths and weaknesses of this method of determining causality (i.e., determining treatment effect) are discussed within the context of the more clinically desirable *ABAB* design.

Strengths and Weaknesses of the ABAB Design

Strengths
1. There is a comparison of what happens to the target problem and/or goal, before and after each intervention period.
2. This design, compared to the *AB* design, offers much more substantive data to support the notion that *B* in fact produced change. The same intervention strategies are applied twice (in the *ABAB* design) producing the same or similar changes.

Weaknesses

1. The more successful the intervention program B_1, the harder it would be to return to baseline conditions in A_2. This may require a complete reorientation on the part of both the client system and action system, something that is difficult to achieve.

2. The withdrawal phase A_2 may contaminate later treatment programs. That is, mixing of desirable and undesirable treatment factors may lead to confusion and measurement error. The client is first introduced to positive change efforts that are later removed and reinstated once again. These procedures may interact with each other, possibly resulting in confusion and error of measurement.

3. If multimodal therapies are offered, this design does not allow one to determine which part of the intervention package was the most effective.

4. Withdrawal procedures cannot, or should not, be used in situations where the target problem is self-putative, destructive, or extremely problematic. In such situations an AB design would be more appropriate, since a withdrawal of treatment (A_2) would verge on unethical activity.

Suggested Design Utility The $ABAB$ design has more limited utility than the AB. As already stated, it is undesirable to return a client system to preintervention behavior under some circumstances. Moreover, the withdrawal phase (A_2) often requires a higher order of control over the treatment environment than the AB design since the $ABAB$ design calls for the person-situation configuration to be as close as possible during both A_1 and A_2 phases. This is often difficult to achieve. Where the action system is so large that numerous individuals are involved in the change process, all of these individuals would have to readjust their activities. This may be hard to accomplish.

Where this design is applied, however, it allows for a stronger causal statement than the AB design does. In view of this strength alone, we would argue that this design should be chosen over the simple AB design when the clinician-researcher wishes to make a strong demonstration of treatment effect and the withdrawal alternative is ethical and feasible. This opportunity would be greater and the control increased if the action system is small and/or the intervention is taking place in an institutional setting.

Finally, note that in clinical practice some unplanned withdrawal of treatment may take place. One example occurs when the event being measured unavoidably reverts to baseline levels, creating the need to reintroduce the intervention. A client is forced to drop out of treatment for a period of time (holidays, illness, etc.). Another originally unplanned reversal may occur when a client has changed "too much" and at least semireversal is needed to return the goal behavior (dependent measure) to within the desired outcome limits. For example, a client in assertiveness training may learn and enjoy aggressive behavior. The clinician-researcher may then find it necessary to focus on the distinction between assertiveness and aggression and move the client back toward assertiveness. Unplanned reversals are not as strong in their causal demonstration of the effect of intervention but often have value in the clinical situation and can provide some useful evaluative and clinical information.

Withdrawal of Treatment and Reversibility of Data: Issues and Procedures Withdrawal and reversibility are discussed here, since they are central manipulations in this design and in a number of clinical research designs that follow.* Withdrawal is simply the removal of intervention, and reversibility is the potential for return to the original preintervention levels. Since the aim of most clinical interventions is to bring about permanent change, as a phenomenon, reversibility poses some interesting questions.

First, what is so good about reversal? Has the intervention been so superficial that its effects can be eliminated with little effort? This is indeed a valid question that can be answered only by explaining the logic behind this procedure. If a given set of circumstances brought about change, then the elimination of these same circumstances and the substitution of different (or original) ones in its place should result in change again. Reinstating the original set of circumstances

---

*Hersen and Barlow (1976) distinguish between "reversal" as an active procedure by the therapist and the data patterns that result from this procedure. We will not always be making this distinction, however, but will sometimes refer to the reversability of the data as a description of the data pattern.

should reintroduce the original state of functioning. One can then argue that, being able to manipulate problem and/or goal levels in this manner, we have essentially demonstrated the primary causal factors, and *ipso facto,* intervention brought about change.

However, we are glossing over many problems when we simply say the "elimination of these circumstances" and "reinstating the original" circumstances. If a problem or goal level cannot be reversed, then how would one know that it was intervention that brought about change? Depending on the situation, some levels cannot be reversed, some circumstances cannot be changed more than once for practical and/or ethical reasons. How would one then know which intervention strategy to employ in a future similar situation? We believe these questions to be significant since these are the ones that the clinician-researcher is striving to answer. To theorize again, the ability to return to the original state of functioning should point out to the clinician-researcher that intervention most likely produced change. This fact can be substantiated further by reapplying the intervention and obtaining the same postintervention results over again. This second manipulation would undoubtedly add credence to the strength of the treatment program.

Yet some ethical and methodological questions arise when this design is used. We delineate some of the basic issues here and attempt to provide pragmatic means (where possible) of coping with them.

1. By definition, reversibility requires that the target levels revert to their original state of functioning if the intervention is removed and the original conditions reinstated. The greatest threat here is irreversibility. Sidman (1960) argues that when irreversibility is encountered the factors responsible for it must be found. While we agree with Sidman from the experimental point of view, for the clinician-researcher, this would quite often mean the application of an inordinate amount of time and effort.

Consider the following example. The clinician-researcher intervenes with a depressed client who has few social contacts. As a result of intervention the depression is reduced, and the client has also developed a small group of friends. As a result of this perceived success, the clinician-researcher may decide to withdraw the treatment program. It is very unlikely that the client will again become depressed and reduce the newly developed social contacts, since these latter will reinforce and support the newly expressed behaviors.

Pragmatics obligate, therefore, a different solution. We believe that the clinician has three options available. First, where reversal appears to be problematic, simply stop the process and immediately reinstate the change conditions. While this is obviously a failure in the experimental process (and the design), it has resulted in clinical success. The second option is one that should be continuously employed but is particularly useful in the present context. When the practitioner is faced with a similar problem situation configuration in the future, reapply only some part of the original intervention. If this procedure is systematically deployed, the causal factors can be isolated with some degree of confidence, resulting in more efficient intervention. Here again, the clinician-researcher must acknowledge the failure of the reversal design, but its usefulness is retained to some extent by repeated applications. The final option is the selection of a nonreversal design for intervention. Obviously, this is not a corrective procedure but a preconceived alternate plan. The implication here is that prebaseline assessment should direct the clinician-researcher toward the selection of an optimum clinical design, rather than the post hoc elimination of prescribed design.

Consider an aggressive child in an institution. During intervention the ward attendants are asked to reinforce the child positively for desirable behaviors. This results in a dramatic improvement in behavior. To ascertain that it is the contingency reinforcement procedures that produced the change, a reversal could be conducted. The attendants are now asked to ignore the child's positive behavior. The chances are the attendants would find it extremely difficult to comply with these new instructions. Even if they did, others in the child's environment (peers, nurses, etc.) who benefited from his improved behavior would likely continue to respond positively to changed behavior. When faced with a situation of this sort, this clinician-researcher would be ill advised to attempt a reversal design.

2. This example can also be used to illustrate the next problem encountered with reversibility—ethics. Should the clinician-re-

searcher ethically, in the interest of determining the effect of the intervention, reinstate undesirable problem levels? This is a difficult question to answer. In many ways this concern can be perceived as raising questions analogus to those group designs employing control groups or wait list controls (e.g. groups not receiving treatment or groups receiving delayed treatment). The reversal procedure would not only help validate the treatment program and the clinician's future effectiveness (since establishing causal relationships now would mean that reversals need not be employed in the future), but it may also sensitize the action system to those factors in their situation that produce problems.

In addition, some authors have argued for the clinical legitimacy of reversal/withdrawal procedures. Keller and Schoenfeld (1950) and Sulzer-Azaroff and Mayer (1977) state that, once a new behavior has been acquired, it can be reacquired more rapidly. Thus, even a short reversal may suffice, since reversal can be thought of as a "test for independence" (Sulzer-Azaroff and Mayer, 1977). That is, reversal/withdrawal essentially "probes" for client functioning in the absence of the intervention program—an artificial situation. Thus, if withdrawing treatment results in the client's returning to baseline, then it could be argued that the client is still in need of support. If, on the other hand, withdrawal does not result in reversal of data patterns, then this is an indication that the client no longer needs support.

In contrast, however, where the target problem is self-destructive or punitive, reversal may not be desirable. Consider an autistic child exhibiting extreme self-injurious behavior. Although these behaviors could be changed, to reinstate the problem behavior by withdrawing the treatment to ensure their effectiveness would, in our opinion, border on the unethical and inhumane. Fortunately, other designs are available to clearly demonstrate the effects of intervention without the use of reversal procedures.

3. The issue of stability poses a particularly difficult question in reversal. It has already been stated that establishing stability is quite often a difficult and time-consuming proposition. To the clinician-researcher, time is critical, and to use two additional periods for the determination of cause and effect is often impossible. Stability can,

however, be assumed with some confidence, if a short reversal period reflects the same data patterns noted during baseline.

The ultimate decision about whether or not to apply a reversal design lies with the individual clinician-researcher. The practitioner's own judgment of the particulars of the case and ethical considerations should provide the necessary guidelines. Whereas reversal designs have empirical strength, their functional utility is somewhat limited by the realities of circumstances, but the availability of alternate designs gives the clinician-researcher a choice.

Design Extensions The design extensions that would be applicable here are much the same as those discussed in chapter 5. The only difference lies in the systematic reversal/withdrawal periods that would be applied after each treatment period.

It is possible, for example, either that a given intervention *B* was not as successful as desired or that part of the *B* package would suffice to attain the desired goal (a question of efficiency). In this instance, as in the *AB* extension designs, the clinician-researcher would simply replace the second *B* intervention with an alternate treatment *C*—where *C* is either a new intervention strategy or a part of the old one. Thus, instead of an *ABAB* design, we would end up with an *ABAC* design, as in Figure 6.3. Theoretically, these alter-

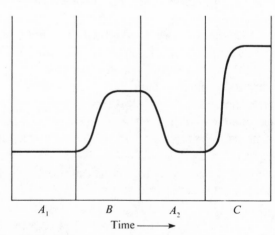

Figure 6.3 The *ABAC* design.

ations could be continued indefinitely, resulting in *ABACADAE* . . . , until the desired goal is reached. The critical notion here, the one that distinguishes these designs from the *AB* extension designs, is the systematic inclusion of the reversal/withdrawal periods after each period of treatment. Further, each treatment alteration must be specifically and uniquely defined in a manner that distinguishes it from the previous treatments and that allows it to be transmitted to other clinician-researchers.

Strengths and Weaknesses of the ABAB Design Extensions

Strengths

1. There is a comparison of what happens to the target problem and/or goal before and after each intervention period.
2. These extension designs, compared to the *AB* extension designs, offer a better opportunity for discriminative analysis, that is, to either break down (strip) or build up (construct) multimodal models of intervention. This is possible by virtue of the return to baseline after each intervention period.
3. The extension designs force the clinician-researcher to be sufficiently specific and concrete to discriminate between the various aspects of treatment.

Weaknesses

1. The more successful the intervention program *B*, the harder it would be to return to baseline conditions in A_2.
2. The withdrawal period may contaminate later treatment programs. That is, "mixing" of desirable and undesirable treatment factors may lead to confusion and measurement error.
3. Withdrawal procedures cannot or should not be used in situations where the target problem is self-putative, destructive, or extremely problematic.
4. As in *AB* design extensions, it is difficult to discriminate "order effects." However, the potential for discrimination between treatments is greater than in the *AB* extension designs by virtue of the reversal/withdrawal periods.
5. As in the *AB* design extensions, it is difficult to discriminate between main effects and interaction effects (see chapter 10). But again, the

availability of the second baseline period offers more credence to the assumption that the effects observed during the C treatment period are "truly" a result of C, rather than a combination of C and residual effects of B.*

Suggested Design Utility All the situational configurations and attributes related to the *ABAB* design would be applicable here. It has, moreover, the added dimension of monitoring change in treatment procedure and measuring the impact of this change. These design extensions, then, allow for a greater degree of flexibility, and in the long run, for more efficiency in the delivery of services.

Effects of Token Economy on Neurotic Depression: an Experimental Analysis

MICHEL HERSEN and RICHARD M. EISLER, Veterans Administration Center and University of Mississippi Medical Center, Jackson, Mississippi, and
GEARY S. ALFORD and W. S. AGRAS, University of Mississippi Medical Center, Jackson, Mississippi

In a recent investigation, Hersen et al. (1972) demonstrated that token reinforcement procedures applied to an experimental ward consisting of young, veteran, psychiatric patients yielded a twofold increase in behavioral output when compared with productivity in baseline periods. During the study clinical staff observed that patients bearing diagnoses of depression appeared markedly less depressed during contingency management phases. Moreover, depressed patients reported to staff that when they were involved in token

---

*Hersen and Barlow (1976) point out that to truly determine the effect of a second intervention, particularly when there is concern for the interaction of interventions, "change *one* variable at a time when proceeding from one phase to the next" (p. 83). Thus, more rigorous (ideal) designs than the *ABAC* could be *A-B-A-B-BC-B-BC*.

Reprinted from *Behavior Therapy*, 4 (May 1973): 392–97. Used by permission of Academic Press and Dr. Hersen.

economy activities they tended to obsess less about themselves and felt an improvement in their conditions. These clinical data fit very well with Ayllon and Azrin's (1968) contention that performance of positive behaviors in a token economy system is essentially incompatible with symptomatic manifestation. In reviewing the effects of their general-ward token economy program, Ayllon suggested that "the symptomatic behaviors by their very disruptive nature were reduced or eliminated because they could not exist side by side with the functional behaviors. In a sense they were incompatible" (p. 23).

Although it is a widely held psychiatric opinion that performance of work is beneficial in counteracting symptomotology in neurotically depressed individuals, there is little of an empirical nature to support this notion. The present study, then, was undertaken to test the hypothesis that work behavior on a token economy program would be incompatible with emission of depressive behaviors. This hypothesis was evaluated in an experimental single base (*ABA*) design with three neurotically depressed patients.

Method

Subjects   The subjects were three neurotically depressed, male patients who were admitted to the Jackson Veterans Administration Center with presenting histories of reactive depression to losses recently sustained. Subject 1 was a 54-year-old, white, married farmer who evidenced sleep disturbances, suicidal ideation, withdrawal, and agitation following the sale of a farm he had owned and managed for 20 years. During the three phases of the study, amitriptyline, 25 mg, t.i.d., was administered to him.

Subject 2 was a 32-year-old, white, married machine operator who evidenced withdrawal, decreased sexual interest, minor accidents at work, and peculiar rituals following his father's heart attack. Just prior to his admission he stopped working. During the three phases of the study trifluoperazine, 2 mg, t.i.d., and chlorpromazine, 100 mg., q.i.d., were administered to him.

Subject 3 was a 53-year-old, white, separated construction worker who reported a 15-pound weight loss, tearfulness, crying episodes, tremulousness, and sleep disturbances following termination of a construction job. During the three phases of the experiment he was medicated with Doxepin, 25 mg, q.i.d.

Token Economy Unit The three neurotically depressed subjects were patients on a token economy unit described in detail elsewhere (Hersen et al. 1972). Briefly, patients were awarded blue index cards (tokens) contingently upon completion of target behaviors under the classification of work, occupational therapy, responsibility, and personal hygiene. All work assignments were off the ward and were administered by nonpsychiatric hospital personnel. Subjects wore street clothes and were expected to plan their days each morning at "banking hours" during all phases of the study.

Measurement of Depression Objective behavioral measures of depression (Behavioral Rating Scale) recently developed by Williams et al. (1972) were used as the dependent variable in the present investigation. Behavioral ratings were obtained surreptitiously on a repetitive time sampling basis by ward nursing personnel in the normative study. Observations of patients were made in terms of presence of absence of behaviors listed under the following three categories: (1) talking, (2) smiling, and (3) motor activity. Each behavior was precisely defined, and a score of 1 or 0 was assigned to the category, depending on its presence or absence at the time of observation.

Williams et al. note that the Behavioral Rating Scale correlates $r = .71$ ($p < .05$) with the Hamilton Rating Scale (Hamilton, 1960) and $r = .67$ ($p < .05$) with the Beck Depressive Inventory (Beck et al., 1961). In addition, the scale was found to be superior to the Beck Depressive Inventory and Hamilton Rating Scale in predicting course of posthospital adjustment for severely depressed patients.

Experimental Design and Procedure During the first baseline period subjects earned tokens contingently upon performance of target behaviors. However, privileges were issued on a noncontingent basis as tokens had no extrinsic value. By contrast, during token economy (contingency management), privileges were issued on an exchange basis according to a predetermined point system. The second baseline period was identical to the first. A reintroduction of the token economy phase (B) was prevented by premature discharge for one subject and changes in medication in the other two subjects. Therefore, the experimental portion of the investigation was terminated at the conclusion of the second baseline phase.

Nursing assistants unfamiliar with the experimental hypothesis were instructed in the use of the Behavioral Rating Scale. Behavioral observations were made surreptitiously by nursing assistants for the three subjects during nonwork-related ward activities between the hours of 0800 and 1600. Eight observations per day were made on a randomly distributed, one-per-hour basis during the baseline and token economy phases of the study.

Results

One set of behavioral measures per experimental phase for the three depressed subjects was rated simultaneously but independently by a second observer. Percentage of agreement between raters for each experimental phase in all three subjects was 100 percent.

Number of points earned and mean behavioral ratings for baseline, token economy, and baseline conditions are presented in Figures 6.4 and 6.5. In

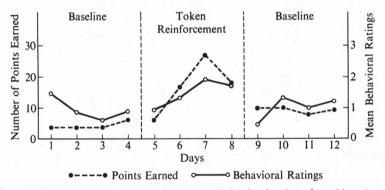

Figure 6.4 Number of points earned and mean behavioral ratings for subject 1.

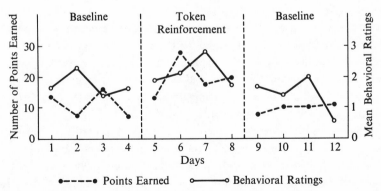

Figure 6.5 Number of points earned and mean behavioral ratings for subject 2.

Figure 6.6 data for the third subject are plotted in blocks of 2 days. Data for all three subjects appear to follow a similar pattern. During baseline there appeared to be concordance between points earned and behavioral ratings in that they both are relatively low. With the introduction of token economy, a dramatic increase in points earned with a concomitant increase in behavioral ratings is noted. The increase in behavioral ratings indicates a *marked diminution of observable depression*. Reinstitution of the baseline phase resulted in a decrease in points earned and an increase of observable depressive behaviors. Clinical impressions by staff were consistent with experimental data in that these subjects were described as "less depressed" during token economy but more "irritable" during baseline phases.

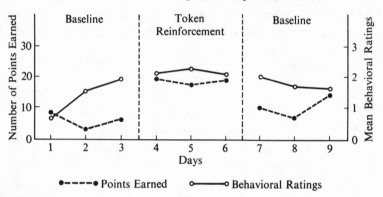

Figure 6.6 Number of points earned and mean behavioral ratings plotted in blocks of 2 days for subject 3.

Discussion

The results of the present investigation indicate that participation in a token economy program which increased work behavior was associated with marked diminution of observable depression in reactively depressed patients. These data lend support to Ayllon and Azrin's (1968) argument that functional behaviors are essentially incompatible with symptomatic manifestation under token economic management.

By increasing the patient's activity level (hospital job tasks, occupational therapy, etc.) via contingent reinforcement, an increased range of social contact was provided. Increased social stimulation probably permitted both the elicitation and reinforcement of target responses of talking, smiling, and activity level. By contrast, in baseline conditions patients decreased their involvement in social situations, thus restricting the availability of reinforcement. Social stimuli which elicited and maintained target responses were absent, and increments obtained under token reinforcement conditions were extinguished. The decrease of positive reinforcement in the genesis and maintenance of depression has previously been documented (Lazarus, 1968; Lewinsohn et al., 1969; Liberman and Raskin, 1971).

The role of the token economy in the treatment of depression should be further examined in both single-case and group design studies. Although token economy programs have been used successfully in the modification of a wide variety of target behavioral problems, few researchers have systematically examined changes appearing in nontarget response classes (see Carlson et al. 1972). Therefore, the concomitant effects of a token economy work program on other behavioral anomalies warrants continued empirical assessment.

References

Ayllon, T. and N. H. Azrin 1968. *The Token Economy: A Motivational System for Therapy and Rehabilitation*. New York: Appleton-Century-Crofts.

Beck, A. T., C. H. Ward, M. Mendelsohn, J. Mock, and J. Erbaugh 1961. "An Inventory for Measuring Depression," *Archives of General Psychiatry*. 4:561–71.

Carlson, C. G., M. Hersen, and R. M. Eisler 1972. "Token Economy Programs in the Treatment of Hospitalized Adult Psychiatric Patients: Current Status and Recent Trends. *Journal of Nervous and Mental Disease,* 155:192–204.

Hamilton, M. 1960. "A rating Scale for Depression." *Journal of Neurology. Neurosurgery and Psychiatry,* 23:56–62.

Hersen, M., R. M. Eisler, B. S. Smith, and W. S. Agras 1972. "A Token Reinforcement Ward for Young Psychiatric Patients." *American Journal of Psychiatry,* 228–32.

Lazarus, A. A. 1968. "Learning Theory and the Treatment of Depression." *Behavior Research and Therapy,* 6:83–89.

Lewinsohn, P. M., M. S. Weinstein, and D. A. Shaw 1969. "Depression: A Clinical Research Approach," in R. Rubin and C. M. Franks, eds.,

Advances in Behavior Therapy. New York: Academic Press Inc. 231–40.
Liberman, R. P. and D. E. Raskin 1971. "Depression: A Behavioral Formulation." *Archives of General Psychiatry,* 24:515–23.
Williams, J. G., D. H. Barlow, and W. S. Agras 1972. "Behavioral Measurement of Severe Depression." *Archives of General Psychiatry,*
27:330–33.

6.2 Summary

Number of Clients Three depressed male patients in a token economy ward in a hospital served as the subjects. The patients were
treated individually within the ward program.

Specification of Goals In defining goals, the authors attempted to
obtain behavioral referents of depression—talking, smiling, motor
activity—rather than rely on some subjective criterion of depression.
As such, these authors subscribed to the theoretical perspective that
the presence of these particular behaviors were incompatible with
depressive behavior; hence, an increase in talking, smiling, and
motor activity would be consistent with the clinically desired goal.

Measurement Strategy The measurement strategy employed here
was a Type C (multiple evaluators) procedure using an interval
record method (presence/absence of goal behaviors within specified
time intervals). The observers in this instance were natural observers
(nurses) who would not be obtrusive in the ward environment. That
the authors report 100 percent interobserver reliability indicates that
the behaviors in question were defined with such a great degree of
specificity that their presence or absence was easily determined.

Within the clinical research model, a multifactorial measurement
strategy beyond the procedures conducted here would have been
desirable. Some type of paper-and-pencil test (subjective measure
of depression) that would have provided additional data confirming
or not confirming the objective findings could have strengthened the
clinical findings. In fact, the authors did get some "clinical impressions" (subjective evaluations) from the staff that corroborated the

findings. This appears, however, to have been an afterthought rather than a planned effort.

Design This study clearly identifies the three phases of the *ABA* design. As indicated earlier, it is not clinically desirable to end treatment with the *A* phase, unless circumstances force such an option. These authors attribute their inability to reintroduce the successful *B* intervention phase (token economy) to changes in the situational context that were beyond their control. This is an example of a proscribed or naturally induced reversal/withdrawal situation, which was discussed earlier in this chapter. While the clients in this instance may not have been the beneficiary of service, it is difficult to deny the possibility that the clinician-researcher may have learned of the value of token economies in dealing with this type of situation. This, then, is the type of accidental situation that would lead to more efficient service delivery in the future.

Data Patterns The data patterns in the three subjects during the three phases (*ABA*) clearly illustrate that the reversal/withdrawal of intervention resulted in a return to baseline behavior. The success of intervention is particularly apparent in the third subject (Figure 6.6) in that the behaviors are relatively stable. In contrast, the reader is also sensitized to the apparent "increasing baseline" with the behavioral ratings during the first baseline period. Similarly, the baseline of the second subject's points earned and behavioral ratings show a distinctly "variable baseline." These data patterns show the desirability of a longer baseline period than was employed here, in an attempt to obtain further stability. Given these data patterns, it is somewhat difficult to demonstrate the effectiveness of intervention with a high degree of confidence. By the same token, however, the reality of intervention often precludes a longer baseline period. Furthermore, the clinician-researcher must also decide whether a score variation between 10 and 20 rating points (Figure 6.5) is indeed variation. Thus, some level of acceptability must be predetermined.

Other observations Some readers may react negatively to the fact that the data (on talking, smiling, and motor activity) were collected "surreptitiously." We believe that this is an individual decision. By surreptitious observation, the authors were able to obtain a "true" (or more accurate) picture of client functioning (on the assumption that client knowledge of measurement may have led to a reactive arrangement and, hence, to a possible change in behaviors being observed). The observation in and of itself was neutral; it did neither harm nor good to the client. As a measurement strategy surreptitious observation allowed for a higher degree of empiricism. As a clinical strategy one could argue that such observations were responsible for determining an effective intervention program for this client in particular, and other clients in the long run.

Reinforcing Self-Help Group Activities of Welfare Recipients

L. KEITH MILLER and OCOEE L. MILLER, University of Kansas

Applied behavior analysis has been defined as the application of behavior analysis to the solution of socially relevant problems (Baer et al., 1968). Socially relevant situations thus studied have included mental hospital wards (Ayllon and Azrin, 1969), classrooms (Hall et al., 1968), preschools (Bushnell et al., 1968), autistic children (Lovaas et al., 1965), and a variety of individual behavior problems. In these situations it has been found that reinforcement procedures can be used to increase the occurrence of "desirable" behaviors. This provided some evidence that behavior analysis can be successfully applied to a wide variety of socially relevant problems.

With its strong emphasis on socially relevant problems, it is not surprising that behavior analysis has begun to be applied to the behavioral components of poverty. For example, a number of studies have been directed at improving the educational attainment of low-income youths (Wolf et al., 1968; Bushell and Jacobson, 1969; Jacobson et al., 1969; Clark et al., 1968; Miller and Schneider, 1968; Hart and Risley, 1968). Another study has been directed at increasing the rate of "desirable" behaviors among institu-

Reprinted from *Journal of Applied Behavior Analysis,* 3 (Spring 1970): 57–64. Used by permission of the Society for Experimental Analysis of Behavior.

tionalized juvenile offenders (Phillips, 1968). These studies provide some evidence that behavior analysis can also be successfully applied to some of the problems posed by poverty conditions.

Poor persons are, however, increasingly rejecting approaches to poverty based solely on changing their behavior to conform to existing institutions. They are demanding that existing institutions be changed and even that new institutions be invented. This demand requires not only behavioral changes on the part of poor persons but also changes on the part of other segments of our society. Thus, a more nearly complete approach to the conditions that cause and maintain poverty may require changing the behavior of both poor persons and others in ways that do not conform to existing institutional requirements.

Part of this more nearly complete approach to poverty has focused on creating new organizations composed and governed exclusively by poor persons and directed toward planning and executing programs for their own benefit (Clinard, 1966). Self-help programs sponsored by these groups include self-improvement through education, cooperatives, and other business enterprises; the organization of pressure groups; and the development of groups to improve neighborhood and housing conditions. The successful establishment of self-help groups requires behavioral change among both the poor and the rest of the community. However, these groups can be a potent force for creating the social change necessary to deal with poverty conditions.

If self-help groups are to be successful agents for social change, they must be capable of attracting and maintaining the participation of poor persons. In behavioral terms this would mean that participation must result in reinforcement if it is to be maintained. One might guess that the long-range and often indirect benefits produced by these groups—such as cleaner neighborhoods, educational improvement, progressive government—would not be sufficiently strong reinforcers to maintain the participation of poor persons. However, there is some evidence from questionnaire and interview surveys that poor persons participate less frequently than the middle class in such voluntary groups as unions, political associations, and churches (Berelson and Steiner, 1964). This suggests that such long-range benefits may not be sufficiently strong reinforcers to maintain the participation of poor persons. If self-help groups are to provide a successful approach to poverty, a method for maintaining participation must be found.

A behavioral approach to maintaining participation requires that "participation" be specified in behavioral terms. However, this is an almost impossible task because participation is a catchall term including attending meetings, speaking, listening, carrying out assignments, keeping minutes, and negotiating with other groups. An alternative behavioral approach is to select a particularly relevant aspect of participation that can be simply specified and investigate methods for maintaining just that aspect. In the present experiment, attendance at meetings was chosen for investigation. It is a particularly relevant aspect of participation because it is an "entry" behavior for most other aspects of participation. If a person attends meetings he can also talk, listen, keep minutes, chair the meeting, and receive assignments. Furthermore, meeting attendance is methodologically convenient in that it has a physically specifiable definition and can be directly observed.

In the present experiment, the use of supplementary reinforcement was examined as a method for maintaining meeting attendance. During two experimental periods, supplementary reinforcement was delivered. In order to assess the effect of this procedure, two control periods were instituted during which no supplementary reinforcement was delivered. Thus, the present experiment evaluates the effectiveness of supplementary reinforcement in maintaining meeting attendance in comparison with the effectiveness of the reinforcers inherent in self-help groups.

Method

Membership Membership in the self-help group was restricted to current recipients in the Aid to Families with Dependent Children (ADC) program of a small midwestern city. In the beginning of the experiment 94 families received ADC; by the end of the study 120 families received it. Of these, 52 family members participated in the self-help groups; 50 were women, 2, men; they ranged in age from 18 to 57 years.

Personnel One author served as a welfare counselor, providing assistance and information to about 50 welfare recipients in the 8 months before the experiment. As a result she was familiar with welfare problems, the welfare agency's response to such problems, and many of the relevant regulations of the agency.

Self-Help Groups Two self-help groups were formed. The membership of each group was determined by its members, who elected a president from among themselves. All meetings except the first one were held in a member's home at a time designated by the president. Members were notified by mail of the date, time, and place of the meeting. Meetings were scheduled monthly.

Meeting Procedures All meetings followed a formal agenda. First, roll was taken and the 25-cent dues collected and recorded. Second, the president using the notes of the previous meeting, found out if all outstanding individual problems had been solved. Each person was specifically asked about any problem that had been described at the previous meeting. If a problem had not been solved, the group decided what further steps to take. Third, the president went over a checklist of welfare problems with each member. This checklist included questions about whether the members received all checks on time last month, received their medical card, and received any increases or decreases in their allowances. Fourth, the members discussed new problems revealed by the checklist or brought up by members. A specific strategy for solving any new problems was arrived at through discussion. Fifth, a general discussion of other community affairs that affected group members was initiated. This ranged over such areas as urban renewal, school board policy, police problems, and city government. If members decided there was a problem, a strategy for dealing with it was decided upon. Finally, additional resources were described. These included services and used goods. Quarterly meetings of all presidents were scheduled in addition to monthly membership meetings. These meetings were designed to exchange information about strategy, agency response, and membership reaction, and to coordinate the different self-help groups.

Procedure During the first phase of the experiment, all ADC recipients were notified by mail before each of three meetings designed to form self-help groups. The welfare counselor was present to explain the purpose of the groups, but there was no supplementary reinforcement for attending these meetings. This phase lasted for three meetings.

At the beginning of the second phase, each recipient was informed in writing of another meeting to form self-help groups. This time, however, they were offered the opportunity to select two free Christmas toys for each child in their family if they attended the meeting. At subsequent meetings of the individual self-help groups, the members in attendance were permitted to ask for any of the types of items listed in Table 6.1. If the item was available, it was given to the recipient on the spot or arrangements were made for its delivery. If the item was not available, the member was permitted to continue making selections. If a member did not select an item, or if no acceptable items were available, then she received none for attending that meeting. Less than 10 percent of the requests were for unavailable items. The goods were solicited from the "concerned" middle-class community by the welfare counselor. Many items were maintained in a storage facility. Services and information were similarly sought out by the counselor. To the extent that the counselor was unsuccessful, these items were unavailable. The second phase lasted eight meetings.

Table 6.1. REINFORCERS AVAILABLE FOR ATTENDING MEETINGS

Goods:
1. Toys
2. Stoves
3. Refrigerators
4. Furniture
5. Clothing
6. Rugs
7. Kitchen utensils

Services:
1. Assistance in negotiating an ADC grievance
2. Assistance in locating a suitable house
3. Assistance in negotiating house improvements with landlord
4. Assistance in clearing up police or court problems
5. Finding odd jobs for teenagers
6. Day camp scholarships
7. Beauty and poise classes

Information:
1. Additional ADC-grant benefits
2. Benefits from other social service agencies
3. Birth control information

The third phase was introduced when the welfare counselor discontinued attendance at meetings due to major surgery, and supplementary reinforcers were not available for attending meetings. This phase lasted for eight meetings.

During the fourth and final phase the counselor again accepted invitations and thereby made reinforcers available to members who attended meetings.

The president of each group was notified of this at the beginning of the first month of this phase. This phase lasted for several meetings.

Results

The average number of ADC recipients who attended the first 26 meetings of the study is shown in Figure 6.7. These data show that an average of about three persons attended meetings during the first phase when the counselor was present but supplementary reinforcers were not contingent upon attending. No recipients attended during the last meeting of this phase. During the second phase, when supplementary reinforcers were given, attendance increased to an average of 15 recipients per meeting. During the third phase, when supplementary reinforcement was not available because the counselor was absent, attendance averaged about three recipients per meeting. Finally, when supplementary reinforcement was again given (during the fourth phase), attendance increased and stabilized at an average of about 16 recipients per meeting. These data show that more recipients attended meetings when supplementary reinforcement was available to them than when it was not.

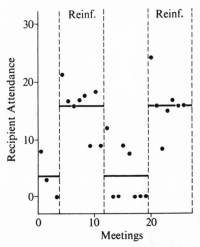 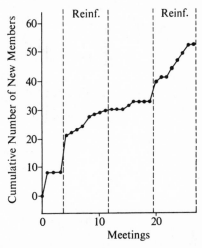

Figure 6.7 Number of welfare recipients attending each of the first 26 meetings of the self-help groups. Recipients were given supplementary reinforcement during the periods labeled "Reinf.".

Figure 6.8 Cumulative number of members attending their first meeting when reinforcement was contingent on attendance (Reinf.) and during periods when it was not.

Figure 6.8 shows the number of new members attending each of the 26 meetings. The data show that seven attended the first meeting of the self-help groups when no supplementary reinforcement was contingent on attendance. The average rate of acquiring new members for the other 10 meetings when no supplementary reinforcement was scheduled was 0.2 per meeting; when supplementary reinforcement was scheduled the average was 2.8 for phase 2 and 2.7 for phase 4. A total of 52 members or about 10 percent of the total persons on welfare were attracted to the groups during the study. The data show, however, that members were attracted primarily when supplementary reinforcement was contingent upon attendance.

The data in Figure 6.8 suggest that the overall effect of supplementary reinforcement may have been to attract new members regularly but not necessarily to keep them. Figure 6.9 shows the attendance rates for phases 2, 3,

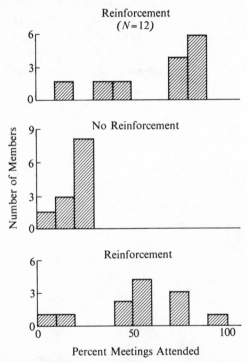

Figure 6.9 Percent of meetings attended by all (12) recipients who were members during these three periods. Arrows indicate mean percent of meetings attended during that condition.

and 4 for the 12 recipients who remained eligible for membership in the group for the entire study. Of the other nine members attending the first reinforced meeting, six moved from town, two dropped out of ADC, and one was dismissed from the club for violating the privacy of group members. The graph shows the number of those 12 who attended N percent of the meetings for a particular phase, for each of the three phases. Thus, during the first phase that supplementary reinforcement was available, six members attended between 80 and 90 percent of the meetings, three membrs attended between 70 and 80 percent of the meetings, and so on. As can be seen from the graphs, most of the members attended more than 50 percent of the meetings when supplementary reinforcement was available. On the other hand, no members attended more than 30 percent of the meetings when supplementary reinforcement was not available. The trends for individual subjects are similar for 10 of the 12 members with only 1 member failing to show an increase during the final reinforcement phase. These data show that the reinforcement contingency maintained attendance among most of these 12 individual subjects.

Another method for exploring the ability of the supplementary reinforcement to both initiate and maintain attendance is to explore attendance of all 52 members between their first meetings and the time at which they become ineligible. If we define the failure to attend four or more consecutive meetings as "dropping membership" in the group, then only seven members voluntarily dropped out. An additional 17 became ineligible for continued membership. Thus, some level of continued attendance was maintained in 86 percent of the total persons who experienced the contingency at least once. Furthermore, counting all the time during which a person remained eligible from his first meeting attended, persons attended an average of 64 percent of all meetings scheduled. (During the periods of nonreinforcement, persons attended about 20 percent of all meetings). These data suggest that the use of supplementary reinforcement maintained a continued participation in the self-help groups among most persons who experienced the contingency.

One further question of interest is whether the involvement in one highly structured self-help group "generalizes." Do members tend to become involved in other civic activities? Unfortunately, data were kept on only one aspect of such "generalization."

Figure 6.10 shows the number of civic groups attended by the presidents of the two self-help groups. While neither president had participated in civic

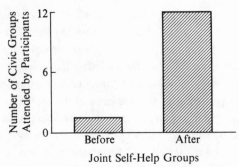

Figure 6.10 Number of civic groups attended by self-help group members before and after joining.

affairs before joining the group, they attended over 10 new groups one or more times after joining. This participation included formal membership in the local OEO governing board, the Model Cities advisory board, a citizen's advisory board, and a school integration committee. It included attendance at meetings of the city council, school board, and mayor's youth advisory committee. The participation of the other members was not systematically observed, but there did seem to be some increase among them too.

Discussion

The results indicate that more persons attended self-help group meetings when supplementary reinforcement was available than when it was not. The low rate when no supplementary reinforcement was scheduled occured whether the counselor was present (phase 1) or absent (phase 3). If the information and services provided by the counselor in these meetings is considerd part of the supplementary reinforcement system (see Table 6.1), it is possible to conclude from this design that the absence of supplementary reinforcement leads to a low rate of attendance. Unfortunately the design does not definitively isolate the role of the counselor's social presence in the group meetings. Her presence in the first phase was not sufficient to maintain attendance, but possibly it would have been after a history of supplementary reinforcement. Furthermore, the presence of the counselor when supplementary reinforcement was scheduled leaves unanswered whether the attendance would continue at a high level if supplementary reinforcement could be scheduled by the group members themselves. Thus, the present experiment cannot be said to have established a procedure for developing and maintaining self-help groups unaided by outside personnel. It does clearly show that self-help groups can be aided in their formation and maintenance by a system of supplementary reinforcement delivered by a technical assistant to the group.

The present procedure did not lead to the involvement of all welfare recipients in self-help groups. In fact, strictly in terms of attendance, less than 20 percent participated in any one group meeting. However, the method was successful in maintaining the participation of most individuals who came into contact with the supplementary reinforcement. Few such individuals voluntarily dropped from the group (14 percent); while most individuals maintained a steady rate of attendance (64 percent attendance including those that dropped). Thus, the problem of generating greater involvement among all eligible recipients would seem to involve devising procedures for getting them to sample the reinforcement at least once. Some extension of the reinforcement sampling procedures explored by Azrin and Ayllon (1968) might be suitable. At any rate, the present experiment would seem to establish the success of the method in maintaining attendance after that first sampling.

There is some evidence that participation in the self-help groups generalized to other forms of self-help; the attendance of the presidents at civic meetings increased from none before their membership in the self-help groups to about 10 groups afterward. Casual evidence also suggested that similar although less pronouned increases occurred among other group members. It was also noted that an increased utilization of tutors for their children also occurred among group members. While evidence of generalization was not generated by an adequate experimental design, it is suggestive of such an effect. If such generalization does occur, it suggests that reinforcing attendance at meetings may have a kind of triggering effect leading poor persons to greater participation in controlling their own lives. Such a possibility clearly warrants further, and more careful, investigation.

Two features of the present procedures may be singled out for additional discussion: (1) the use of attendance as the target behavior (2) the use of supplementary reinforcers.

The first major feature of the present procedure is the use of attendance as a target behavior. We see it as the first step in solving a difficult methodological problem: how to measure the success of a procedure in forming a self-help group. Previous approaches to this type of problem have relied on attitude scales and various subjective measurements (Hyman et al., 1962) or "membership" (Clinard, 1966), which need not require participation. The use of attendance provides a directly observable approximation to success that can also have reinforcement contingencies applied to it. It suggests further approximations to defining a successful self-help group.

Thus, the use of attendance as a target behavior might be extended to group programs other than "meetings"; e.g., attendance in adult education programs, at projects that create income for the self-help groups, and at neighborhood rehabilitation projects. The attendance of a new member at one or more meetings may also be used to define "recruitment," and the recruiter can be reinforced. Thus, as simple a behavior as attendance can be elaborated to a wide variety of projects within self-help groups, including even the growth of membership itself. Each added project would permit a closer approximation to a successful self-help group.

Attendance might be used as a target behavior with respect to programs outside the self-help groups as well. Thus, attendance at city council, school board, and urban renewal meetings provides a further elaboration of the success of self-help groups.

These examples suffice to suggest that attendance could be used to measure the participation of members, not only in discussion meetings, but also in a wide variety of projects within the self-help groups and between them and the broader community. Further, since it is an objective behavior, reinforcement contingencies could be specified to increase the attendance in these projects. Taken together, these elaborations of the present study would represent a significant approximation to community development goals within a behavior modification framework.

Further elaborations of the present work might take either or both of two directions. First, further specification might be undertaken of target behaviors when self-help group members meet together. Thus, different dimensions of attendance at group meetings might be specified, such as coming on time, paying dues, and bringing membership materials. Further specification might involve defining different roles within the meeting: taking attendance, recording dues payments and making a treasurer's statement, recording on a checklist individual welfare problems, making an agenda, recording minutes, and sending out notices of the next meeting. All of these target behaviors are easily observed and reinforcement criteria could be specified.

A second elaboration would involve measuring the effect of the self-help group in relation to the broader community. Thus, the effect of membership on the size of welfare benefits could be measured. The reassignment of recipients to new caseworkers, or even the termination of caseworkers could be determined. The size of the group's treasury and the size of its used-item stockpile could be additional measures. Membership in community groups such as War on Poverty and, perhaps ultimately, the election to local office provide further measurable criteria of the success of self-help groups.

The second major feature of the procedure is the use of supplementary reinforcers. It may be thought that the low-income individual lives in a subculture which displays feelings of despair, defeatism, and powerlessness (e.g., Clinard, 1966; Harrington, 1962). Consequently, community organizers sometimes emphasize the formulation of relatively minor initial goals that may be achieved immediately. This emphasis on quick success may be one way to increase the chance that the participation of the individual group member will be reinforced. The present procedure was an attempt to guarantee that members' participation would be reinforced by utilizing reinforcers that were not necessarily intrinsic to long-range group goals. These supplementary reinforcers allowed for the systematic scheduling of meaningful consequences that would maintain individual participation until other naturally available reinforcers can develop control. Such supplementary reinforcers may be imperative during the initial phases of an organization when it is not yet strong enough to guarantee group success.

Potential supplementary reinforcers can be readily obtained by organizers in almost any community. Such items as used clothing, furniture, appliances, and toys are readily available as donations from the more affluent members of the community who are "concerned" about poverty. Information about welfare policy regulations can frequently be obtained from a sympathetic caseworker or by accompanying a recipient to the welfare office to inspect the policy book. Other potential reinforcers such as tutoring services, free summer camp or day camp scholarships, admission to recreational facilities, as well as arts and crafts workshops are often available without charge.

Greater flexibility in the management of such supplementary reinforcers may be achieved through the use of a token system (Ayllon and Azrin, 1969). A self-help group might award a token to each member who attends a meeting. The members might then decide, for example, that a used refrigerator could be exchanged for 40 tokens. Four tokens (say) might be given to a person who brings a potential member to a meeting: five tokens might be given for attending a relevant public meeting (e.g., school board, city planning) and reporting back to the group. Such procedures would allow reinforcement contingencies to be attuned more sensitively to the needs of the group.

References

Ayllon, T. and H. H. Azrin 1969 *The Token Economy*. New York; Appleton-Century-Crofts.

Azrin, H. H. and T. Ayllon 1968. "Reinforcer Sampling: A Technique for Increasing the Behavior of Mental Patients." *Journal of Applied Behavior Analyis*, 1:3–20.

Baer, D., M. Wolf, and T. Risley 1968. "Some Current Dimensions of Applied Behavior Analysis," *Journal of Applied Behavior Analysis*, 1:91–97.

Berelson, B. and G. A. Steiner 1964. *Human Behavior*. New York: Harcourt Brace.

Bushell, D. and J. Jacobson 1969. "The Simultaneous Rehabilitation of Mothers and Their Children." *Boston Association for the Education of Young Children Reports*, 1:85–90.

Bushell, D., Patricia Ann Wrobel, and Mary Louis Michaelis 1968. "Applying Group Contingencies to the Classroom Study Behavior of Preschool Children," *Journal of Applied Behavior Analysis*, 1:55–61.

Clark, M., J. Lachowicz, and M. Wolf 1968. "A Pilot Basic Education Program for School Dropouts Incorporating a Token Reinforcement System," *Behavior Research and Therapy*, 1:183–88.

Clinard, M. 1966. *Slums and Community Development*. Toronto: Collier-Macmillan.

Hall, V., D. Lund, and D. Jackson 1968. "Effects of Teachers' Attention on Study Behavior," *Journal of Applied Behavior Analysis*, 1:12.

Harrington, M. 1962. *The Other America*. Baltimore: Penguin Books.

Hart, B. and T. Risley 1968. "Establishing Use of Descriptive Adjectives in the Spontaneous Speech of Disadvantaged Preschool Children." *Journal of Applied Behavior Analysis,* 1:109–20.

Hyman, H., C. R. Wright, and T. K. Hopkins 1962. *Applications of Methods of Evaluations.* Berkeley: University of California Press.

Jacobson, J., D. Bushell, and T. Risley 1969. "Switching Requirements in a Head Start Classroom." *Journal of Applied Behavior Analysis,* 2:43–47.

Lovaas, I., B. Schaeffer, and J. Simmons 1965. "Building Social Behavior in Autistic Children by Use of Electric Shock." *Journal of Experimental Research in Personality,* 1:99–109.

Miller, L. K. and R. Schneider 1968. "The Use of a Token System in Project Head Start." Paper read at meetings of American Psychological Association, San Francisco.

Phillips, E. 1968. Achievement Place: Token Reinfocement Procedures in a Home-Style Rehabilitation Setting for Pre-delinquent Boys," *Journal of Applied Behavior Analysis,* 1:213–23.

Wolf, M., D. Giles, and V. Hall 1968. "Experiments with Token Reinforcement in a Remedial Classroom," *Behavior Research and Therapy,* 1:51–64.

6.3 Summary

Number of Clients The client system in this case is actually a group of clients—52 ADC welfare recipients who were involved in a group program in an attempt to generate self-help activities.

Specification of Goals A primary goal of the study was to maintain the recipients' attendance at self-help groups. The implicit contention, of course, is that in order to benefit from the group, the member must attend. A secondary goal was to investigate whether participation in a highly structured self-help group would generalize to involvement in community groups. This secondary goal can then be viewed as an indicator of the group's success in developing self-help activities.

Measurement Strategy Given the simplicity of the objectives, a simple count was kept of the number of members attending the group meetings. Since one goal of the program was to increase attendance, the more members that attended the meetings, the greater the success.

The secondary goal of generalized participation in other community groups was also easily measured by a simple count. Here, the authors simply counted the number of civic groups attended by the participants after the program began.

It may be argued that these counts are very rough indicators of program success and do not measure real change. At the same time, however, the counts are direct measures of the defined goals, and this, in fact, is the prime purpose of measurement. Depending on one's theoretical bend, additional measures (such as self-esteem) could be incorporated, provided that the decision to include these was made prior to treatment.

Design This is an example of an *ABAB* design, this one being, however, conducted with a group. As in the *ABA* design presented earlier, this is an unplanned and opportunistic reversal—the welfare counselor required surgery, and the reinforcement program had to be discontinued, but the group continued without her presence and the reinforcement program. The counselor was present during the first baseline period, but not the second. This leads one to believe that it was the availability of the reinforcements that led to the maintenance of attendance, rather than the presence or absence of the counselor.

Data Patterns The data patterns clearly illustrate three alterations in attendance trends, all of which covary with the presence or absence of reinforcement. Thus, this study illuminates the value of tangible reinforcers in working with groups of welfare recipients.

Figure 6.10 substantiates the secondary goal, that the behaviors generated by the planned meetings generalized into other community activity and thus supported the intervention procedures employed by the counselor.

Other Observations It is questionable whether the reversal/withdrawal could have been accomplished in this instance if the counselor had not fallen ill. We stated earlier that, quite often, reversal/withdrawal designs are more opportunistic rather than deliberate—unless unique appropriate conditions are present. When such an opportunity does arise, however, an opportunity that adds validity to the treatment process, it should be taken advantage of for developmental purposes. Such a procedure could not be incorporated unless the clinician-researcher was already collecting data. Hence the value of continuous application of clinical research designs.

This study also illustrates the simplicity of collecting data. Only the counselor was involved. If the counselor so desired, the generalization effects could have been strengthened further by involving the leaders of the civic groups as evaluators (Type C). This may have provided a stronger intervention and more data but, at the same time, would have complicated the activities of the counselor. Such a decision becomes more a pragmatic one based on time/cost factors, work load, and the like. As a rule of thumb, however, the proposed Type C procedure is more desirable.

Chapter Seven

MULTIPLE-BASELINE DESIGNS

7.1 Multiple Baseline Design A_1B
A_2A_2B
$A_3A_3A_3B$

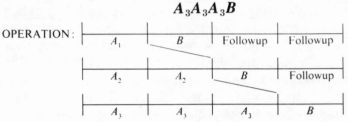

A_1 = baseline period of first problem/goal, situation, or individual.

A_2 = baseline period of second problem/goal, situation, or individual.

A_3 = baseline period of third problem/goal, situation, or individual.

THE MULTIPLE-BASELINE design involves the sequential application of an intervention strategy to two or more problems/goals, situations, or individuals, while concurrently taking measurements on all the target problems/goals, situations, or individuals. This design is particularly useful when more than one problem/goal, situation or individual need to be intervened with at a given point in time. Also, unlike the *ABAB* designs, no reversal/withdrawal is necessary to demonstrate the impact of intervention. The multiple-baseline design is illustrated by the schema above. Time is represented by movement from left to right; therefore, A_1, A_2, and A_3 occur simultaneously.

Superficially then, it appears that the multiple-baseline design is simply a series of *AB* designs. In a sense this is true. The critical difference between this design and two or more sequentially applied *AB* designs (where the same intervention package is used) is that here, measurement is begun at the same time for all problems/goals situations or individuals. This measurement is continued concurrently for all targets until the end of all treatment periods. Furthermore, the application of intervention with the second problem/goal

172

and so on, does not occur, until a period of intervention has already taken place with the first problem/goal, and so forth. Thus, although the intervention is introduced to each separate problem/goal, and so on at different points in time, the measurement periods are concurrent. If change occurs in each measured area during the period of intervention (and only during this period), the logic of the design argues that the intervention produced the change (on the principle of unlikely coincidences).

Before the alternate forms of the multiple-baseline design are discussed, the following points are important in understanding this design:

1. A_1, A_2, and A_3 represent baseline data on three different problems/goals, situations, or individuals. For example, the clinician-researcher may be gathering baseline data on a couple's sexual relationship (A_1), communication patterns (A_2), and decision-making patterns (A_3). This represents the gathering of baseline data across behaviors on the same client system. (Presumably, these three behaviors have been targeted as problems that need to be changed.) On the other hand, the clinician-researcher may be working with three alcoholics in an outpatient clinic and is concerned with how they are adjusting. Here, the worker may apply a "family relations scale" to Jim (A_1), John (A_2), and Jerry (A_3). By simultaneously working with all three alcoholics and measuring their relative adjustment, the clinician-researcher is employing the multiple-baseline design across individuals. Finally, in working with a delinquent child, the clinician-researcher may be interested in finding out whether his interventions at home would result in better behavior at school and in the community. Thus, the clinician-researcher would evaluate the child's behavior at home (A_1), at school (A_2), and in the community (A_3). This example illustrates the application of the multiple-baseline design across situations. It is extremely important to realize, however, that only one of these modes may change within a design. Thus, if the clinician-researcher elects to change situations, the individuals and problems/goals must be held the same across all situations, and so forth.

2. The intervention package and the measurement strategy B remain the same throughout all intervention phases. The clinician-

researcher, in essence, is repeatedly testing the efficacy of the intervention program with each successive application. Thus, there is internal replication (over time) of the intervention package B, adding validity to its effectiveness or noneffectiveness.

3. Note that, while intervention is taking place with problem A_1, baseline data are being collected on problems A_2 and A_3. Thus the clinician-researcher would end up with different durations of baseline data for the different problems/goals, and so forth.

4. Finally, a critical point concerns the relative interdependence between target problems/goals, situations, or persons (that is, the dependent variables). The higher the degree of interrelatedness, the greater the likelihood that change in one of the target problems/goals, situations, or persons will simultaneously result in change in another. In general, this problem is particularly sensitive when one is working with multiple behaviors.

For example, when one is working with an alcoholic, the multiple-baseline design would lose much of its power if one were to measure his "frequency of drinking," as well as his "quantity of consumption," since the two are probably highly related. As illustrated in Figure 7.1, reducing the frequency of drinking would more than likely result in reduced consumption. The clinician-researcher, in this instance, would be hard pressed to state that intervention produced change rather than some other unknown factor. In this instance, we have in effect a simple AB baseline design with a Type B measurement strategy, showing one alteration in data pattern.

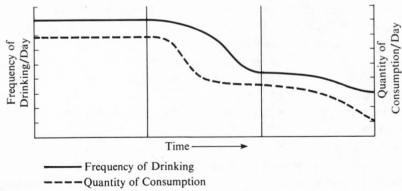

Time ⟶

——— Frequency of Drinking

– – – – Quantity of Consumption

Figure 7.1 A simple *AB* baseline design with a Type B measurement strategy.

In contrast, increasing communication between a marital couple may or may not increase their sexual contact. The latter may require a separate application of the same intervention program. In general, to implement a multiple-baseline design across behaviors, there must be reasonable assurance that the target behaviors are relatively independent, if any cause-effect statement is to be made, that would have a higher degree of validity than the simple *AB* design. If on the other hand there is reason to believe that the behaviors are related, then the multiple-baseline design can be used to test for generalization.

When multiple-baseline designs are used across situations or individuals, the question of interrelatedness may be less of a factor. Different persons and situations are less likely to be affected than different behaviors within the same person. Nonetheless, interrelatedness remains a possibility, and it must be considered in the application of any multiple-baseline design.

5. In view of the possibility of interrelatedness and to maximize the power of the multiple-baseline design, Hersen and Barlow (1976) and Wolf and Risley (1971) offer the following rule of thumb: When employing the multiple-baseline designs across problems/goals, situations, or individuals, monitor at least *three different* problems/goals, situations, or individuals. The power of the three-criteria notion can be viewed under the same probability concepts discussed earlier regarding causality. That is, the more opportunities one has to test the effectiveness of a given intervention program within the same situation, the more information one has to confirm or disconfirm its probable impact. By the same token, however, the three-criteria perspective should be viewed as the guideline it is meant to be, and the clinician-researcher should not hesitate to employ the multiple-baseline designs across two alternatives.

7.2 Multiple Baseline Across Problems/Goals

Here, two or more problems/goals are targeted for change, and baseline data gathered. Figure 7.2 illustrates the ideal data pattern that may be attained with this design. In this approach, the clinician-researcher applies intervention to one target problem/goal at a time

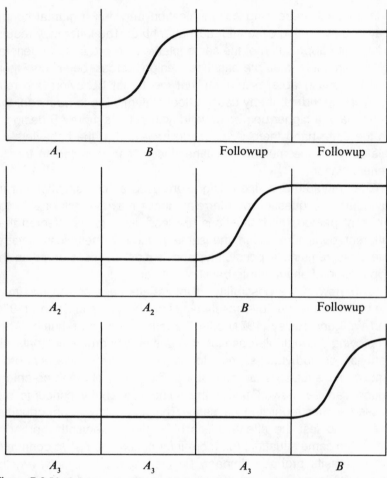

Figure 7.2 Ideal data pattern for multiple baseline across problems/goals.

(on the basis that the assessment criteria show that this problem is the one with the highest priority), while continuing data collection on the others. If this problem shows improvement and others do not, then there is beginning evidence in support of the power of the intervention as a change agent. The next problem is then intervened with, and so on. Each successive intervention that produces change adds more and more evidence toward a cause-effect relationship, following the principle of unlikely successive coincidences.

Design Utility The multiple-baseline design across problems/goals is particularly useful when the client system presents a multiproblem situation. This design allows for the simultaneous gathering of data across all the target problems—an option that has not been available in either of the two design alternatives discussed in the previous chapters.

7.3 Multiple Baseline Across Situations

In the multiple-baseline design across situations, data on a given problem/goal for a client system are collected across two or more physical situations (such as a school, home, or office). As in the across problems/goals alternative, intervention is applied in one situation at a time, with the assumption that change will be seen in that situation and in no other. Obviously, the concept of independence between situations plays a central role.

Design Utility This is one of only a few clinical research designs discussed in this text that allows the clinician-researcher to compare the effects of treatment across different situations. Thus, when problems appear in two different physical contexts (home and school, for example), the clinician-researcher can intervene in both contexts, all the time gathering data and thus ensuring that intervention is effective across both situations.

7.4 Multiple Baseline Across Individuals

In applying the multiple-baseline design across individuals, baseline data on a given problem/goal are collected across two or more individuals. However, the intervention is begun with only one person at a time, while baseline data are gathered on the others. If the one individual with whom intervention took place shows desired change, the second individual is intervened with, and so on. Identical intervention strategies and measurement procedures must be employed across all individuals.

According to Sulzer-Azaroff and Mayer (1977), "the object is to show that, regardless of time, specific subject, and environmental factors, the behavior of each client changes substantially when—and only when—the intervention is introduced" (p. 454). The notion of independence may not be as obvious here as it is in the two previous design options, but it is equally important. The greater the contacts between the target individuals, the more likely it is that the treatment procedures would be conveyed to others and thus contaminate the baseline data and affect the validity of the multiple-baseline design.

Not that the multiple-baseline design across individuals deviates somewhat from the "own control" notion of the clinical research approach. In baseline intervention designs and reversal/withdrawal designs, each client served as his or her own control (preintervention data being compared with postintervention data). Here, not only is there "own control," but also there is the comparison across individuals. Such a procedure would naturally add even more reliability to the process of intervention.

Design Utility The optimum utility of this design would lie in situations where the clinician-researcher is required to work simultaneously with a number of individuals. For example, a teacher at school and a parent at the agency complains of children who "never pay attention." The clinician-researcher may then suggest an intervention strategy to the parent and teacher (two clients) to try at home and at the school respectively.

As in the previous two design alternatives, the individuals participating in the across-persons multiple-baseline design must not be "related." That is, there must be minimal contact between the individuals in treatment—on the assumption that contact would lead to interrelatedness. This design may therefore have less utility in group treatment situations, where there is considerable contact between group members. This design is best when the target problem is something that does not require immediate intervention, since some of the individuals are in effect "denied treatment" for a short period of time. Here, however, the same arguments that were brought up in the context of assessment and procedural efficacy could be reiterated to justify the so-called withholding of treatment.

Strengths and Weaknesses of the Multiple-Baseline Designs

Strengths

1. There is a comparison of what happens to the target problem/goal, before and after intervention.
2. This design, compared to the *AB* baseline intervention design, offers more substantive data to support the notion that *B* in fact produced change. The same intervention strategies are applied over time, producing same or similar results.
3. Although the cause-effect statements are not as strong as in reversal/ withdrawal designs (Hersen and Barlow, 1976; Howe, 1974), these designs offer a powerful alternative where reversibility is problematic.
4. Although the design specifically requires independence between the target problems/goals, situations, or individuals, it can be used as an instrument for the analysis of generalization effects, or covariation among related problems. Thus, when intervention with one problem produces change in another problem (presumably related), or when intervention with one individual produces change in another individual (presumably owing to contact), or when intervention in one situation produces change in another situation (presumably owing to similarity), the possibility of generalization effects must be assumed. When this occurs, the multiple-baseline procedure is no longer a viable design alternative to demonstrate intervention effect. But its very failure has provided valuable information on generalization.
5. The multiple-baseline procedure also offers an opportunity to observe "contravariation," that is, the possibility that, as the intervention produces desirable change in one behavior, it may produce undesirable change in another.

Weaknesses

1. Where multimodal therapies are offered, this design does not allow for discriminative analysis; that is, it would not be possible to isolate the more effective parts from the less effective parts of the intervention program.
2. The requirement that there be independence between the target problems/goals, situations, or individuals often suggests an unrealistic clinical context. As stated earlier, however, nonindependence does not and should not mean that the design has to be abandoned—although its empirical value has been minimized.

3. The design requires the "withholding" of treatment when employed across individuals. Therefore, the utility of this particular option of the multiple-baseline design is delimited by the nature of the problems encountered.

Design Extensions One alternate design extension that is related to multiple-baseline designs: the "changing-criterion design" (Hall, 1971; Weiss and Hall, 1971). In this design extension, baseline data are gathered on a given target problem and/or goal. In the typical paradigm the clinician-researcher would define steps leading up to the final goal. For example, the client who is reinforced for achieving a given subgoal (step 1) must keep achieving more desirable levels (higher order steps) to obtain the same reinforcement. A simple example would be a situation where a child is given a candy bar for doing 10 problems in 15 minutes the first time, but now must do 15 problems within 10 minutes to obtain the same candy bar! Thus, each period of treatment (attainment of first subgoal) serves as the baseline for the next period of treatment (attainment of second subgoal) (Hartmann and Hall, 1976). The ideal pattern for the changing-criterion design is presented in Figure 7.3.

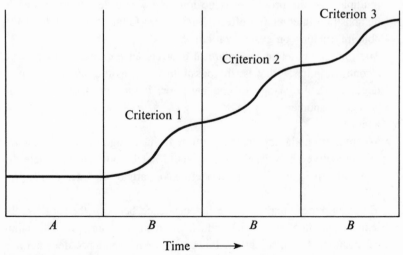

Figure 7.3 Ideal pattern for the changing-criterion design.

Strengths and Weaknesses of the Changing-Criterion Design

Strengths
1. There is a comparison of what happens to the target problem and/or goal, before and after intervention.
2. This design, compared to the *AB* baseline intervention design, offers more substantive data to support the notion that intervention in fact produced change. The same intervention strategies are applied over time, producing increasingly better performance.
3. Although the cause-effect statements are not as strong as in withdrawal/reversal designs, this design offers a powerful alternative where reversibility is problematic.
4. This design offers the unique opportunity to observe the systematic achievement of subgoals. Thus, the design offers the intrinsically desirable clinical quality of positive progress in defined and achievable steps.

Weaknesses
1. Where multimodal therapies are offered, this design does not allow for discriminative analysis. That is, it would not be possible to isolate the more effective parts from the less effective parts of the intervention program.
2. If multiple problems and/or goals are to be intervened with, then the design configuration would get somewhat complicated, and the notion of independence between the target events would come into force.

Suggested Design Utility This design is particularly applicable when the clinician-researcher is using "shaping" procedures, that is, situations where the ultimate goal is broken down into a series of subgoals, and the attainment of each subgoal is a prerequisite for the attainment of the next subgoal, all of which are "successive approximations" to the desired ultimate goal.

Alleviating Marital
Communication Problems

ELEANOR R. TOLSON, University of Chicago

The major purpose of the study reported in this chapter was to evaluate the effectiveness of a set of task-centered methods, the Task Implementation Sequence (Reid, 1975), in alleviating specific problems in face-to-face communication between marital pairs.[1] It is assumed that such problems are a common source of difficulty in marriages and that they contribute to other difficulties (referent problems) in the relationship. That is, if marital partners cannot talk to one another in a mutually satisfying and effective manner, the quality of their marriage is diminished as a result, and they can be expected to have difficulty in working through problems of common concern in respect to children, finances, sex, and so on.

Previous Research

Literature pertinent to the study at hand appears to be scant. In an exploratory project reported by Carter and Thomas (1973), twelve couples were tape recorded while discussing two predetermined topics. From these discussions the researchers prepared a written statement describing their communication strengths and problems and making recommendations. After sharing this analysis with the couples, the researchers requested that they discuss one of the previous topics again. The experimenters selected four problems for the purpose of examining the effects of intervention and concluded, "The results for the two cases reported are encouraging with regard to the efficacy" of this technique (p. 108).

Two studies by Richard B. Stuart (1968 and 1971), are tangentially related to mine. The sample in the first study was composed of five married couples. The wives' major complaint was a deficit in communication and the husbands' complaint was a deficit in sexual activity. The wives specified the

Reprinted from William J. Reid and Laura Epstein, 1977. *Task-Centered Practice* (New York: Columbia University Press), pp. 100–12. Used by permission of the Press.

kinds of communication they wanted from their husbands. The husbands were rewarded with tokens when they engaged in these communicational acts. The tokens could then be exchanged for physical contact ranging from kissing to intercourse. The weekly intercourse rate increased from an average of zero to over three times per week; the daily conversation rate increased from less than 1 hour to almost 5 hours. Tape recordings were made for all seven treatment sessions with two couples. When these were analyzed to determine the number of positive and negative statements made about the spouse, they revealed that verbal behavior became "markedly more positive" (p. 225).

In the second study, Stuart attempted to increase the number of positive statements made in the interaction of four mother-son pairs where the son was a delinquent. A signaling device called SAM was utilized whereby each of the conversationalists could signal the other by means of lights. Positive or negative statements were indicated by the lights. During the first four sessions the therapists signaled to each after a positive or negative speech. During the last five sessions the mother and son signaled to one another. The increase in positive statements ranged from 20 to 47 percent.

One study (Reid, 1975) tested the effectiveness of the proposed treatment strategy. The design was implemented and the data gathered by twenty first-year students enrolled in the task-centered sequence. Each student treated a control and an experimental case. In both cases they developed a task which was intended to alleviate the target problem. In the experimental case, they then utilized a package of procedures, the Task Implementation Sequence (TIS), which included planning task implementation, establishing commitment, resolving obstacles, modeling, rehearsal, planning recording of task progress, and summarization. In the control case nothing further was done following task formulation. Significantly more experimental than control clients completed the task. While this work supports the efficacy of the TIS, none of the experimental cases were married couples with communication problems, and so its success with this kind of sample and problem is yet to be demonstrated.

Study Plan

I decided to test the efficacy of the TIS as a method of treatment for marital communication problems in a single case. A multiple-baseline design was used in an attempt to isolate the effects of treatment. The logic of the design, as I used it, called for collection of baseline data on a set of problems followed by treatment of each problem in sequence. If each problem showed greater change following treatment than during the baseline period, then one could infer that the change was the result of treatment as opposed to other factors, such as spontaneous recovery or external circumstances. The layout of the design in the present study is presented in Table 7.1 During phase 1, baseline data were obtained on all communication problems. During phase 2, the TIS was employed with respect to the first problem. During phase 3, the TIS was used to work on the second problem, and so on. Once a problem had been treated, the couple was left to work on it largely on their own, as attention shifted to the next problem.

Table 7.1. MULTIPLE-BASELINE DESIGN

Communication Problem	Phases				
	I *Week 1*	*II* *Week 2*	*III* *Weeks 3, 4*	*IV* *Weeks 5, 6, 7*	*V* *Week 30*
1	Baseline	Treatment	Followup	Followup	Followup
2	Baseline	Baseline	Treatment	Followup	Followup
3	Baseline	Baseline	Baseline	Treatment	Followup

The Case

The study was conducted as a part of treatment of a marital pair, the Ts. The couple, both college teachers, had been married 14 years and had three children, ranging in age from 4 to 13. They were referred to me as an independent practitioner from an outpatient psychiatric clinic, where Mr. T. had called requesting marital treatment.

The bulk of the study was conducted during the first portion of treatment (in seven interviews over a 9-week period). Treatment, largely task centered, continued for about 5 months with focus primarily on child rearing and sexual problems. No further attention was given to the communication problems dealt with during the first 9 weeks. At the conclusion of this period, followup data on these communication problems were collected.

Problem Identification and Data Collection During the first 7 weeks, communication problems were identified and monitored by having the *T*s tape record three 7-minute episodes of face-to-face communication each week, one immediately after the session and the other two at home at approximately 2-day intervals.

I tentatively identified the problems after listening to these tape-recorded segments. The unit of analysis used in problem identification was the "speech," which consisted of what each partner communicated while he or she "held the floor." Problems selected for treatment consisted of (1) interruptions, which were defined as occurrences in which one partner began to talk before the other had finished his speech, or in which both partners talked simultaneously; (2) monopolization, defined as the occurrence of speeches in excess of eighty words[2]; (3) topic changes, which were defined as a partner's making shifts or digressions from the topic of the other partner's preceding speech.[3] It was found that the frequencies of all problems could be determined from typescripts with a satisfactory degree of reliability.[4]

Data revealing the frequency of occurrence of the problems were shared with the Ts, along with examples of each problem. The problems were introduced in sequence: after the first problem was identified, treated, and had begun to decrease in frequency, the second problem was introduced, and so on. Although I assumed more responsibility for problem identification than is suggested by the task-centered model, the Ts did agree that each of these problems was a source of difficulty and in fact selected the third (topic changes) from a list of several problems which I prepared. Exploration of other problem areas of concern to them were deferred until later in treatment—another deviation from procedures called for by the model.

Treatment The treatment of the identified communication problems consisted of an application of the TIS. My use of this approach in the present case is outlined below.

Establishing rationale and commitment In Reid's articulation of the TIS, this step pertains to establishing a rationale for the commitment to implementing the task. In this study, this activity was applied to the problem rather than the task. This was necessary because the problems were not originally identified by the Ts and, thus, motivation for altering them could be assumed. My attempt to help the Ts develop a rationale for and a commitment to modify the communication problems differed somewhat from problem to problem.

The first communication problem, interruptions, was addressed in the second interview. It was described as a manifestation of the struggle for control in which the Ts were engaged. Support for the existence of a struggle for control was provided by reminding them of some information they had shared during the baseline or intake interview and by current behavior: namely, that they had difficulty locating any specific problems but were, nevertheless, not getting along with one another. This was supported by explaining a little of communication theory: that a message, in addition to containing content, defines a relationship (Watzlawick et al., 1967). Their frequent interruptions were a way of arguing about who held the floor, or the control in this relationship. Thus, the attempt to build commitment to alter the seemingly trivial problem of interrupting was based on a theoretical explanation. Monopolization became more of a problem after the Ts had made some progress on reducing their rate of interruptions. Although one might expect the length of their speeches to increase if they interrupted each other less, the amount of increase, particularly in Mrs. T's speeches, could not be accounted for by this reason alone. The rationale presented for working on monopolization was that, if one symptom of the control struggle was simply replaced with another, no progress would have been made. Emphasis was placed on the effects of a monopolizing speech, such as the feelings aroused in the listener (impatience and anger) and the loss of content.

Less time and effort was spent on increasing the Ts' commitment to modifying the third communication problem, topic changes. This problem was addressed in the fifth interview. By this time the Ts had already observed that the conversations which began for the purpose of solving a problem dwindled to haggling over unrelated or tangentially related matters. They were reminded of this.

The attempts to develop a rationale for working on the communication problems and, hence, increase the Ts' commitment to modify them differ along what would seem a logical, albeit unanticipated, progression. The progression appears to be based on the ever-increasing knowledge of the clients. In the initial phase of treatment, problem rationales were based on theory. In the middle phase, they were based on a combination of theory and behavioral repercussions for the Ts. Late in treatment the rationale came from the shared experience between therapist and clients. Mr. T, who was primarily concerned about difficulties in their face-to-face interaction, seemed more committed to working on the communication problems than

Mrs. T, who seemed to think the difficulties lay more in their attitudes and feelings toward each other and in other problems, although it was hard for her to be specific.

Task-Formulation This activity began once the problem had been specified and the Ts acknowledged that the problem seemed worth altering. (For the first two problems, it was implied by the act of selecting the problem from a list of problems.)

The activity of formulating a task was begun by a direct question: "What do you want to do about this?" Usually very little additional input was required. Suggestions for a task for each problem were prepared in the event that the Ts were unable to develop one. The Ts seemed to have trouble constructing a task for monopolizing, so one was suggested. The Ts eventually rejected it, however, and constructed their own.

The tasks designed to alter the number of interrupting and monopolizing speeches consisted of each making hand signals to the other when he or she wished to speak. The task for altering topic changes was for each to paraphrase the idea of the other's preceding speech in order to achieve continuity in their dialogue.

A guide to evaluate the potential effectiveness of a task was developed with the Ts. It consisted of the requirement that the task differ sufficiently from normal interaction so that it would be noticed and yet was not so absorbing that it would be difficult to use or would interfere with the ongoing conversation. This guide was necessary to facilitate arbitration of their individual responses to the problem of task development. Mr. T, originally, tried to avoid formulating specific tasks and wanted to cope with the problem "when it comes up." Mrs. T, on the other hand, tended to plan complex tasks which seemed, in themselves, to contain whole new areas for debate. This guide was not anticipated but developed while watching the Ts attempt to formulate the first task. It was articulated at that time.

Analyzing and Resolving Obstacles The tasks developed were interactional; that is, they were designed to effect reciprocal change. Tasks of this sort with couples experiencing marital difficulties present special problems and potential obstacles. First, the relationship is one in which each individual is unlikely to respond positively to attempts by the other to influence his behavior. Thus, it is important to try and design tasks which would avoid, to the extent possible, the arousal of negative feelings. Second, the individual employing the task is likely to become discouraged if using the task doesn't result in some benefit. (This also applies to clients whose tasks are not interactional, but with individual clients one seldom has the opportunity to directly influence the behavior of others in his environment.) This potential obstacle is overcome by planning not only the task but also the response.

The Ts needed only a little help in overcoming these two potential obstacles. With regard to interruptions, Mrs. T directly asked Mr. T if he would become angry when she used the hand signal. He said he would not. Mr. and Mrs. T talked about responses. They discussed questions such as, "Do I stop speaking immediately or do I finish my sentence?"

A couple with less foresight might be helped to eliminate these obstacles by considering two questions: What feeling is the task likely to arouse in this particular responder? What behavior is the task intended to stimulate in the responder?

Modeling, Rehearsal, Guided Practice The Ts began practicing the tasks within the interview without prompting. Since two of the three tasks were nonverbal, the amount of practicing could not be assessed from tapes of the interviews. (Evidence of practicing exists on the tape, however, in the form of inappropriate-sounding laughter from all concerned. The laughter is induced by the hand signals rather than psychoses.)

Planning Client Recording of Task Progress A form had been devised for the purpose of assessing the frequency with which the tasks were utilized. This was given to the Ts, and its usage was explained.

Summarization The task, including when it was to be employed and the response it was to evoke, was restated at the end of the interview in which it was formulated.

The pattern of results revealed in Tables 7.2 through 7.4 suggests that the TIS had an immediate impact on the communication problems. All problem measures show some degree of positive change from the preceding baseline period after the TIS was applied (starred cells), although problem occurrence was not always reduced below earlier baseline measures. In all instances effects persisted at least one phase beyond the treatment phase.

Table 7.2. PERCENTAGES OF INTERRUPTING SPEECHES, MR. AND MRS. T.

Phase	Weeks	Condition	Mr. T	Mrs. T	Combined
I	1	Baseline	67	47	57
II	2	Treatment	26*	30*	28*
III	3, 4	Followup	23*	35	29
IV	5, 6, 7	Followup	17	29	25
V	30	Followup	20	28	24

Table 7.3. PERCENTAGES OF MONOPOLIZING SPEECHES

Phase	Weeks	Condition	Mr. T	Mrs. T	Combined
I	1	Baseline	4	3	4
II	2	Baseline	9	13	11
III	3, 4	Treatment	4*	8*	6*
IV	5, 6, 7	Followup	4*	10	7
V	30	Followup	13	9	11

Table 7.4. PERCENTAGES OF SPEECHES CONTAINING TOPIC SHIFTS

Phase	Weeks	Condition	Mr. T	Mrs. T	Combined
I	1	Baseline	49	52	50
II	2	Baseline	34	34	34
III	3, 4	Baseline	36	53	45
IV	5, 6, 7	Treatment	28*	47*	31*
V	30	Followup	21	30	26

*Point at which TIS was applied.

Results

Data on change in the three communication problems are presented in Tables 7.2–7.4.

Effects seem to be the most clear-cut in respect to interruption, which showed a dramatic decrease after the TIS was introduced; the effects persisted through all subsequent phases. Monopolization has a more complex pattern. As was noted, an increase in lengthy speeches was expected as a result of a decrease in interruptions; thus the phase 2 baseline for monopolization was apparently influenced by the experimental intervention. Percentage of long speeches declined again after the TIS was used but still remained above the initial baseline. It may be that the "optimum" percentage of lengthy speeches is closer to the percentages observed during the treatment phases than to the initial baseline. In appraising these findings it should be noted that the second baseline period contained several instances of excessively long speeches, 180 words or more. Speeches of this length did not recur after the treatment started. The relative frequency of the third problem, topic changes, is less following treatment than for any of the baseline periods (with the exception of the phase 2 baseline for Mrs. T).

Comparing the two partners, one finds that Mrs. T's communication problems showed the greater amount of change immediately following treatment and, for the first two problems, a greater degree of persistence in the phase following. With the exception of the first problem, Mrs. T made relatively more progress than her husband between the end of the treatment period and the final follow-up. In fact, in respect to the third problem, Mrs. T showed more positive change during the 5-month followup period than she did immediately after treatment.

Finally, decreasing amounts of change were achieved during the treatment periods as we moved from problem one to problem three. Examining the data for Mr. and Mrs. T combined, we see that a 68-percent reduction in interruption occurred between the baseline and the treatment period; the comparable reduction for problem two was 45 percent and, for problem three, only 12 percent. The same pattern can be discerned when data for Mr. and Mrs. T are analyzed separately.

Evaluation of Impact and Practice Implications The TIS appeared to be an effective means of reducing specific communication problems. In respect to two of the problems, changes were still evident approximately 5 months after the problems had been treated. At the same time, the study demonstrates the importance of viewing efforts to change such problems in systems terms. Decrease in interruptions may have contributed to the increase in monopolization during the second baseline period and to its lack of persistence in the posttreatment period. This may be an example of "symptom substitution," a much-discussed but little-documented phenomenon. The finding suggests that clinicians who try to affect specific problems in marital interaction need to be aware that their efforts may lead to possible negative side effects need to be appraised in the light of gains achieved. In the present case, it may be argued that some increase in monopolizing speeches was outweighed by the benefit resulting from the decrease in interruptions, which had been a serious obstacle to any meaningful dialogue. Also it is possible that longer speeches are less of a source of strain if they are related to the topic at hand; and there is evidence that the Ts' conversations were becoming more focused with alleviation of their problem of topic changing.

The differences between the partners in speed and amount of problem change may have been related to differing orientations and motivations. Mr. T frequently stated his belief that working on surface interaction was the place to begin. The problems he identified in his marriage concerned face-to-face interaction and the type of treatment which he believed possessed the greatest likelihood of success was one which focused on behavior, especially interaction. Mrs. T, however, was eager to move on to other kinds of problems. While she acknowledged the interrelatedness of feelings and behavior, she believed that changes in feelings must precede changes in behavior. As Mrs. T's communication behavior did change more slowly and erratically than Mr. T's, it is likely that the attributed sources of their discomfort and their beliefs about the most effective treatment approach combined to determine the degree of their motivation for working on communication problems. This, in turn, may have affected changes in the frequency of the problematic communication behavior.

One treatment implication is obvious and supports the task-centered treatment model: work on problems selected by the client is more likely to bear fruit. A second is somewhat more subtle: it may be strategic to use methods which the client believes will successfully solve the problems. Perhaps we should spend less time and effort persuading clients of the efficacy of our methods, and instead offer them referrals to therapists whose methods are in harmony with the clients' beliefs. The versatile therapist could, of course, employ the method most compatible with the client's notions.

The progressive decrease in amount of change in the problems may be accounted for, in part, by Mrs. T's growing resistance to exclusive focus on communication problems. Another partial explanation may be found in the fact that the definitions of the communication problems became less and less distinct. Interruptions are largely an "either-or matter," and both parties are aware or can easily be made aware of their occurrence. Monopolizing is a matter of degree and is affected by the content. If one partner is talking at length about an issue of interest to the other, the listener is less likely to define this speech as monopolizing than if the speaker is talking about something which seems irrelevant. Topic changes are a matter of definition, as evidenced by the fact that it takes trained raters to achieve reliability when measuring their frequency. Certain lessons can be learned from the foregoing: when communication problems are the focus of treatment, the problems should be defined as explicitly as possible. Efforts should be made to select problems, whatever their type, in a way that maximizes the motivation of each partner. Depending on time constraints, the latter can be done by alternating the focus of treatment between problems identified by each spouse. Thus, a specified number of weeks could have been spent working on communication problems (of primary concern to Mr. T), and then a specified number of weeks working on problems identified by Mrs. T. The alternative would have been to balance the time in each interview between the problems of each partner.

In conclusion, task-centered methods appear to have promise as a means of bringing about positive change in specific marital communication problems. There is need for further work of this kind guided by a systems view of marital interaction. In so doing, it will be necessary to develop systematic connections between treatment of separate communication problems and between work on such problems and work on other aspects of the marital relationship.

References

Carter, Robert D. and Edwin J. Thomas 1973. "Modification of Problematic Marital Communication Using Corrective Feedback and Instruction." *Behavior Therapy*, 4:100–109.

Navran, L. 1967. "Communication and Adjustment in Marriage." *Family Process*, 6:173–84.

Reid, William J. 1975. "A Test of Task-centered Approach." *Social Work*, 20:3–9.

Stuart, Richard B. 1968. "Token Reinforcement in Marital Treatment." In Richard D. Rubin et al., eds. *Advances in Behavior Therapy*, vol. 6. New York: Academic Press;——1971. "Assessment and Change of the Communication Patterns of Juvenile Delinquents and Their Parents." In *ibid.*, vol. 8.

Tolson, Eleanor Reardon 1976. "An Evaluation of the Effectiveness of the

Task Implementation Sequence in Alleviating Marital Communication Problems.'' Unpublished Ph.D. dissertation, University of Chicago.

Watzlawick, Paul, Janet H. Beavin, and Don D. Jackson 1967. *Pragmatics of Human Communication*. New York: Norton.

Notes

1. The study is reported in full in Tolson (1976).

2. The 80-word criterion is arbitrary but has the following justification: speeches of that length "stand out" in the Ts' dialogue. Less than 5 percent were of this length in the initial baseline period. A review of a variety of typescripts of family communication suggests that speeches over 80 words in length are generally uncommon in dialogues among family members.

3. As might be expected, a fairly elaborate set of criteria needed to be developed to decide which speeches reflected topic changes. (See Tolson, 1976.)

4. Reliability coefficients for the three variables based on duplicate coding of transcripts of conversations between Mr. and Mrs. T were as follows: interruptions, $r = .85$, monopolization, $r = .97$, topic changes, median percent of agreement = 83.

7.5 Summary

Number of Clients The client system in this study consisted of a husband and wife who had been married for 14 years and had three children. They were seeing the therapist for marital problems.

Specification of Goals The global problem area was defined as one of poor communication. By analyzing tape recordings, the author identified several specific behaviors within the communication process that needed to be changed: interruptions, monopolization of speech, and topic changes. These three target behaviors were specified concretely (for example, interrruption, being defined as "occurrences in which one partner began to talk before the other had finished his speech") and resulted in reliability coefficients of .85, .97, and .83 respectively when duplicate recordings were done. The goal of treatment was to reduce the occurrence of each of these undesirable behaviors.

Measurement Strategy The marital couple was asked to tape record a series of face-to-face communications. These were then transcribed, and the transcripts were analyzed for the frequency of occurrence of the target behaviors. The tape recordings were made at 2-day intervals, resulting in a multiple-point measurement strategy.

In the multiple-baseline, across-behaviors design being used, interruptive behavior was baselined for 1 week, monopolizing speech for 2 weeks, and topic changes for 4 weeks—all baseline data collection being started at the same point in time. The author employed a Type A measurement strategy. It may have been additionally desirable to have obtained some other indicator of marital satisfaction, such as a global rating using a self-report measure.

Design This study illustrates the across-behaviors application of a multiple-baseline design. Here we see the simultaneous measurement of three separate and unique behaviors that occur within the global problem area of communication. The same intervention strategy is being applied successively to all the behaviors resulting in some change. Note the "withholding" of treatment from monopolizing and topic changes while the effect of intervention is being evaluated with interruptive behavior—hence the differing lengths in baseline. Presumably, there is a conscious decision about which specific behavior is to be intervened with first (by virtue of irritability of problem, probability of success, etc.).

Data Patterns As evidenced in Table 7.2, the author in this study chose a somewhat different method of presenting the data. This presentation, while perhaps not as clear as graphic illustrations, provides the same information. All the target behaviors show some change as a result of intervention, the most clear-cut results being exhibited with interruptive behavior. The multiple-point frequency count has been aggregated, and the data are presented in terms of "percentage of occurrence" at given weeks into baseline and intervention.

Given the somewhat weak results (that is, the lack of a definitive trend in data) obtained in this study, it is difficult to note whether or not treatment with the first problem led to any kind of generalization to the other problem areas (the issue of independence). Given the fact that no statistical tests were performed, we have to rely on "eye-balling" (see chapter 10) the data. On this basis, no distinct trends can be seen that would suggest generalization. Thus, it appears that the multiple-baseline design was effectively implemented in this instance across behaviors.

Other Observations The fact that data were collected during the essentially artificial communication exercise suggests that the entire data-gathering process is obtrusive. By the same token, that intervention produced some change despite this artificiality is perhaps an indication of the power of the intervention and the design. Moreover, although the author employed a somewhat rigorous and complicated method for the analysis of the communication information, its clinical value from the perspective of client learning is well demonstrated by the client's comments reported by the author.

Case Study: Implementation of Behavior Modification Techniques In Summer Camp Settings

GEORGE J. ALLEN, University of Connecticut

A growing number of institutions provide summer camping programs as part of a total treatment approach. In line with this trend, summer camps are performing rehabilitative as well as recreational functions. However, simply providing an individual with exposure to opportunities available in such settings does not guarantee amelioration of problematic behaviors. Recognizing this problem, the Society for the Psychological Study of Social Issues (1957) called for extensive research into the efficacy of remedial behavioral procedures applied in camp environments. Response to this call has been less than overwhelming. Although camps offer worthwhile opportunities for imple-

Reprinted from *Behavior Therapy*, 4 (1973):570–75. Used by permission of Academic Press.

mentation of operant behavioral techniques, little research has been conducted. Rickard and his associates have provided a carefully designed, systematic research program which included shaping adaptive social responses in 11 boys (Rickard & Dinoff, 1965), and demonstrating operant control of "clean-up" behavior (Rickard & Saunders, 1971).

Application of behavior modification techniques in camp settings can further actualize the rehabilitative potential of such environments for individuals who are unresponsive to normal camp routines, and provide a convenient locale for conducting controlled research in naturalistic settings. Camp environments possess five characteristics which may be used to enhance therapeutic behavior change. First, physical facilities of camps provide potentially powerful reinforcers which are not readily available in home or school situations. Second, research suggests that both fearful and aggressive children respond to social reinforcers delivered only by a limited number of individuals (Patterson, 1965; Wahler, 1969a). Camp routines provide for large numbers of social interactions between children with problematic behaviors and adults who have the potential to shape adaptive responses by administering or withholding reinforcers such as food, beverages, privileges, praise, or attention. Since initial opportunities for reinforcing approximations toward adaptive behaviors are numerous, teaching such skills may be conducted more efficiently.

Third, since behavior change may be facilitated by training conducted in novel environments (McReynolds, 1969; Wahler, 1969b), the initial novelty of entering camp settings suggests that remediation of problematic acts may be further enhanced. A fourth dimension involves the ease with which interested staff members can be trained to apply behavioral principles. Most camps employ students who do not possess strong (mis)conceptions about the etiology of maintenance of disordered behavior. Positive changes in problem targets as a result of behavior modification techniques often quickly increases staff acceptance of this approach. Finally, camp environments allow for use of both adults and children as models for positive behavior change in targeted individuals.

The paucity of well-controlled studies in camp settings may be a result of the erroneous notions that treatment and research demands are incompatible, rigorous experimental control cannot be guaranteed, and problems in staff coordination make systematic programming impossible. While pressure to provide treatment without proper evaluative procedures is sometimes brought to bear upon camp personnel, delineation of the parameters of *effective* treatment must be based upon analysis of behavior change. Use of within-subject designs, including reversals and multiple baselines (Baer et al., 1968), can provide strong causal inferences relating behavior change to environmental manipulations. Such designs dovetail with the philosophy of individualized programming found at many camps. Programming naturally occurring reinforcers avoids limited generality, which afflicts much laboratory-based research. An additional advantage exists in the relative unobtrusiveness of behavioral observation, which can be made during ongoing activity periods. Coordination of staff activities does take effort but can be effectively accomplished through meetings and memos. A case study illustrates these points.

Elimination of Bizarre Verbalizations

Subject and Setting Mike was an 8-year-old boy, diagnosed as being "minimally brain damaged," attending a sleep-in summer camp. This was his first camping experience. His parents had reported that he "fantasized about penguins for up to 8 hours every day." His menagerie included such colorful characters as "Tug-Tug," "Junior Polkadot," and "Super-Penguin."

Behavioral Observation Two counselors accompanied Mike's group throughout camp from the first day to assist the bunk counselors and record the frequency with which "penguin verbalizations" occurred. A response was scored whenever Mike mentioned the word *penguin* or the names of his "pets" in a sentence. Observation also revealed that listener responsiveness to lead-in questions, such as "Guess what?" "Want to know something?" and "Do you know what?" was invariably followed by a penguin statement. The frequency of these questions was also recorded beginning on the fourth day of camp.

Experimental Phases
Baseline The observers were instructed to simply record every penguin statement without responding to or encouraging their occurrence. No other counselors received any instructions concerning how Mike's verbalizations

should be responded to. A number of counselors actually reinforced Mike's penguin talk, apparently considering it to be "cute." Baseline data were collected for 6 days.

Ignoring The high frequency of penguin statements was deemed as interfering with Mike's ability to relate well with adults and other children. Consequently, a systematic program designed to extinguish this behavior by withdrawal of attention was instituted. A 1-hour meeting was held with Mike's bunk counselors, activity counselors, and administrative staff. Baseline data were presented and theory and practice of extinction procedures discussed. Since some counselors expressed reservations that using extinction might produce "symptom substitution," use of a multiple-baseline design was suggested as a method of demonstrating that his verbalizations were being maintained by environmental reinforcement.

All staff members were instructed to drop Mike's hand immediately and turn away from him whenever he mentioned penguins or asked one of his lead-in questions. Staff attention was immediately reinstituted whenever he discussed his feelings, home, or camp activities. He was also praised for appropriately interacting with other children. Additional staff members were briefed in the procedures whenever ignoring was extended to different part of the camp. Although the program soon became general knowledge, close supervisory contact was maintained with the 12 counselors who had most frequent contact with Mike.

A multiple-baseline design was used to assess the effectiveness of ignoring Mike's bizarre verbalizations. The physical camp environment was divided into four settings, and the remaining 22 days of the camp session were blocked into four units. During the first time block, ignoring was done only in the setting in which the target response had occurred most frequently during baseline. During the second time block, ignoring was maintained in the first setting and introduced into a second setting. This strategy was followed until the target behavior was being ignored in all four settings.

Results

Interobserver reliability was determined by computing the number of agreements found within 20 half-hour intervals daily and dividing by the total number of intervals in which either observer scored a response as occurring.

Time blocks in which both raters recorded no statements were not counted as agreements. Observer agreement ranged from 81 to 100 percent with an average of 94 percent agreement found for the 27 days of observation. No discrepancy of more than two responses between raters or statements-per-day was found. A Pearson r on ratings of statements-per-day was .96.

The number of penguin statements that Mike made in each of four camp settings daily is presented in Figure 7.4. A rate-per-minute measure of bizarre verbalizations during each of the 6 baseline days was computed separately for each setting. A setting × days analysis of variance of these data yielded an F ratio of 1.12 ($df = 3.20$, $p > .10$), suggesting that setting differences in frequency of penguin statements were a function of the amount of time Mike spent in each setting rather than rate of verbalization. The target response decreased from an initial frequency of 116 to less than 1 per day during the last week of camp. This decrease was apparently the result of the experimental manipulation. Ignoring penguin statements on camp trails and during evening activities produced a rapid fourfold response suppression within these settings. When applied in the subsequent settings, ignoring led to rapid response reduction, with generalization across settings occurring in the latter phases of the study. Slight response suppression apparently occurred in the cabin before ignoring was instituted in this setting. Spontaneous suppression in the educational situation was more pronounced. Ignoring also led to a breakdown of the invariant relationship between lead-in questions and penguin statements. During the final 8 days of the program, only 6 percent of the questions were followed by penguin talk. Increases in appropriate social interactions were noted and ultimately frequently reinforced by the counselors.*

Discussion

Implementation of both treatment programs led to additional changes in staff behavior. Total time spent training and coordinating staff averaged less than 15 minutes a day for each program. Although extensive introduction to the philosophy of using behavior modification was initially time consuming, the

---

*A second program involving teaching an aquaphobic boy to swim by shaping entry into the water and approximations to swimming strokes was also successfully conducted. A brief report of this experiment may be obtained by writing to the author.

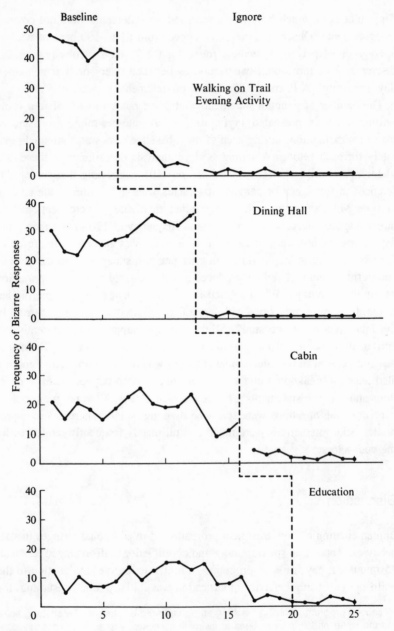

Figure 7.4 Daily number of bizarre verbalizations in specific camp settings.

treatment procedures themselves were easily learned. Progress charts, used to provide staff feedback on program effectiveness, kept interest high and served to reinforce staff cooperation (Fielding et al., 1971; Panyan et al., 1970). Ethical issues of behavior control became a heatedly debated topic among staff. A majority of those most directly involved in either program expressed favorable attitudinal changes toward use of applied behavioral approaches. Four counselors expressed interest in obtaining graduate training in behaviorally oriented psychology graduate programs.

Both experiments add further documentation of the utility of conducting behavior modification research in naturalistic settings (Gruber, 1971; Lazarus, 1971). Therapeutic behavioral procedures may be applied in camp settings without diminishing the strength of causal relationships between treatment and outcome variables. Most reported demonstrations have involved remediation of specifically defined behaviors in targeted individuals or small groups, with evaluation by means of within-subject designs (Lattal, 1969). However, researchers are not limited to the exclusive use of within-subject designs in camp settings.

Campers are often grouped according to ability levels, skills, or homogeneity of problematic behavior. These groups may be employed to assess effectiveness of behavioral treatment procedures within factorial group designs. Behavioral measures of athletic competence, motor coordination, or interpersonal functioning may be made at the beginning and end of camp sessions to provide evaluative data. Further research in camp settings can provide better answers to practical problems relating to amelioration of social and motoric behavior problems and theoretical issues regarding the degree of applicability of behavior modification in naturalistic settings.

References

Baer, D. M., M. M. Wolf, and T. Risley 1968. "Some Current Dimensions of Applied Behavior Analysis," *Journal of Applied Behavior Analysis,* 1:91–97.

Fielding, L. T., E. Errickson, and B. Bettin 1971. "Modification of Staff Behavior: A Brief Note" *Behavior Therapy,* 2:550–53.

Gruber, R. P. 1971. "Behavior Therapy: Problems in Generalization," *Behavior Therapy* 2:361–68.

Lattal, K. A. 1969. "Contingency Management of Toothbrushing Behavior in a Summer Camp for Children." *Journal of Applied Behavior Analysis,* 2:195–98.

Lazarus, A. A. 1971. "Reflections of Behavior Therapy and Its Development: A Point of View," *Behavior Therapy* 2:369–74.

McReynolds, L. V. 1969. "Application of Timeout from Positive Reinforcement for Increasing the Efficiency of Speech Training," *Journal of Applied Behavior Analysis,* 2:199–206.

Panyan, M., H. Boozer, and N. Morris 1970. "Feedback to Attendants as a Reinforcer for Applying Operant Techniques," *Journal of Applied Behavior Analysis,* 3:1–4.

Patterson, G. R. 1965. "A Learning Theory Approach to the Treatment of the School Phobic Child." In L. P. Ullmann and L. Krasner, eds. *Case Studies in Behavior Modification.* New York: Holt.

Rickard, H. C. and M. Dinoff 1965. "Shaping Adaptive Responses in a Therapeutic Summer Camp." In L. P. Ullmann and L. Krasner, eds. *Case Studies in Behavior Modification.* New York: Holt.

Rickard, H. C. and T. R. Saunders 1971. "Control of Clean-Up Behavior in a Summer Camp." *Behavior Thrapy,* 2:340–44.

Society for the Psychological Study of Social Issues 1957. "Therapeutic Camping for Disturbed Youth," *Journal of Social Issues* 13:1–62.

Wahler, R. G. 1969a. "Oppositional Children: A Quest for Parental Control." *Journal of Applied Behavior Analysis,* 2:159–70.

Wahler, R. G. 1969b. "Setting Generality: Some Specific and General Effects of Child Behavior Therapy," *Journal of Applied Behavior Analysis,* 2:239–46.

7.6 Summary

Number of Clients An 8-year-old minimally brain damaged boy served as the object of this intervention program in a summer camp setting.

Specification of Goals Inappropriate verbalizations by the boy (Mike) were identified as the target problem. Specifically, the verbalizations were tied to Mike's utterances around the topic of penguins, which was identified as an inappropriate fantasy that interfered with his ability to interact with adults and peers. The goal of intervention was identified as the reduction of such inappropriate penguin verbalizations.

Measurement Strategy A simple frequency count of the problem verbalizations was used. Two primary counselors were employed to observe and record Mike's verbal behavior (Type C). The observations were carried out extensively across all aspects of the camp environment. Thus, the author was able to obtain a fairly accurate and representative picture of the child's functioning with regard to the target problem prior to intervention.

The apparent specificity with which the target problem was defined is reflected in the 94 percent agreement reported between the two observers. While it is not particularly clear, it appears that as many as 12 counselors may have been involved in the intervention program. This does not, however, affect the reliability measurement noted, since the frequency of occurrence of the target problem was observed across time by the same two observers.

The author divided the camp setting into four distinct units: trail/evening activity, dining hall, cabin, and education. These four units, that is, distinct physical contexts, served as the different situations across which the specified problem needed to be changed. Thus, the guidelines of the multiple-baseline approach being followed, the target problem (penguin verbalizations) was recorded across all four units simultaneously.

The author reports increased "appropriate verbalizations" as a result of intervention. In this instance, it would have been beneficial to have observed and recorded the increases in the defined appropriate behaviors as complementary products of the intervention program. This could have been done by including a Type B measurement procedure in the study.

Design This is an example of the application of a multiple-baseline design across situations. The target problem is simultaneously measured across all four situations during baseline, and the same intervention program is successively administered across each separate physical context (Figure 7.4). Note that the author specifically chose to start the intervention program within the physical context in which the problem was judged (by virtue of baseline data) to be the most prevalent.

Data Patterns Figure 7.4 clearly demonstrates the impact of intervention in each successive application of the treatment. Note, however, the apparent generalization of treatment effects. With the trail/evening activity and dining hall interventions, we see little generalization with the baseline data. That is, the data patterns during baseline remain fairly constant. But toward the latter part of treatment, within the cabin and education contexts, an apparent decreasing baseline is being recorded. Thus, while the situational contexts appear to be unique (superficially), there appears to have been some generalization of treatment effects. That is, the latter two contexts showed change even before intervention was begun. Given the independence issue referred to earlier, the power of the multiple-baseline design to establish cause-effect relations is reduced by virtue of this apparent interrelationship.

Other Observations The data-gathering process used in this study is essentially nonobtrusive, since the counselors were natural elements in the camp environment. From an "eyeballing" perspective, we see the two graphs depicting the target problems in trail/evening activity and dining hall behavior dramatically illustrate the impact of intervention. Here the data patterns show a sudden and precipitous change from the baseline data in the desired direction. While the other two graphs are perhaps not as dramatic, they essentially support these findings. This study is a clear example of successive replication of the same intervention strategy. Thus, if the trail/evening activity graph were to be treated as a simple *AB* baseline intervention design, it clearly shows impact—but it is just one alteration in data pattern, perhaps coincidental. The fact that three or more applications of the same intervention program on the same target problem show similar results strengthens our ability to make a causal inference and attribute change to the treatment—again, on the basis of the principle of unlikely successive coincidences.

Training Predelinquent Youths and Their Parents to Negotiate Conflict Situations

ROBERT E. KIFER, MARTHA A. LEWIS, DONALD R. GREEN,
and ELERY L. PHILLIPS

One problem contributing to the delinquency of many youths is their behavior in conflict situations with authority figures such as parents and teachers. Conflict situations are interpersonal situations in which the youth and authority figure have opposite desires; e.g., the youth wants to spend summer job money on a bike, but his mother wants him to spend it on clothes.

Many youths make inappropriate responses to conflict situations (such as fighting, tantrums, or destructive behavior) that ultimately bring them into contact with courts, clinics, and other agencies. In many of these situations, negotiation is a possible response that is likely to produce more acceptable consequences for both parties. Unfortunately, negotiation is a much more difficult response to execute, but its benefits warrant investigation of procedures to train this behavior.

Previous work in this area may be classified into two general approaches, arbitration or mediation of specific conflicts and modification of communication processes. Behavior contracting is the most prevalent example of the arbitration approach. This procedure has been described in detail elsewhere (Patterson et al., 1972; Stuart, 1971) and involves the therapist in the role of a mediator or arbitrator who facilitates mutual agreements beween opposing parties about reciprocal exchanges of specific behaviors, reinforcers, and punishers. This approach has been successfully used with marital (Stuart, 1969) and parent–youth conflicts (Stuart, 1971).

The work of Bach and Wyden (1968) and Carter and Thomas (1973) exemplifies the second approach. While not aimed specifically at the negotiation process, these procedures were designed to modify problem behaviors that are relevant to negotiation (e.g., abusive criticism, failure to express opinions, complaining). Verbal instructions, practice, and feedback are the

Reprinted from *Journal of Applied Behavior Analysis*, 7 (Fall 1974):35–64. Used by permission of the Society for the Experimental Analysis of Behavior.

major techniques used to modify communication processes. Much less experimental evidence exists on this approch.

The procedures described in this paper are also attempts to modify communication processes, but differed in two respects. First, the emphasis was entirely on learning new adaptive behaviors, rather than eliminating problem behaviors. Second, these techniques were primarily educational, rather than therapeutic. The training was designed to teach one specific skill, and was not a comprehensive treatment package. The procedures involved analyzing the negotiation process into component behaviors and using instructions, practice, and feedback to train these behaviors. The goal of the training was to enable clients to resolve their own conflicts without outside intervention.

The purpose of this experiment was to determine if negotiation skills could be simultaneously taught to youths and their parents, and if so, the effect of these skills on mutually agreeable solutions to conflict situations, and the extent to which these skills would generalize to discussions of real conflict situations at home.

Method

Subjects Two mother–daughter pairs and one father–son pair served as subjects. The youths (aged 13, 16, and 17) had at least one contact with the County Juvenile Court. The boy and one girl were in Achievement Place homes (Phillips, 1968), and the other girl was a candidate for Achievement Place. Only one parent was involved in each case because two of the youths were living with only that parent, and the father of one of the girls declined to participate. All subjects were volunteers for this project and freely signed informed-consent forms.

Setting All training procedures were conducted in a small (12-by-14-foot—3.6-by-4.5-meter) windowless classroom containing table and chairs, video-tape recording equipment, and a cassette tape recorder.

Procedures Each parent–child pair experienced three main phases of this study. The first was a *home observation* conducted 1 week before classroom sessions and consisted of collecting sample data regarding each subject pair's behavior in discussing actual conflict situations in their home. The second phase consisted of *classroom sessions*. The third period was another *home observation* to measure generalization of trained behaviors into the home. The first two authors functioned as trainers and made all experimental contacts with subjects.

Home observations

Trainers visited subject's homes and asked them to identify "the three most troublesome problem situations between the two of you at this time." Any conflict situations identified by both parent and youth were discussed. In case different situations were identified, at least one selected by the parent and one by the child were discussed.

Subjects were instructed to discuss each situation for 5 minutes without help from trainers and were told to "try to reach a solution acceptable to both of you." At the end of the first discussion, trainers gave brief general praise for discussing the situation, restated the next cnflict situation, and repeated the instructions.

Classroom sessions

Each parent–child pair attended their own weekly session. The same three-step format was used in all sessions: (1) presession simulation, (2) discussion and practice simulations, and (3) postsession simulation.

1. *A presession simulation* was conducted as soon as subjects arrived. Trainers described a hypothetical parent–child conflict situation and instructed them to role play that situation to the best of their ability. No other instructions were given. This and all other simulations were stopped by trainers after 5 minutes unless subjects indicated they were finished before that time.

2. *Discussion and practice* followed a standard procedure known as the Situations—Options—Consequences—Simulation (SOCS) model originated by Roosa (unpublished). After the presession simulation, trainers passed out copies of a sheet (see Table 7.5 for an example) containing a description of the same situation that subjects had just simulated, a list of response options, and a list of consequences. First, this situation was read again by trainers. Then, trainers and subjects took turns matching each option with its probable consequences. Additional options and consequences were added if they occurred to anyone. After all options were related to their probable consequences, the parent and the child selected the consequences that were most desirable to them. By noting which options led to desired consequences, subjects selected the best response to the situation. Finally, practice simulations were conducted in which each subject practiced his selected option.

Table 7.5. SITUATION SIMULATION

Situation

You have worked all summer for money and your mother insists that you spend it on clothes, but you want to spend it on something else.

Options
1. Tell her it is your money and it is none of her business what you spend it on.
2. Spend it on ugly clothes you know she hates.
3. Since she will not let you spend it the way you want, give it to charity.
4. Do not spend it on anything; put it in savings and let it collect interest.
5. Spend some on clothes she wants you to get and some on what you want.
6. You buy clothes if she will buy what else you want.
7. Sell them to a friend after you buy them.
8. It is easier to buy the clothes than hassle with mother.

Consequences
1. Get her mad at you and maybe have money taken away.
2. You have to wear the clothes you bought.
3. Feel good in helping a worthy cause.
4. End up with more money than you originally had.
5. Find out the clothes were a good thing.
6. Be miserable about the whole thing.
7. Never learn how to negotiate.

Typically, the child played the role of the youth for the first few times; then subjects switched roles. The trainers rarely took part in these practice simulations. They functioned like directors of a film, providing instructions before simulations, quietly observing simulations, signaling the beginning and the end of simulations, and providing feedback.

3. Finally, a postsession simulation was conducted exactly like the presession simulation.

The same pool of hypothetical situations was used for each parent–child pair, but situations were counterbalanced across pairs. Negotiation was a possible option in all situations. Subjects were encouraged to use their own real-problem situations, but these were never volunteered except by the father–son pair during their last two classroom sessions.

All simulations were videotaped unless subjects preferred not to use the equipment that day. Videotapes were not replayed after each simulation because of the extra time involved. Replays were made only to check the occurrence of a behavior if there was any doubt, or to show subjects an especially good performance.

Behavior definitions.
Two response classes were measured: negotiation behaviors and agreements. Negotiation was separated into three component behaviors: complete communication, identification of issues, and suggestion of options.

1. *Complete communications:* statements that indicate one's position (what one thinks or wants) regarding the situation being discussed and that are followed in the same verbalization by a request for the other person to state his position or respond to the position just expressed. Examples: (a) "I want to spend my summer job money on a bike. Is that O.K. with you?" (b) "I want you to run for Student Council. What do you think about it?"

2. *Identification of issues:* statements that explicitly identify the point of conflict in the situation. This statement may contrast the two opposing positions, or try to clarify what the other's position is if this is unclear, or identify what one thinks the conflict is really about. Examples: (a) "You want to buy clothes, but I want to buy a bike." (b) "The real issue is that I want you to learn responsibility." Subjects were encouraged but not required to use the word *issue* when performing this behavior to make its occurrence more explicit.

3. *Suggestion of options:* statements that suggest a course of action to resolve the conflict but are not merely restatements of that person's original position. Examples: (a) "How about if I spend some on clothes and use the rest to buy a bike if you'll help pay for it?" (b) "I could get a part-time job and learn responsibility that way." Subjects were encouraged but not required to pose options in the form of questions to increase the likelihood of receiving an answer to the option.

Agreements, the end result of negotiation, were recorded as one of two types: Compliant or Negotiated.

1. *Compliant agreements:* agreements by one person to the original position of the other. Example: "All right, I'll spend all my money on clothes."

2. *Negotiated agreements:* agreements to a suggested option that is not merely the original position of either person. Such agreements can take the form of a compromise, a deal (*A* gets his way but must in turn do something for *B*), or a new alternative (a different course of action). Example: "O.K., I guess a job would be fine." Agreements need not restate the course of action agreed upon. This was done in the examples to preserve the identity of situations.

Training procedures

Instructions, practice, and feedback were used to train subjects to use all three negotiation behaviors in practice simulations. Instructions consisted of telling the subject to perform all three behaviors, e.g., "Use complete communication, remember to identify the issue, and then suggest some options." Practice involved each subject's rehearing all three negotiation behaviors in practice simulations. Feedback consisted of social reinforcement such as praise, smiles, and head nods. Instructions were given before practice simulations, nonverbal feedback such as smiles and head nods were given during these simulations, and verbal praise occurred after these role plays.

First one subject was instructed, then practiced these behaviors until he performed all three in the same simulation. Then, the other subject went through the same procedure. Subjects were taught to use the negotiation behaviors in the order in which they were defined. A typical sequence occurred as follows. First, trainers instructed the youth before his first practice simulation to use all three negotiation behaviors. Then, trainers signaled subjects to begin the simulation and smiled or nodded approval after any negotiation behavior used by the youth. Usually, the youth did not use all three behaviors in the first attempt, and so he was praised for those behaviors he did use and reminded to use the behaviors he did not use. Next, the youth was instructed to use all three behaviors, and the second practice simulation was started. This sequence occurred until the youth performed all three negotiation behaviors in the same practice simulation. At that point, subjects switched roles and the parent went through the same sequence. After the parent met the criterion of all three behaviors in the same simulation, that session was ended and the postsession simulation was conducted.

During the first training session, the three behaviors were chained together in the following manner. After the situation—options—consequences discussion, the behavior definition of the first behavior was read and a rationale given for its use. Next, trainers modeled that behavior in the context of that day's situation. Then, subjects participated in practice simulations until each had used the behavior. This procedure was repeated, the second, and finally the third behavior being added, until each subject had used all three behaviors in the same simulation.

Experimental conditions and design

A multiple-baseline design across subject pairs was used to evaluate the effects of the training procedures on the occurrence of negotiation behaviors and the number and type of agreements reached. Baseline data on these behaviors were taken on each subject pair. Training procedures were then begun with one pair while the other two pairs remained in baseline conditions. Then, the second subject pair entered training while the first pair remained in baseline conditions. Then, the second subject pair entered training while the first pair remained in training and the third remained in baseline conditions. Finally, the training procedures were applied to the third subject pair. The two experimental conditions are described below.

1. Baseline. During baseline sessions no instructions or praise were given for negotiation behaviors. Subjects were given minimal and general instructions before simulations. They were told to remain on the topic under discussion, use a pleasant tone of voice, or look each other in the eye, according to their particular interaction pattern. General praise (e.g., "Good job") and praise for general instruction following were given after simulations. Baseline sessions typically lasted 45 minutes.

2. Training. The only difference between baseline and training sessions was the addition of instructions and praise for the negotiation behaviors. Praise for these behaviors was given after presession and postsession simulations. Instructions and praise were used for practice simulations as previously described. Training sessions typically lasted 75 minutes owing to a greater number of practice simulations.

During all classroom sessions, subjects were never instructed to reach agreements and were inadvertently praised for doing so only three times. Agreements were not trained, to determine what effect the negotiation behaviors had on this desired goal behavior.

Training was terminated after two consecutive presession simulations in which subjects used all three negotiation behaviors between the two of them; for example, the parent could use two of the behaviors and the youth could use the third. Subjects were informed of this termination criterion at the time indicated by the arrow in Figure 7.5.

Measurement technique and observer agreement

All classroom sessions and home observations were recorded with a small cassette recorder operated by trainers and visible to subjects. These tapes were listened to by an observer in her home on another recorder. The observer recorded occurrences of instructions, negotiation behaviors, agreements, and praise.

Table 7.6. SUMMARY OF RELIABILITY DATA

| | Reliability | |
Behavior	Range (%)	Mean (%)
Complete communication	50–100	89.5
Identification of issues	67–100	91.6
Suggestion of options	67–100	85.3
Compliant agreements	87–100	95.7
Negotiated agreements	77–100	90.3
Instructions	73–100	89.8
Praise	85–100	95.9

Observer agreement was checked at least once in each classroom condition and home observation for each parent–child pair (a total of 12 checks were made). These checks consisted of another observer's listening to the tape and recording data in the same way. Observers' records were compared point by point across all simulations in that session. Instances in which both observers recorded occurrences or both recorded nonoccurrence of each behavior were counted as agreements. Any other combination was counted as a disagreement. Overall reliability was computed for each behavior with the following formula.

$$\text{Per cent reliability} = \frac{\text{No. of cells of agreement}}{\text{Total number of cells}} \times 100$$

Observer agreement averaged 85 percent for all behaviors. Table 7.6 summarizes these data.

Results

Figure 7.5 shows the percent of the three component negotiation behaviors emitted during the presession and postsession classroom simulations by the three parent–child pairs. Solid bars represent presession simulations. Striped bars represent postsession simulations. The letter C above a bar indicates that a compliant agreement was reached in that simulation. The letter N designates a negotiated agreement. Absence of any letter indicates no agreement was reached in that simulation. The arrows indicate when subjects were informed of the termination of training criterion.

Under training conditions, all three subject pairs substantially increased their use of the negotiation behaviors over baseline levels in postsession sim-

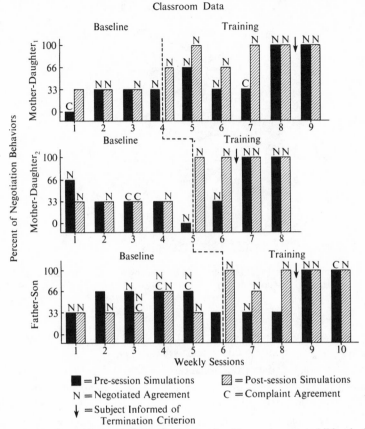

Figure 7.5 Percent of negotiation behaviors emitted by each parent-child pair during pre- and postsession classroom simulations.

ulations. However, only the first mother–daughter pair showed a similar increase in presession simulations before being informed of the criterion for termination. After learning of this criterion, both pairs promptly improved their presession performance to the required level.

The father–son pair reached both types of agreements in the presession simulations of sessions 4 and 5, and in the postsession simulation of session 3. They first reached a negotiated agreement but continued to discuss the situation until the son complied with his father's original position. The end result was a compliant agreement. For all subject pairs a slightly greater per-

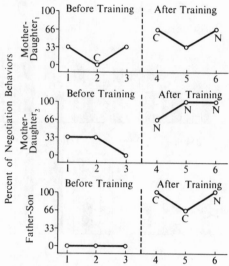

Figure 7.6 Percent of negotiation behaviors emitted by each parent-child pair during home observation discussions of actual conflict situations.

centage of training condition presession and postsession simulations ended in negotiated agreements as compared with baseline.

Figure 7.6 presents data from home observations before and after training. Each data point represents the percent of the three component negotiation behaviors used during discussion of each real-conflict situation in subjects' homes. Agreements are indicated as in Figure 7.5. Except for situations 2 and 5 of the second mother–daughter pair, all situations discussed after training were different than those used before training.

Posttraining home observations of all three subject pairs showed substantial increases over pretraining observations in both performance of negotiation behaviors and agreements reached.

After an appropriate time period determined by the nature of the agreements, each parent–child pair was contacted and asked if agreements reached during home observations had been kept. Only one of the nine situations discussed in pretraining observations ended in any kind of agreement, and this agreement was reportedly kept. Eight of the nine situations discussed after training resulted in agreements, and five of these were reportedly kept.

Discussion

The training procedures produced substantial increases in negotiation behaviors during postsession simulations. However, it seemed that presession simulations constituted a more appropriate test of the degree to which subjects had learned these behaviors, because presession performance involved using the behaviors in a new conflict situation after 1 week had elapsed after the previous training session. Presession simulations were tests of generalization to a new conflict situation in the same setting. Generalization to new conflict situations did not occur with two subject pairs until after they were informed of the termination criterion. This criterion seemed to be responsible for improvements in presession simulations for these two subject pairs.

The trained negotiation behaviors generalized to discussions of actual conflict situations without instructions or any other contingency placed on their occurrence by trainers. More importantly, each parent–child pair reached agreement in more of these real conflict situations after training than before. Lack of an untreated control group prevents the conclusion that these improvements were due to the training procedures, although classroom data support this conclusion. These improvements could also have been due to the use of different conflict situations, but use of the same situations seemed inappropriate. It seemed more important for subjects to resolve current conflicts than to "settle" past issues that no longer presented problems. It is clear that generalization to actual conflicts can occur without using real situations in classroom training sessions.

Classroom data demonstrate, and home observations data support the conclusion, that use of these negotiation behaviors leads to agreement in a greater percentage of discussions of conflict situations. To this extent the behaviors had their desired function. Other behaviors that enhance the negotiation process can and should be identified in future research.

Although subjects sometimes appeared angry or emotional during home observation discussions, these discussions always occurred after the situations had already emerged as problems. Probably many of the unfortunate consequences of inappropriate discussion of conflict situations occur in the "heat of battle" when the situations first become conflictual. It is likely that these negotiation behaviors would be even more difficult to emit during states of extreme emotional upset, which may accompany the onset of serious conflict situations. This issue was not attended to in this study, because the procedures were designed for people who already had their emotional behavior under reasonable control. Future work in this area should attend to this issue. Several strategies for dealing with this problem have been suggested. Ferseter et al. (1962) suggested a strategy of gaining control over the temporal occurrence of a behavior before attempting other modification procedures. Bach and Wyden (1968) discussed some interesting ideas for regulating the time and place of fights. For example, a particular time and place could be set aside for discussing conflicts which arose during the day. The self-government system at Achievement Place (Fixen et al., 1973) incorporates such a procedure. Youths are expected to comply with disagreeable requests when they occur but are encouraged to discuss and negotiate their grievances at a daily meeting.

The present study provides encouraging evidence that relatively inexpensive procedures can be developed that change parent–child interaction during conflict situations from disagreement to negotiation and agreement. The procedures required from 9 to 10 hours per subject. Future research should (1) investigate procedures that train these and other aspects of negotiation in less time, (2) evaluate effects of these procedures on other specified problem behaviors, (3) develop ways of reducing the aversive effects of emotional responses on negotiation, and (4) use long-term followup data collection to measure durability of effects.

References

Bach, G. R. and P. Wyden 1968. *The Intimate Enemy*. New York: Morrow.

Carter, R. D. and E. J. Thomas. 1973. "Modification of Problematic Marital Communication Using Corrective Feedback and Instruction," *Behavior Therapy*, 4:100–109.

Ferster, C. B., J. I. Nurenberger, and E. B. Levitt 1962. "The Control of Eating." *Journal of Mathematics*, 1:87–109.

Fixen, D. L., E. L. Phillips, and M. M. Wolf 1973. "Achievement Place: Experiments in Self-Government with Predelinquents." *Journal of Applied Behavior Analysis*, 6:31–47.

Patterson, G. R., J. A. Cobb, and R. Ray 1972. "A Social Engineering Technology for Retraining the Families of Aggressive Boys," In H. Adams and L. Unikel, eds. *Georgia Symposium in Experimental Clinical Psychology*, Vol. 2 Springfield, Illinois: Charles C Thomas.

Phillips, E. L. 1968. "Achievement Place: Token Reinforcement in a

Home-Style Rehabilitation Setting for Pre-delinquent Boys.'' *Journal of Applied Behavior Analysis*, 3:213–23.

Roosa, J. B. 1973 "SOCS: Situations, Options, Consequences, and Simulation: A Technique for Teaching Social Interaction.'' Unpublished paper presented at the American Psychological Association, Monteal, Canada, August 1973. (Reprints may be obtained from Dr. Jan Roosa, Suite 107, 3700 W 83rd., Prairie Village, Kansas 66206.)

Stuart, R. B. 1969. "Operant Interpersonal Treatment of Marital Discord.'' *Journal of Consulting and Clinical Psychology*, 33:675–82.

—— 1971. "Behavioral Contracting Within the Families of Delinquents.'' *Journal of Behavior Therapy and Experimental Psychiatry*, 2:1–11.

7.7 Summary

Number of Clients Three youths aged 13, 16, and 17 and their parents (two mothers and one father) served as the subjects in this study. Each parent–child pair was treated as a client system.

Specification of Goals The goal of the study was to teach each parent–child pair to negotiate conflict situations and arrive at a mutually acceptable solution. The process involved several classroom sessions with simulations, home observations, and training. In general, the goals were somewhat broadly defined.

Measurement Strategy Two aspects of communication were measured—negotiation behaviors and agreements. All the classroom sessions and home observations were audiotaped, and the tapes were then analyzed for the occurrence or nonoccurrence of the target behaviors. These recordings were randomly cross-checked by a second coder to ensure the reliability of coding procedures.

We see a Type B measurement process employed in this study. That is, several different behaviors are seen as the indicator of the occurrence of the goal. As such, multiple measures are employed to evaluate the achievement of a given goal.

Design A multiple-baseline design across subjects has been employed in this study. Note, however, that each parent–child pair serves as one subject. Figure 7.5 clearly illustrates the application of the multiple-baseline procedures across the three subjects. Note the successive applications of the training procedures while baseline measurement is going on across all subjects.

Data Patterns This study utilizes both bar graphs and line graphs in the presentation of the data. Both Figures 7.5 and 7.6 illustrate visually the relative impact of treatment. Note, however, the relatively stable baseline in the bar graphs and the relatively variable baselines in the first two parent–child pairs in Figure 7.6.

In this instance, the authors established a criterion level performance and moved toward its attainment. Thus, while pure eyeballing may not appear to show dramatic change from pretreatment to posttreatment, the data do clearly indicate the achievement of the criterion level.

Other observations This is a good example of the application of a multiple baseline across subjects where the subjects are defined as a family unit. Thus, the flexibility of the design approach across different size systems becomes apparent.

Note also the generally broad goal definition—increased negotiation and agreements—and the somewhat specific measures used to index their achievement. Thus, while it is sometimes possible to state a goal in broad terms, it must be specified in unique terms if its achievement is to be measured at all.

Decreasing Inappropriate Classroom Behavior

MARK JAY SKLAR

Reinforcement procedures have been used effectively to encourage children to stay in their seats and pay attention (Becker et al., 1969). Birnbrauer and Lawler (1964) suggest that immediate and delayed rewards can be employed to teach new skills as well as eliminate inappropriate behaviors.

Reprinted from *School Applications of Learning Theory,* 3 (1971):33–36.

The purpose of this study was to decrease or eliminate the inappropriate out-of-seat behavior of an adolescent male. This behavior greatly hindered the student's academic progress. For this study, immediate token reinforcement coupled with peer pressure served to decrease the inappropriate behavior by strengthening new, incompatible, appropriate behaviors.

Subject

The subject (S) was a 12-year-old male student in a public school center for children with learning disabilities. He was characterized as a good-natured boy who was eager to please, but who had problems with a lack of "impulse control." He was hyperactive, had a short attention span, and had a very poor "self-image." His academic functioning was at the 2nd + grade level in reading and in arithmetic. He did not write well, since he had not learned to hold a pencil properly. His full scale IQ on the WISC was 96.

During the past 2 years, S had reportedly had several very traumatic experiences at home. His mother passed away when he was 10 years old, and his father subsequently remarried. The next year, his stepmother died, apparently at her own hand. When confronted with his son's behavior and progress, S's father was uninterested and uncooperative. Despite numerous recommendations from the counselor, the psychologist, the principal and several teachers, the father refused to allow the boy to use medication or to receive outside therapy.

Procedure

The study was conducted in a classroom of eight children, all diagnosed as having learning disabilities. Baseline data were collected for a total of 10 days over a 2-week period. The student was observed by the classroom aide for approximately 2 hours on each of these days. The observation period lasted from the time S entered the classroom (9:15) until morning break time (11:10). This time period included morning drill, first and second periods.

Tokens, which could be exchanged for chocolate chip cookies at break time, served as reinforcers. One token would be earned for every 15 minutes that the subject remained in his seat. The purpose of the study was explained to the other seven students. They agreed that S's behavior needed improvement and that cookies might be the reward he would work for. The class was also told that they would receive a treat of cookies each day that S earned three or more tokens.

During treatment period one (the first week of experimental treatment), tokens and verbal praise were given to S every 15 minutes that he remained in his seat. During treatment period two (the second week), tokens were given every half hour for the same time period. In the final week (treatment period three), tokens were given on a variable-interval basis, with a bonus of three tokens if S remained in his seat for the entire observation period. If the criterion was met he and the rest of the class received their cookies at break time (11:10).

Results and Discussion

The data (Figure 7.7) indicate the number of times S was out of seat without permission during the daily period from 9:15 to 11:10.

Inappropriate out-of-seat behavior was markedly decreased with the implementation of the token system. However, another variable worth considering might be S's sudden position as center of attention and "hero" of the class. At this point the implementation of a reversal procedure by withdrawing just the token system might have been helpful in determining if the token system alone was responsible for the behavioral change. Whatever the reasons, not once during the study did S fail to earn the required three tokens necessary for the class to receive their treat.

It was a successful study because it decreased the out-of-seat behavior sufficiently to permit appropriate learning behavior to occur. Because S was successful at this new and exciting task, he seemed to "shine" during the final days of the treatment period, and this was reflected in his work, his behavior and his own "self-image." Several other members of the class also caught the good-behavior spirit from the example set by S. This was a benefit that the examiner did not count on.

The peer pressure (cues, approval, and disapproval) have had as much effect as the tokens or cookies. Further studies in this area could exclude the peer pressure as a variable to see how much S's good behavior carried over to other students, and to see just how important peer pressure alone might be in modifying behavior.

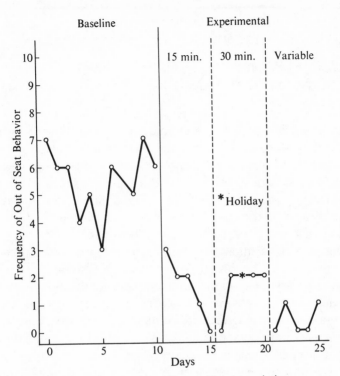

Figure 7.7 Number of times S was out of seat without permission.

References

Becker, W. C., D. R. Thomas, and D. Carnine 1969. *Reducing Behavior Problems: An Operant Conditioning Guide for Teachers*. Illinois, n.p.

Birnbrauer, J. S. and J. Lawler 1969. "Token Reinforcement for Learning." *Mental Retardation*, 2:275–79.

7.8 Summary

Number of Clients A 12-year-old boy, low IQ, hyperactive, and with a learning disability, served as the subject of this intervention. In reality, however, one could argue that the entire class was in some sense truly the subject in that they were all directly involved, and their behavior was also altered, in the intervention program.

Specification of Goals The purpose of this study was stated quite explicitly: to decrease or eliminate inappropriate out-of-seat behavior within a given class.

Measurement Strategy A simple frequence count of this truly "obvious" out-of-seat behavior was made by a teacher's aide. Perhaps owing to the obvious nature of the behavior in question, the author does not report a reliability count. From the perspective of the clinical research model, including such a reliability count is one of a number of ways that this study could have been bolstered. Another problem is the use of the same time frame (9:10 to 11:00 A.M.) for observation was used throughout the study. This was not a representative sample of the child's school behavior. A more accurate picture could have been obtained by sampling behavior at other times of the day. Such a "total" assessment of the target problem would have been desirable since there is really no way of knowing whether this behavior was idiosyncratic to this class, or whether it was a generalized inappropriate behavior.

The measurement strategy employed in this study was a unitary procedure—that is, one behavior being measured by one scale. It could easily have been expanded to a Type A multifactorial measurement procedure and thus elicited some clinically valuable data. For example, the author reports that the child had a "short attention span" and a "very poor self-esteem image." It would have been desirable to administer a self-esteem measure before and after treatment (single point), and similarly, the attention span could easily have been tracked by the same teacher's aide (since out-of-seat behavior is a relatively infrequent behavior). The importance of these measures both from a clinical and evaluative perspective becomes significant when we realize that the author has to depend totally on clinical judgment when he reports improved work and better self-image at the end of treatment.

Design This study is a good example of a changing-criterion design. Whereas in the first treatment phase, the required time for in-seat behavior was 15 minutes (first criterion), during the second treatment phase, it was raised to 30 minutes (second criterion). That is, while the intervention strategy remained the same, the time considered desirable for in-seat behavior was raised. Similarly, there was even a higher requirement (goal behavior) for the appropriate performance in the third and final phase. Thus, while the intervention program remained the same (more or less), the goal that had to be achieved by the client was gradually changed.

Data Patterns As in the previous example, the data patterns in this study are indeed dramatic. The implementation of the intervention program resulted in immediate positive change, and this desired behavior change was maintained in each successive phase.

Other Observations Statistical tests are not considered necessary, as there is a clear visual demonstration of the power of intervention in bringing about and maintaining behavior change. (As we note in chapter 10, however, a visual impression of change may *not* always be statistically significant.)

As in the previous design example where the data were altered so dramatically, the technique of "eyeballing" appears to be more than sufficient in this instance (unless the clinician-researcher *wants* to establish statistical significance for his or her own edification). In this study, there is a reduction in frequent occurrence of the problem behavior from an average of 5 incidents before treatment to an average of 0.5 after treatment—a result that requires little questioning.

Chapter Eight

COMPONENT ANALYSIS DESIGNS

IN THIS CHAPTER we have clustered together the "successive treatment designs" (AB and ABAB extension designs), the "simultaneous-treatment designs," and "strip/construction designs." Unlike the design alternatives presented in the three previous chapters, this chapter on component analysis designs includes designs that have a unique characteristic: they are specifically suited to analyze the impact of multimodal therapies. By definition, component analysis designs are geared to the analysis of multiple strategies within a given intervention package or the comparative analysis of different treatment packages. Since each design alternative is unique, no single operation can be clearly stated to encompass all the component analysis designs. Thus, each design alternative is presented separately.

8.1 Simultaneous-Treatment Designs

$$\text{DESIGN: Simulaneous-treatment design} \quad A\text{--}\overset{D}{\underset{C}{B}}\text{--}C \text{ or } D \text{ or } B$$

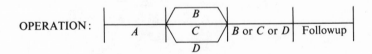

OPERATION:

A = baseline period of target problem and/or goal

B or C or D = unique treatment packages and/or identified strategies of treatment. Each of the packages and strategies must be distinct and separate from each other.

In the simultaneous-treatment design, the clinician-researcher applies a multimodal therapy, a combination of a number of treatments, simultaneously on one target problem. Out of this combined application, the one strategy or package that appears to produce the most amount of change is then continued with the client, while the others are discontinued (Figure 8.1). Basically, this design offers an oppor-

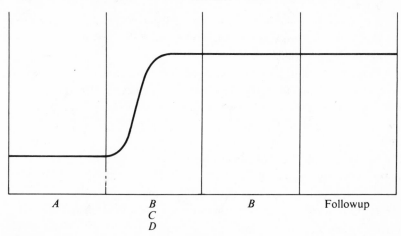

A	B	B	Followup
	C		
	D		

Figure 8.1 Pattern of the simultaneous-treatment design (B is selected as the treatment of choice).

tunity for the internal comparison of the efficacy of several methods of intervention, which ultimately would result in the more efficient delivery of services.

For example, an alcoholic may be treated with three distinct packages: methadone, aversive conditioning, and reevaluation therapy. Here we see the simultaneous application of three distinct strategies, each of which is expected to produce positive results in and of itself. The goal of the design, however, is to evaluate their relative effectiveness while at the same time to provide a strong intervention. Similarly, a clinician-researcher may employ communication exercises, role-playing strategies, and contingency contracting in working with a marital couple. Together, the three strategies form a treatment package. The simultaneous-treatment design would allow this clinician-researcher to evaluate the relative efficacy of each of these three components.

The following points are of importance in understanding this design:

1. *A* signifies the baseline period; no intervention has taken place up to this period.
2. *B, C,* and *D* in the vertical order indicate that all three of the different treatments are being administered simultaneously on the same target problem.
3. *B* or *C* or *D* in the horizontal order indicates the chosen alternative— that is, the one treatment strategy or package that was decided upon as the treatment of choice.
4. Note that the ability to apply just one of the treatments implies that they are uniquely and distinctly defined and administered. Thus, there is the implicit notion that the applied strategies and packages are indeed independent of one another.

Comment Some clarification of the term *simultaneously* is in order. In the example given, the clinician-researcher cannot literally administer role playing, communication exercises, and contingency contracting all at the same point in time. The implication is that, during a given *phase* of treatment, all three strategies are administered in a successive order. For example, a 3-week period of intervention may be employed by the clinician-researcher to test the efficacy of all three of these procedures. During this period the clinician-researcher applies the three treatments in a "counterbalanced" manner. The important thing to remember is that *all* treatments are administered within the same phase of intervention.

The notion of counterbalancing is important in this design. It merely states that the three treatments must be alternated so that the manner of presenting the treatments does not confound the results. Thus, in the design example by McCullough et al. (presented later in this chapter), we see the teacher and teacher's aide alternating the applications of two treatments. Both treatments are administered simultaneously, in that both are offered in one treatment phase, but their actual implementation is alternated between the two individuals and time of day. In this particular design, by counterbalancing, the authors have also tried to avoid order effects as well as any interaction between one individual and one treatment (since in this example two individuals are involved in the treatment program). It is less likely that a repeated demonstrated effect that could be attributed to one treatment is due either to its being used by one individual or to its being applied consistently first in the day. The entire 4-day period constitutes the treatment phase.

Frequent alterations in data patterns where the treatment is or is not present in different situations allow the clinician-researcher to have greater confidence in making causal attributions. As in the reversal/withdrawal design, one's confidence in relating a particular change to a given treatment is related to the number of measurement changes that correspond to the introduction and removal of that treatment.

Strengths and Weaknesses of the Simultaneous-Treatment Design

Strengths

1. There is a comparison of what happens to the target problem and/or goal before and after intervention.

2. This design, compared to the previously discussed designs, allows for the comparison of simultaneously applied treatments—that is, the proportional efficacy of the treatment packages or strategies.

3. Where time is a factor, this design takes considerably less time to implement than either the reversal/withdrawal designs or the multiple-baseline designs, while offering more information than the *AB* baseline intervention design.

4. Unlike the *ABAB* reversal/withdrawal designs, treatment does not have to be removed for any period of time.

Weaknesses

1. This design requires the clinician-researcher to apply two or more uniquely distinct treatments. The greater the relationship that may exist between the treatment packages or strategies, the greater the confounding that may enter into the interpretation of the data.

2. Since the treatments are administered simultaneously, there may be carry-over effects from one treatment to another, and thus the uniqueness of the results may be confounded; that is, the effects of one treatment may add on to or subtract from the next treatment and thus create in inter-action effect.

3. This design requires careful planning on the part of the clinician-researcher to manipulate the various components in a manner that would minimally effect contamination across treatments—that is, the counterbalancing arrangement.

4. To determine the unique effects of a given treatment, a fairly complicated statistical analysis may be required (Benjamin, 1965; Browning, 1967; Browning and Stover, 1971). Otherwise, the distinction between main effects and interaction effects may be relatively unclear. When this occurs, the whole purpose of the design in providing an opportunity for discriminative analysis among treatments can be lost.

5. There may be contrast effects, as demonstrated in the article by Kendall, Nay, and Jeffers (see chapter 9). Here the recipient of treatment may compare what was received during the first application of a treatment with that received during another phase of treatment. Thus, there may be a reaction to this difference rather than to the treatment per se, a reaction that would be difficult to detect and discriminate.

6. Note that, unlike the strip/construction designs (see chapter 8.3), this design does not allow for the analysis of the effectiveness of combined treatment strategies or packages. In fact, it is specifically designed to discriminate between treatments.

7. Perhaps as a function of these design complexities, there are only a handful of instances of the application of this design in the literature.

Suggested Design Utility The major advantage of this design lies in its broad-range approach. The simultaneous application of a number of different treatment strategies, if they complement each other, should result in relatively fast improvement. Thus, from an efficiency perspective, this design takes a shorter time to administer and may rapidly produce the desirable effects. Like the *AB* design, this design could be easily implemented in virtually any situation or with any problem—with the added advantage that one may be able to isolate the more effective components from the less effective ones. Presumably, all treatments *alone* would have brought about positive results; the simultaneous-treatment design offers an opportunity to isolate the more potent procedures.

8.2 Multiple-Schedule Designs

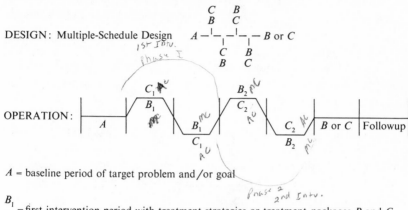

DESIGN: Multiple-Schedule Design

$A = $ baseline period of target problem and/or goal

B_1
C_1 = first intervention period with treatment strategies or treatment packages B and C

B_2
C_2 = second intervention period with treatment strategies or treatment packages B and C

This is a rather complex design in which two or more treatments are offered by different therapists or rendered in different settings in an alternating manner. The client may thus receive treatment B_1 under one condition and treatment C_1 under another condition during the first phase of treatment—where a condition could mean situations, therapists, family members, and so on—and these treatments are then alternated between conditions in successive treatment phases.

For example, two clinician-researchers may work with an alcoholic. During phase one, the first therapist offers marital counseling (B_1) and the other aversive conditioning (C_1) in separate sessions. In the second treatment phase, the first therapist now conducts an aversive conditioning session (C_2) while the second offers marital counseling (B_2). This alternating pattern between therapists is continued in subsequent treatment phases. This example illustrates the application of a multiple-schedule design across therapists.

Alternately, the multiple-schedule design may be administered across settings. For example, a clinician-researcher may use group treatment (B) and individual counseling (C) strategies with an institutionalized client who is gradually being readied for release. In the first treatment phase the two treatments are offered within the institution, and in the second treatment phase, in a halfway house. Thus, the same therapist administers the same treatments in two different contexts. The two treatments could be alternated within each phase of the contexts to counterbalance order effects. Note that the two treatments are never offered simultaneously.

The following points are of importance in understanding this design:

1. *A* signifies the baseline period and no intervention has taken place up to this period.
2. *B* and *C* in the vertical order means that the two treatments are being administered during the same phase of treatment, but they are not being administered simultaneously.
3. *B* and *C* in the staggered vertical order indicates that the treatments are being administered alternately and successively on the target problem.
4. *B* and *C* in the horizontal order indicates the chosen alternative, that is, the one treatment package or strategy that was decided upon as the treatment of choice.
5. Note that the ability to apply just one of the packages or strategies implies that the treatments are uniquely defined and administrable. Thus, there is the implicit notion that the applied strategies or packages are indeed independent of one another.
6. B_1 is identical to B_2, and C_1 is identical to C_2. The successive numbers identify the notion that the treatments are being offered in successive periods of treatment.

This design has similarities to the simultaneous-treatment design in that it allows for the internal comparison of various treatment strategies or packages. However, it also differs in one significant manner. Whereas in the simultaneous-treatment design the treatments are applied *concurrently* within the same situation by the same clinician-researcher throughout intervention, in the multiple-schedule design, the treatments are administered by different therapists or in different situations, the treatments being *alternated* between the therapists or situations, with no simultaneous application.

At this point both design alternatives employ the counterbalancing procedures. In the simultaneous-treatment approach, the counterbalancing occurs within the same treatment period. In the multiple-schedule design, the counterbalancing occurs across different treatment phases.

The major value of the multiple-schedule design in comparison to the simultaneous-treatment design would be its ability to compare across individuals or situations, which makes it similar to the multiple-baseline design. However, the multiple schedule design differs from the multiple-baseline design in that it compares two or more treatments, whereas the multiple-baseline designs are geared to study the impact of one intervention package or strategy. One other significant difference lies in the baseline procedure. In the multiple-baseline procedures, the baseline data gathering is continued on one behavior, individual, or situation while intervention is taking place with another. In contrast, with multiple-schedule designs, baseline data gathering occurs only until the beginning of intervention (unless these are combination designs with reversal/withdrawal procedures as described in chapter 9).

Strengths and Weaknesses of the Multiple-Schedule Design

Strengths
1. There is a comparison of what happens to the target problem and/or goal before and after intervention.
2. Like the other designs in this chapter, this design allows for the comparison of proportional efficacy of different treatment packages or strategies.
3. Unlike the *ABAB* reversal/withdrawal designs, treatment does not have to be removed for any period of time.
4. This design allows for the comparison of treatment effects across persons, situations, or therapists.

Weaknesses
1. Since the treatments are administered successively, there may be carryover effects from one treatment to another, and thus the uniqueness of the results may be confounded. That is, the effects of one treatment may add on or subtract from the next treatment and thus create an interaction effect.
2. This design requires careful planning on the part of the clinician-

researcher to manipulate the various components in a manner that would minimally effect contamination across treatments. This is the counterbalancing arrangement referred to earlier.

3. There may be contrast effects. Here the recipient of treatment may compare what was received during the first application of treatment with that received during another phase of treatment. Thus, there may be a reaction to this difference rather than to the treatment per se, a reaction that would be difficult to discriminate.

4. Like the simultaneous-treatment design, this design does not allow for the comparative analysis of combined treatment packages or strategies.

5. Finally, this is a relatively complex design, requiring considerable control over the treatment situation. Hence, it is found rather infrequently in the literature.

Suggested Design Utility This design has many of the same advantages of the simultaneous-treatment design as far as the discriminative analysis of treatment packages or strategies is concerned. It also has some of the advantages attributed to the multiple-baseline design by virtue of its applicability across individuals and situations. It is, however, restricted by the control necessary over the environment for its application.

8.3 Strip/Construction Designs

DESIGN: Strip/Construction Designs

Strip: $A-(BC)-A-C-A-B-B$ or C or (BC)

Construction: $A-B-A-C-A-(BC)-B$ or C or (BC)

OPERATION:

The strip/construction designs were originally labeled and discussed by Thomas (1975). The essence of these designs is the systematic deletion (stripping) or addition (construction) of various treatment strategies or packages. In his original conceptualization of these designs, Thomas argued that there should be a return to baseline conditions between the administration of each successive treatment program, whether it be one of deletion or addition. In the literature, however, we find numerous studies implementing various modifications of these "pure" design alternatives—one of which is presented later in this chapter. The tendency has been, not to return to original baseline conditions, but rather, to return to an earlier treatment context (perhaps for clinical and heuristic reasons). For example, in an A–B–A–C–A–(BC) construction design, instead of returning to baseline, one finds instances of returning to former treatments—A–B–A–C–B–(BC). Such modifications pose serious problems in analysis, as there are no comparable phases before and after the C or (BC) intervention phases.

In essence, strip/construction designs have components of simultaneous-treatment designs (in that two or more treatments can be offered at a given time), and reversal/withdrawal designs (in that reversal procedures are required between treatments). (See Figures 8.2 and 8.3.) Note also that these designs have similarities to the administration of successive treatments (such as AB and ABAB design

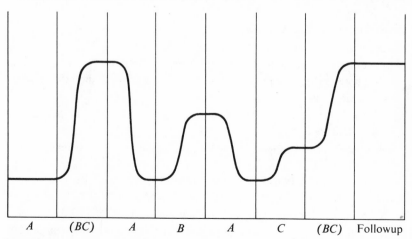

A   (BC)   A   B   A   C   (BC)   Followup

Figure 8.2 The "strip" model.

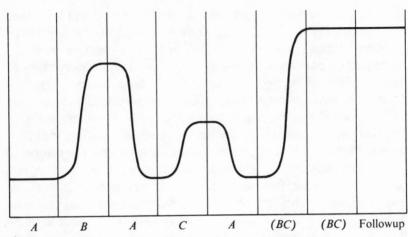

    A   *B*   *A*   *C*   *A*   *(BC)*   *(BC)*   Followup

Figure 8.3 The "construction" model.

extensions), but they differ to the extent that, at some point in time, there is the application of two or more treatments simultaneously.

The following points are of importance in understanding this design:

1. A_1 signifies the baseline period; no intervention has taken place up to this period.
2. *B* and *C* signify unique treatment strategies or packages.
3. *(BC)* signify the combination of two unique treatment strategies or packages.
4. $A_2, A_3,$ and A_4 are reversal/withdrawal periods. Theoretically, the conditions surrounding this measurement period should be identical to the conditions surrounding the measurement of baseline (A_1). The implication here is that, each time intervention is withdrawn, the effects of intervention will somehow be reversed.
5. The final selection of a treatment strategy or a treatment package is dependent on the data. That is, the strategy or package that showed the most amount of change will be retained as the treatment of choice.

Comment These designs are very appealing in that they allow for the implementation of more than one method of treatment while at the same time offering an opportunity to compare them. But this multimodal application combined with the reversal/withdrawal procedures introduces some major problems with regard to the analysis and interpretation of data.

Strengths and Weaknesses of the Strip Construction Designs

Strengths

1. There is a comparison of what happens to the target problem and/or goal before and after intervention.
2. This design allows for the comparison of different treatments—that is, the proportional efficacy of the treatment strategies or packages.
3. By virtue of return to baseline procedures, this design offers more support for the notion that treatment produced change rather than some unknown artifact.
4. Furthermore, return to baseline procedures minimizes the potential interaction between the different treatments.

Weaknesses

1. This design requires the clinician-researcher to apply two or more uniquely distinct treatments. The greater the relationship that may exist between the treatment packages or strategies, the greater the confounding that may enter into the interpretation of the data.
2. There may be contrast effects. Here the recipient of treatment may compare what was received during the first application of treatment with that received during another phase of treatment. Thus, there may be a reaction to this difference rather than to the treatment per se, a reaction that would be difficult to discriminate.
3. The more successful each intervention package or strategy is, the harder it would be to effect a return to baseline.
4. Reversal/withdrawal procedures cannot or should not be used in situations where the target problem is self-putative, destructive, or extremely problematic.
5. In design modifications where the reversal is to a previously administered treatment (rather than to baseline conditions), the question of interaction becomes somewhat acute, and the design may lose its power.

Suggested Design Utility Like the *ABAB* reversal/withdrawal designs, the requirement that one return to baseline conditions delimits the utility of the strip/construction designs. All the problems inherent in the application of *ABAB* designs are applicable here. The

strip/construction designs offer, however, the option of refining multimodal therapies.

Utilization of the Simultaneous-Treatment
Design to Improve Student Behavior
in a First-Grade Classroom

JAMES P. McCULLOUGH, JOHN E. CORNELL,
MAX H. McDANIEL, and ROYCE K. MUELLER, University of
Southern Mississippi

A single-case study is presented to demonstrate the utility of the simultaneous-treatment design. The case involved one first-grade student, a first-
grade teacher, a teacher's aide, and two treatments applied simultaneously
following a 5-day baseline period. The treatment × teacher administration
was counterbalanced over a 4-day period. The goal of the program was to
decrease the disruptive behavior of the child in the classroom. The authors
were also interested in testing the efficacy of the design itself.

Method

Subject and Behavior Cedric was a 6-year-old Negro male from a poor
rural community in a class of 36 first-grade students from the same neighborhood. His teacher complained that he refused to cooperate with many of
the scheduled classroom activities. His uncooperative-disruptive behaviors
took the form of roaming around the classroom, sleeping, daydreaming,
fighting with other children in the class, and playing at the desk with pen-
cils, erasers, and other school materials. These behaviors are labeled *un-*
cooperative by the experimenters. A second target behavior, *cooperative be-*
havior, was to be modified and was defined as the class assignments and not
engaging in any uncooperative behavior. The authors hypothesized that

Reprinted from *Journal of Consulting and Clinical Psychology*, 42 (1974):288–92.
Used by permission of the American Psychological Association.

some of Cedric's uncooperative behavior was indvertently reinforced by his teacher; for example, the teacher frequently asked him to perform some simple chores as he roamed around the room (e.g., run an errand for her). He usually accomplished these tasks successfully, which resulted in praise by the teacher.

Contingencies Two experimental treatments were compared. The contingencies for experimental condition A paired social reinforcement (verbal praise, physical contact) with cooperative behavior, while uncooperative behavior was ignored. The experimenters predicted that praise and physical contact from the teacher would, when delivered following the occurrence of some behavior, increase the frequency of that behavior. This had, in fact, been observed to occur during the base rate period. The literature also supported the hypothesis that teacher attention functions as a positive reinforcer for elementary-age children (e.g., Hall et al., 1968; Thomas et al., 1968). Withdrawing teacher attention from Cedric for uncooperative behavior was judged to be a potentially punishing consequence. Experimental condition B paired social reinforcement with cooperative behavior but administered "time out" for uncooperative behavior. Specifically, Cedric was removed from the classroom by either the teacher or teacher's aide and was placed in an empty adjacent room to remain alone there for 2 minutes. Both teachers continued to manage their large class while the study was run. The scope of the project was necessarily limited by the classroom demands imposed on the teachers. Thus, no control groups were run to investigate the differential effects that punishment might have had when delivered without any administration of social reinforcement. Time was another important consideration. The teachers wanted to know, as quickly as possible, the best strategy to take with Cedric. The present design, and the extinction and counterconditioning program, were constructed to answer their question.

Procedure Each classroom day was subdivided into morning (9:00–11:00 A.M.) and afternoon (12:00–2:00 P.M.) sessions for measurement purposes. Each session was further subdivided into eight 15-minute observation periods. A minus was recorded for an observation if during that 15-minute period Cedric exhibited any uncooperative behavior (e.g., roaming, sleeping). A *plus* was recorded for the period to indicate cooperative behavior if Cedric did the assignment and emitted no uncooperative behavior.

Table 8.1. SPECIAL LATIN SQUARE DESIGN

	Treatment*			
Time	Day 1	Day 2	Day 3	Day 4
AM	A_{T-1}	B_{T-2}	A_{T-2}	B_{T-1}
PM	B_{T-2}	A_{T-1}	B_{T-1}	A_{T-2}

*T-1 = the teacher; T-2 = the teacher's aide.

The study consisted of three phases. During the first phase, 5 days of baseline data were obtained. Recording procedures remained constant throughout all phases. The two experimental treatments were compared during the second phase. The teacher and the teacher's aide, after having been trained in the administration of the treatment strategies, alternated between 2 days as the teacher administered treatment A and the teacher's aide administered treatment B. During the last 2 days, the teacher conducted treatment B and teacher's aide administered treatment A again while alternating between morning and afternoon sessions. The special Latin square design employed here is illustrated in Table 1. The more effective set of contingencies was chosen on the basis of the analysis of data from phase 2 and was then applied solely during the third phase. The experiments predicted that the significantly more effective treatment would continue to have a facilitative effect on Cedric's cooperative behavior. Phase 3 lasted 8 days. Followup data were obtained on Cedric's behavior in the classroom 1 week, 1 month, and 2 months after termination of phase 3.

The teacher and the teacher's aide were trained and encouraged to administer contingently positive reinforcement for cooperative behavior "as frequently as was appropriate for them." Neither teacher had difficulty in contingently reinforcing the target behaviors in the manner outlined by the experimenters. The teachers were encouraged to report daily any extraneous events that occurred during their class sessions. This daily log was viewed as additional information that might help the authors evaluate any target behavior irregularities.

Results

An 84 percent agreement was obtained between the teacher and the teacher's aide when their observational data were used as an estimate of interobserver reliability. No extraneous events were reported in the log by either the teacher or teacher's aide, both of whom apparently thought classroom procedure functioned as usual.

Figure 8.4 illustrates the baseline data. Cooperative behavior occurred during approximately 30 percent of the observation periods. The sequen-

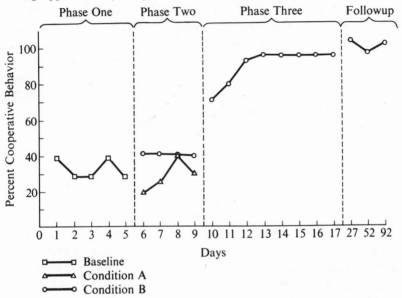

Figure 8.4 Percentage of observation periods in which Cedric emitted cooperative behavior.

tially counterbalanced order in which the teachers administered the treatments for each successive day during phase 2 meets the requirements for a 2×2 special Latin square for the use of each subject as his own control (Benjamin, 1965). Table 2 summarizes the results of this analysis. Treatment B was significantly more facilitative than treatment A ($p < .05$). When

Table 8.2. LATIN SQUARE ANALYSIS OF DIFFERENTIAL EFFECTS OF TIME, EXPERIMENTERS, AND TREATMENT CONDITIONS FOR COOPERATIVE BEHAVIOR

Source	SS	df	MS	F
Experimenters	1.56	1	1.56	2.14
Error$_1$	4.38	6	.73	
Treatments	5.06	1	5.06	6.93*
Days	.06	1	.06	.08
Error$_2$	4.37	6	.73	

*$p < .05$.

treatment *B* was administered, cooperative behavior occurred during approximately 44 percent of the total observation periods. During treatment *A* administration, cooperative behavior occurred during approximately 30 percent of the total observation periods. Since treatment *B* was significantly more effective than treatment *A*, the former treatment was exclusively during the third phase. Cooperation behavior increased to 94 percent on day 12 and remained at that level for the final 5 days.

Followup data were obtained on Cedric 1 week later. Cooperative behavior occurred during 100 percent of the observation periods. Two subsequent followup days were taken 1 month and 2 months later. Cedric's cooperative behavior was being maintained at the 87 percent and 94 percent levels, respectively.

Discussion

The results appeared to strengthen the hypothesis that Cedric's behavior varied as a function of teacher reinforcement behavior. Cedric's case demonstrated the utility of the simultaneous-treatment design in examining a client's behavior change over time and in suggesting which of two possible treatment strategies might be most effective. The design was efficient timewise. In a matter of 4 days, two sets of treatment conditions were compared in such a way as to control partially for sequence and experimenter effects. The confounding of the various interactions did not seem too severe a limitation, since the treatment outcome in phase 3 was consistent with the statistical results of the data analysis at the end of phase 2. Treatment *B* was found to be statistically more effective than treatment *A*, and treatment *B* appeared to exert this facilitative effect throughout the remainder of the study.

Figure 8.4 may be somewhat confusing when one initially observes the sudden jump in cooperative behavior during phase 3. A cumulative percentage total is obtainable from phase 2 data. Both lines on the graph represent cooperative behavior under varying treatment conditions. Cedric's cumulative percentage totals for cooperative behavior on days 6–9 were as follows: 62, 67, 79, and 67 percent. Seen from this perspective, the jump to 71 percent on day 10 is not extraordinary. However, the authors were not able to explain why the target rate increased as it did during the remainder of the third phase. Information from the teacher's daily log shed no light on this problem. The authors and teachers were confronted with a treatment outcome that, though pleasing, could not be thoroughly evaluated. The time-series design is an effective indicator of trends within data over some period of time, but it does not allow the experimenter to effectively assess other topographical characteristics of the curve.

The present study also precluded an evaluation of the differential effects of social reinforcement when compared to punishment. As was previously mentioned, Cedric was treated within an applied setting. It appeared to the authors, at least during the base rate phase, that teacher attention exerted a facilitative effect on Cedric's classroom behavior. The major problem was in finding an effective punishment procedure to complete the treatment package. Unlimited time and experimental flexibility were not available, since the teachers had the dual roles of functioning as observers and behavior modifiers for Cedric and classroom leaders for the remaining 35 children. That the program was a success, in spite of these experimental limitations, was further evidence of the utility of the simultaneous-treatment design.

References

Benjamin, L. S. 1965. "A Special Latin Square for the Use of Each Subject 'As His Own Control,' " *Psychometrika*, 30:499–513.

Hall, R. V., D. Lund, and D. Jackson 1968. "Effects of Teacher Attention on Study Behavior." *Journal of Applied Behavior Analysis*, 1:1–12.

Thomas, D. R., W. C. Becker, and M. Armstrong 1968. "Production and Elimination of Disruptive Classroom Behavior by Systematically Varying Teacher Behavior." *Journal of Applied Behavior Analysis, 1:35–45.*

8.4 Summary

Number of Clients A 6-year-old child in a classroom situation served as the subject of this intervention program.

Specification of Goals The goal of the intervention program was to decrease disruptive behavior in the classroom. This global goal of reducing disruptive behavior was defined by the authors in more precise and measurable terms, such as sleeping, fighting, and the like, that is, a series of behaviors considered disruptive in the classroom environment. The authors also specified and monitored cooperative behavior, those incompatible behaviors that would presumably increase in frequency as a function of decreasing the undesirable behaviors.

Measurement Strategy This study demonstrates again the use of the common form of interval record measurement within a multiple-point measurement strategy. Within the classroom period, observation times were broken down into sessions of 15 minutes. The occurrence of a target behavior during each session was recorded as a plus (+) and its nonoccurrence as a minus (−). The occurrence of both disruptive and cooperative behaviors was recorded.

Note the relatively long period (15 minutes) of observation sessions in contrast to some of the earlier studies where the interval record method was employed. Here we are concerned with a relatively infrequent (but sufficiently frequent to be disruptive) behavior. Thus the clinician-researcher must have some preliminary notions about the relative frequency of the target behavior to determine an appropriate observation period.

Two natural observers, the teacher and a teacher's aide, served as coders. The teacher had the dual responsibility of conducting the class while at the same time gathering this information. This, perhaps, illustrates adequately the potential ease in applying the interval-record data-gathering approach. Since the time intervals of observations were relatively long, and the behaviors in questions relatively obvious and infrequent, the ability to record the occurrence or nonoccurrence of a target behavior was not a difficult task. When such procedures are used, however, it is generally desirable to have at least a second observer so that reliability can be ascertained, as in this instance. In this study, the teacher and teacher's aide agreed 84 percent of the time.

Design This is an example of a simultaneous-treatment design. By the authors own report, this study was partially conducted to test the efficacy of the design in addition to helping the teacher cope with a problem child.

If the application of several treatments simultaneously is nothing new, the application of these treatments in a "counterbalanced" order certainly is. (The term *Latin square* merely refers to the way in which this counterbalancing occurs.) While the phenomenon of counterbalancing is often difficult to achieve in typical treatment settings (particularly in the natural environment), it is a straightforward notion. It simply means that the different treatments must be offered across all behaviors, individuals, and situations in a random manner, at the same time. That is, each behavior, individual, or situation must experience each of the treatments in a different order of presentation. As illustrated in Table 8.1, on day 1, the teacher administered the treatment A in the morning while the aide administered the treatment B. In contrast, on day 2, the teacher administered the treatment B while the aide administered the treatment A.

The power of the design lies in its multiple applications of the different treatment packages or strategies in this counterbalanced order. Whereas in the strip/construction designs, and in the AB extension designs, there is the possibility of order effects (that is, the possibility that the impact of B following C may be different from the impact of C following B), this design minimizes these artifacts as possible sources of error since all treatments are ordered in all sequences.

This design must be carefully articulated before its implementation. All sequences must be thought through, and the application must follow a previously determined logical order. It is perhaps this relative rigidity in design needs that has resulted in the lack of use of this desirable component analysis design.

Data Patterns The data patterns graphed in Figure 8.4 dramatically illustrate the value of the simultaneous-treatment approach. Phase two of the design saw the application of the two treatments A and B simultaneously. The authors, concluding that treatment B produced better results than treatment A and, therefore, proceeding to administer only treatment B during the third phase, thus fulfilled the basic goal of this design, that of isolating the more effective treatment strategy.

Other Observations This is a valuable design alternative for those clinician-researchers interested in testing the efficacy of different treatment strategies or packages. While the intervention in such a situation must be carefully planned (following the counterbalanced order), it is not difficult to do so, provided the number of treatments are not many. As the number of treatments to be compared within one design increases, so does the complexity of the design and analysis. As a rule of thumb, this is an excellent choice when the number of treatments to be compared does not exceed three.

Increased Communications of Chronic Mental Patients by Reinforcement and by Response Priming

FRANK O'BRIEN, NATHAN H. AZRIN, and K. HENSON, Anna State Hospital, Illinois

A major problem in treating chronic mental patients is their failure to communicate their needs, desires, problems, and possible solutions to the treatment staff. Methods of dealing with this problem have been "patient governments" (Greenblatt et al., 1955), suggestions boxes (Roberts, 1960), open-door policy regarding access to the therapist's office (Sarwer-Foner et al., 1960), and encouraging patients to talk out their problems (Rogers, 1951). The present study attempted to apply principles of operant conditioning to the problems of inadequate communication by chronic schizophrenics, specifically, to their making suggestions.

A straightforward method of applying reinforcement principles to increasing suggestions would be to reinforce suggestions immediately and consistently. Accordingly, a reinforcing event such as a cigarette, a token, or

Reprinted from *Journal of Applied Behavior Analysis,* 2 (1969):23–29. Used by permission of the Society for the Experimental Analysis of Behavior and Dr. O'Brien.

praise could be given to the patient when a suggestion was made. An alternative type of reinforcing event is suggested by the analysis of verbal behavior by Skinner (1957). Suggestions are considered as "mands," which are verbal statements that specify their own reinforcers. This analysis suggests that the event to be used as the reinforcer be the very one specified in the mand and predicts the likelihood that suggestions will be a direct function of the frequency with which they are granted. The present study evaluated the utility of this analysis by varying the consistency with which staff members made the changes suggested by the patients.

Another method of increasing patients' communications is suggested by the "reinforcer exposure" procedure, which is a method for increasing the frequency with which mental patients utilize a known reinforcer (Ayllon and Azrin, 1968a; 1968b). This reinforcer exposure procedure was based on the principle that control by reinforcement is greater in stimulus situations that are in temporal proximity to the one in which reinforcement is given (Kelleher, 1958; Kelleher and Fry, 1962). In the previous reinforcer exposure studies, the procedure was to have the patient request the known reinforcers at the location of reinforcement, rather than elsewhere. As applied to the present problem of increasing patients' suggestions, the above rationale suggests that the ward staff require, rather than await or invite, attendance at the location where the suggestions would be immediately reinforced. Since the required attendance also would constitute an interruption of competing behaviors, any change in the patients' requests might be attributable to this interruption, rather than the patients' presence in the reinforcement situation. Accordingly, a control procedure was used in which the competing behaviors were similarly interrupted but without required attendance in the reinforcement situation. Changes in the patients' suggestions might also be attributed to imitation if the suggestions were made in a group situation. Accordingly, the response priming procedure was also evaluated in a situation where only one patient was present at a given time.

It seemed superfluous to many of the patients and staff to require attendance at the suggestion meeting; intuitively, the patient would naturally enter the meeting if she had any suggestions to make. Also, required attendance would not matter if the patient had nothing to say. The rationale for using the priming procedure, however, was that the presence of the patient in the suggestion situation would prime communications that otherwise would not have been made.

Method

Subjects Thirteen chronic mental patients, living in the token reinforcement ward environment described elsewhere (Ayllon and Azrin, 1965; 1968b), earned token points for various adaptive behaviors during the normal working day; they exchanged these points for various consumables, articles, and activities after working hours and on weekends and holidays. Their ages ranged from 29 to 69 years with a mean age of 50. Their mean duration of hospitalization was 18 years, with a range of 6 to 35 years. Ten were diagnosed as schizophrenic and three as mentally retarded with psychosis. Six patients were receiving maintenance doses of phenothiazine-derivative drugs. These patients were chosen for the study because of their long institutional history had resulted in a passive acceptance of their hospital environment.

Response Definition and Reliability A suggestion was defined as a direct and unequivocal request for an addition to, or change in, the ward treatment procedure. Several steps were taken to assure impartial recording. First, the patient was required to state the request fully such as, "I would like to have an appointment with the dentist next week." The meeting leader, one of three staff members then, repeated the request and asked the patient if that was indeed her desire. Only if she answered affirmatively was the patient's statement scored as a suggestion. Secondly, present at all meetings was a recording secretary whose only responsibility was to record the suggestions; the secretary was unaware of the experimental nature of the meeting. Thirdly, three ward attendants independently scored the recording secretary's transcript at the end of the study to determine whether or not each item was a suggestion as defined above.

Procedure During each suggestion meeting, the meeting leader asked three questions of each patient: "Are you feeling well?" "Is there anything about the ward program that upsets you or is there anything about the program that you would like changed"? and "Is there anything you would like to earn that is not available now?" These three questions were designed to prompt suggestions regarding improved medical, administrative, and reinforcement procedures, respectively. All suggested changes were granted by the meeting leader's saying "Yes" if the change held any hope of improved treatment for the patient. If the change was for an additional reinforcer, as specified in the third question, the leader also stated the cost in token-points at the time the request was granted. For reinforcers that had to be purchased (a new dress), the cost was equal to about 1 cent per token-point. For reinforcers that did not require purchase (e.g., attending a local rodeo of which the staff had not been aware), the standard cost for equivalent events was assigned.

Table 8.3 outlines the principal features of the procedure. Experiment I compared the response priming procedure with a non-priming procedure in an *ABA* design during a meeting held on the ward at the same time each weekday. All other ward activities and programs were discontinued for that time of day. Chimes sounded on the ward, and all patients were required to assemble in a room where an attendant read a statement that a discussion and suggestion interview would now be held in a nearby room. For the non-priming procedure, the statement invited the patients to attend. The statement was: "Mr. —— will spend the next 25 minutes in his office. During this time you *may* meet with him alone about anything you wish to discuss with him" (repeat). The priming procedure differed only in that the statement was: ". . . you *will* meet with him . . . ," and all patients were required to attend the meeting in the psychologist's office.

The procedure for experiment II was identical to that of experiment I, except that the patients met as a group (each patient was still asked the three prompting questions). The patients, the meeting leader, the recording secretary, and the ward schedule were the same. The sequence of conditions was, again, *ABA:* 5 days each of non-priming, then priming, and then non-priming, again.

Experiment III evaluated the importance of the consistency with which the patients' suggestions were followed. A multiple schedule (see Ferster and Skinner, 1957) was arranged in which two meeting leaders served as the discriminative stimuli. Both leaders were supervisory personnel, and had the requisite administrative authority to make changes in the ward procedure. The two leaders conducted the meetings on alternate days. During the first 8 days, leader *A* followed all suggestions made by the patients during his four meetings; leader *B* followed none during his four meetings. To control for the manner in which the leaders asked the three questions and conducted the meetings, their roles were reversed during the next 8 days, days 9 to 16. On days 17 to 24, leader *A* followed 25 percent of the suggestions; leader *B* fol-

Table 8.3. PROCEDURAL OUTLINE AND SEQUENCE OF THE THREE EXPERIMENTS

	Experiment I, Private Interview			Experiment II, Public Meeting			Experiment III, Public Meeting							
	No Priming	Priming	No Priming	No Priming	Priming	No Priming	Priming		Priming		Priming		Priming	Priming
Meeting Leader	A	A	A	A	A	A	A	B	A	B	A	B	C+A	C+B
Percent Reinforcement	100	100	100	100	100	100	100	0	0	100	25	75	100	0
Days	2	14	4	5	5	5	4	4	4	4	4	4	4	4

lowed 75 percent. During these intermittent schedules, a table of random numbers was used to determine which suggestions would be followed. During the final 8 days the procedure was identical to the first 8 days, except that an individual with no prior knowledge of the study conducted the meetings. The leaders remained silent except to reply affirmatively or negatively after a suggestion was made. The introduction of a naive individual to conduct the meetings served as a further control for the manner in which the leaders conducted the meetings.

Results

Throughout the study 192 suggestions were recorded by the recording secretary. Only three of these were considered by the meeting leader as unfeasible or whimsical. Of the remaining suggestions, 5 percent were concerned with the medical program, 24 percent with the therapeutic program, and 71 percent with the reinforcers. Every patient made at least one suggestion. When the list of 192 suggestions was scored by the three independent and naive attendants, their agreement with the recording secretary was 100, 99.5, and 99 percent, respectively, about whether the statement was a suggestion and was of potential benefit. Questioning of the recording secretary, after the study, revealed that she was still unaware of the experimental nature of the meetings and the scheduled manipulation of the experimental variables. She did note that the patients responded more frequently when the group leader was "agreeable."

Figure 8.5 shows that the mean number of suggestions during the private interview of experiment I increased from zero to about three per day when response priming was introduced. This increase occurred for 11 patients; the other 2 remained unchanged. This difference was statistically significant ($p < 0.005$) according to the Wilcoxin Matched-Pairs Signed-Ranks Test (Siegel, 1956). When response priming was eliminated, the mean number of suggested improvements decreased to 0.3 per day ($p < 0.005$). This decrease occurred for 11 patients; the other 2, again, remained unchanged. The number of suggestions in the second no-priming condition was significantly greater than in the first.

Figure 8.6 shows that the mean number of suggestions during the group meeting of experiment II increased from 0.4 to 3.0 when response

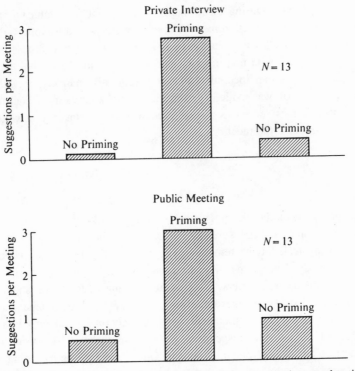

Figure 8.5 Number of suggestions per meeting made by 13 chronic mental patients when they were invited to attend the meeting (no priming) and when attendance at the meeting was required (priming). The upper graph presents the data for Experiment I, during which the 13 patients met with the meeting leader individually and in private; the lower graph is for Experiment II, during which the 13 patients met with the meeting leader as a group.

priming was introduced ($p < 0.01$). Of the 13 patients, this increase occurred for 7, 5 remained unchanged, and 1 patient decreased. When response priming was eliminated, the mean number of suggested improvements decreased from 3.0 to 1.2 ($p < 0.025$). Of the 13 patients, this decrease occurred for 7, 5 remained unchanged, and 1 patient increased. Again, the number of suggestions during the second no-priming condition was not significantly greater than the first.

Figure 8.6 shows the day-by-day changes in the number of suggestions made in the presence of each meeting leader in each phase of the multiple

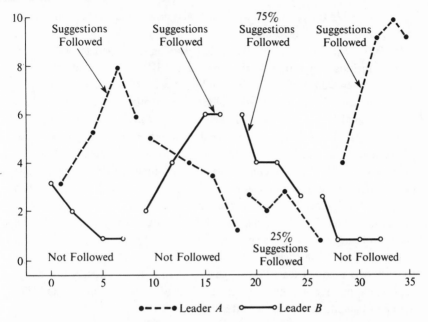

Figure 8.6 The number of suggestions made by 13 mental patients daily, during the multiple schedule of Experiment III. The schedule stimuli were the two meeting leaders, A and B, who conducted the meetings and reacted to the suggestions as noted.

schedule of experiment III. Initially, the same number of suggestions was made to each of the meeting leaders. During the next 6 days, the number of requests gradually increased for leader A, who followed 100 percent of the suggestions and gradually decreased for leader B, who granted 0 percent of the suggestions. When the meeting leaders reversed their roles on day 9, the number of suggestions to leader A gradually decreased to one per day; those to leader B gradually increased to six per day. When leader A followed 25 percent instead of 0 percent of the suggestions on days 17 to 24, the suggestions increased from one to about two per day. When leader B followed 75 percent instead of 100 percent of the suggestions during the same period, the suggestions gradually decreased from six to three per day. During the last 8 days, the suggestions again changed as a function of the change in the consistency of following the suggestions, even though the naive discussion leader conducted the meetings. Suggestions gradually increased in the presence of leader A, who granted 100 percent instead of 25 percent, and gradually decreased in the presence of leader B who now granted 0 percent instead of 75 percent of the suggestions.

In Figure 8.7, both the number of suggestions made and the number of patients making suggestions during experiment III are presented as a function of the percentage of suggestions followed. The mean number of suggestions per meeting was based on the last four meetings of each phase and thereby included two meetings for each meeting leader. The data points for 0 percent and 100 percent are based on six meetings each; the data points for 25 percent and 75 percent are for two meetings. The mean number of suggestions per meeting increased as a direct function of the percentage granted from about one suggestion when none were granted to about seven when all were granted. Similarly, the mean number of patients who made a suggestion increased from about 1.0 to 4.5 per day. The differences in the number of suggestions between 0 percent and 100 percent, and 25 percent and 100 percent values were statistically significant ($p < 0.025$). Of the nine patients who made at least one suggestion during this portion of the study, eight made more when all were granted than when none were granted. For the ninth patient, there was no difference.

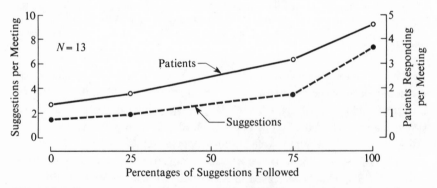

Figure 8.7 The number of suggestions made by 13 patients and the number of patients making suggestions per meeting as a function of the percentage of suggestions followed. The data are based on the last 4 days of each 8-day phase of the multiple schedule of Experiment III.

Discussion

Patients' suggestions were increased by the response priming procedure, which consisted of requiring, rather than inviting, the patient to be present in a structured response situation where suggestions were reinforced. Suggestions increased when priming was used and decreased when it was discontinued. A lingering effect of priming was seen in the slightly higher level of suggestions after the priming than before it. The increase was obtained for most of the patients whether the suggestion procedure was a group meeting or a private interview. The frequency of suggestions by patients was a direct function of the probability of the staff member's following that suggestion. When one staff member followed the suggestions, and a second one did not, a high frequency of suggestions occurred in the presence of the member who did reinforce and a low frequency in the presence of the one who did not. The priming procedure was complementary to the reinforcement procedure in that few suggestions were made when priming was used without reinforcement or when reinforcement was used without priming.

The rationale for the priming procedure was that control by a reinforcer is greatest during the terminal portion of a response sequence and weakest at the early portion. This phenomenon is indicated by the increasing response rate with increasing proximity to reinforcement during a fixed-interval or fixed-ratio schedule of reinforcement (Ferster and Skinner, 1957). When the stimulus situation changes as proximity to reinforcement changes, it has similarly been found that control by the reinforcer is weakest during the initial stimuli and greatest during the terminal stimulus. This is indicated by the low response rate in the initial stimuli and the high rate during the last stimulus of a chain schedule (Kelleher and Fry, 1962). This phenomenon has also been widely studied with rats in runways and is referred to as the "approach gradient": the strength of a response increases as the distance from the goal box decreases (Miller, 1944). These findings suggest a general response priming rule for increasing low-frequency behavior: do not require an individual to initiate a response sequence when he is in a stimulus situation remote from reinforcement, but rather, arrange or require his presence in a terminal portion of the sequence at the time for response initiation. The present study demonstrated that this priming procedure effectively increased the response of making suggestions. Response priming had previously been found to increase utilization of many types of reinforcers (Ayllon and Azrin, 1968b) and has more recently been applied in the development of a behavioral engineering apparatus (Azrin and Powell, in press). It may, therefore, be concluded that priming, as defined here, is a general procedure for increasing behavior involved in the response-reinforcer relation.

Several other interpretations of the priming effect may seem plausible but were not supported by the specific findings. The increased suggestions during priming cannot be attributed to the interruption of competing activities, because no other activities were scheduled at that time; in addition, the nonpriming control procedure interrupted competing activities but in a different location. The increase of suggestions during priming might have been caused by imitation of the other patients during the required attendance at the group meeting; the same increase occurred, however, during the individual meetings where no other patients were present. Simple familiarization resulting from the required attendance could not have been responsible, because the suggestions decreased when priming was discontinued and after familiarization had already taken place.

The increase of suggestions when the suggestions were followed demonstrates that the act of following a suggestion constitutes a reinforcer in accord with Skinner's (1957) analysis of mands. Two other properties of reinforcement were found to apply. First, the suggestions increased as a function of the frequency with which they were carried out; this relation conforms to the general findings that the frequency of a response is a direct function of the frequency of reinforcement (Skinner, 1938; Catania and Reynolds, 1968). Secondly, a stimulus discrimination based on reinforcement could be established, as evidenced by the high frequency of suggestions in the presence of whichever meeting leader was following them but a low frequency in the presence of the meeting leader who was not. The correspondence of these findings with general reinforcement principles confirms the theoretical value of this analysis of verbal behavior.

The present results indicated that the priming procedure was of clinical value to the patient. The number of suggestions was large (about six per session) when one considers the withdrawn and passive condition of these chronic schizophrenic patients. The importance of obtaining these suggestions can be estimated by the efforts of clinicians to elicit them by other methods, such as "patient governments" and having patients "talk out" their problem. Examples of their importance were seen here in suggestions which revealed medical disorders that were otherwise overlooked, as well as treatment possibilities that were not apparent. For example, several patients requested a home visit for the first time in several years. Also, many new reinforcers were requested, each of which the patient later obtained by engaging in adaptive behaviors that earned the required number of token points. The alternative procedures of simply inviting suggestions or having group meetings for that purpose were found to be relatively ineffective as compared to the combined priming and reinforcement procedure. Few suggestions were made unless the suggestions were primed and reinforcement was given by granting the requests almost without exception. Subjectively, the effect was to impart a feeling of initiative and assurance to the patients as well as a feeling by the attendants that the program was continuously responsive to the desires and best interests of the individual patient.

References

Ayllon, T., and N. H. Azrin 1965. "The Measurement and Reinforcement of Behavior of Psychotics" *Journal of the Experimental Analysis of Behavior*, 8:357–83.

Ayllon, T., and N. H. Azrin 1968a. "Reinforcer Sampling: a Technique for Increasing the Behavior of Mental Patients." *Journal of Applied Behavior Analysis*, 1:21–34.

Ayllon, T., and N. H. Azrin 1968b. *The Token Economy: A Motivational System for Therapy and Rehabilitation.* New York: Appleton-Century-Crofts.

Azrin, N., and J. Powell 1969. "Behavioral Engineering: The Use of Response Priming to Improve Prescribed Self-Medication." *Journal of Applied Behavioral Analysis*, 2:39–42.

Catania, A. C., and G. S. Reynolds 1968. "A Quantitative Analysis of the Responding Maintained by Interval Schedules of Reinforcement." *Journal of the Experimental Analysis of Behavior*, 2:327–82.

Ferster, C. B., and B. F. Skinner 1957. *Schedules of Reinforcement.* New York: Appleton-Century-Crofts.

Greenblatt, M., R. H. York, and E. L. Brown 1955. *From Custodial to Therapeutic Patient Care in Mental Hospitals.* New York: Russell Sage Foundation.

Kelleher, R. T. 1958. "Fixed-Ratio Schedules of Conditioned Reinforcement with Chimpanzees." *Journal of the Experimental Analysis of Behavior*, 1:281–9.

Kelleher, R. T., and W. Fry 1962. "Stimulus Functions in Chained Fixed-Interval Schedules," *Journal of the Experimental Analysis of Behavior*, 5:167–73.

Miller, N. E. 1944. "Experimental Studies of Conflict." In J. McV. Hunt, ed. *Personality and the Behavior Disorders*, vol. 1. New York: Ronald Press, pp. 431–65.

Roberts, L. M. 1960. "Group Meetings in a Therapeutic Community." In H. C. Denber, ed. *Therapeutic Community*. Springfield, Illinois: Charles C Thomas, pp. 129–46.

Rogers, C. R. 1951. *Client Centered Therapy*. New York: Houghton-Mifflin.

Sarwer-Foner, G. L., W. Ogle, and T. E. Dancey 1960. "A Self-Contained Women's Ward as a Therapeutic Community." In H. C. Denber, ed. *Therapeutic Community*. Springfield, Ill.: Charles C Thomas, pp. 79–96.

Siegel, S. 1956. *Nonparametric Statistics for the Behavioral Sciences*. New York: McGraw-Hill.

Skinner, B. F. 1938. *The Behavior of Organisms: An Experimental Analysis*. New York: Appleton-Century-Crofts.

Skinner, B. F. 1957. *Verbal Behavior*. New York: Appleton-Century-Crofts.

8.5 Summary

Number of Clients Thirteen institutionalized patients, diagnosed as schizophrenic or retarded, and living in a token economy chronic ward, served as the targets of this intervention program.

Specification of Goals Passivity resulting from long institutionalization was chosen as the area of general concern. As a result of this institutionally learned passivity, the patients were dependent on the ward staff for virtually all their daily needs and were incapable of making even their basic needs known to the ward staff. The specified goal of intervention, then, was to increase communication between the patients and ward staff, and specifically, to increase the making of suggestions for changes in the ward environment.

Measurement Strategy Preliminary assessment revealed that ward staff were inconsistent in following through with the suggestions made by their patients. The treatment procedure tested the efficacy of consistency in meeting the suggestions of the patients as a possible inducement for increased communication.

The suggestions made by the patients took place during a series of meetings that were either primed (required) or not primed (not required). A recording secretary recorded each suggestion made by the patients, provided the suggestions were made in a defined manner (precise definitions were used in an attempt to minimize the possibility of "reading-in" to statements made by the patients). Reliability of these records was checked independently by three ward staff who also kept records and thus ensured, not only the accuracy of the data, but also the fulfillment of the suggestions.

Since the meetings were for prescribed periods of time, a large number of suggestions could occur. The measurement employed was thus a simple frequency count of the number of suggestions made and by whom.

Design The study illustrates the use of the multiple-schedule design. This particular study is a fairly complex one, comparing situations in which meeting attendance was required with meetings where attendance was essentially voluntary. In addition, within these structural formats, the study attempted to evaluate the impact of two group leaders' following or not following the suggestions of the patients.

Figure 8.5 illustrates the impact of priming and nonpriming as far as the number of suggestions are concerned. The bar graph clearly demonstrates the effectiveness of priming as a desirable strategy to increase suggestive behavior.

Note also the multiple-schedule counterbalancing procedures employed by the two leaders in the study. During the period that leader A followed all suggestions, leader B followed none. Alternately, during the next phase, leader B followed all suggestions while leader A followed none and thus counterbalanced any possible effect that may be attributed to the "leaders" rather than to the reinforcement of suggestions per se. Other variations of this format were conducted in this study, and in each instance, both group leaders alternated their responsibilities.

Data Patterns Figure 8.6 clearly demonstrates the value of the multiple-schedule design as a discriminative analyzer. Note that the

number of suggestions varied directly with whether or not suggestions were followed and had nothing to do with who the leader was.
In essence, the design succeeded in isolating the treatment that
worked—priming the patients to come to meetings and reinforcing
their suggestions in that context—while simultaneously minimizing
the possible impact that a particular leader may have in the explanation of the results.

Other Observations The complexity and control necessary for the
implementation of this multiple-schedule design is quite evident in
this study. On the other hand, a multiple-schedule design does not
necessarily have to be as complex. As the number of groups or individuals in treatment increases, and when there is more than one
clinician-researcher participating in the program, the counterbalancing of the treatments and individuals requires considerable
forethought and planning. Despite these mechanistic hurdles, the
value of the multiple-schedule design as a desirable component
analysis design is indeed high.

Effect of Positive Reinforcement, Informational Feedback, and Contingency Contracting on a Bulimic Anorexic Female

PETER M. MONTI, BARBARA S. McCRADY
and DAVID H. BARLOW,
Brown University and Butler Hospital

Behavior modification procedures incorporating selective positive reinforcement have proved effective in treating anorexia nervosa (Blinder et al.,
1970; Leitenberg et al., 1968). Although most studies suggest that reinforcement leads to weight gain, only two studies have attempted to isolate the
role of reinforcement. In the first study, Leitenberg et al. (1968) demon-

Reprinted from *Behavior Therapy*, 8 (1977):258–63. Used by permission of Academic
Press and Dr. Monti.

strated that, although positive reinforcement increased caloric intake and weight gain, weight gain continued after withdrawal of reinforcement. In the second, Agras et al. (1974) demonstrated, in a series of single-case experiments, that reinforcement, informational feedback, and meal size all contribute to increased eating.

Although the above studies have demonstrated the effectiveness of behavioral treatment for anorexia nervosa, none of the patients in the studies cited were bulimic anorexics. This is unfortunate since bulimia (morbidly increased appetite) is often a problem which alternates with anorexia. Also absent from the literature are reports of post-hospitalization followup on anorexic cases treated with behavior modification (Feinstein, 1974). Lack of followup data has made evaluation of long-term effectiveness of behavioral treatment for anorexia nervosa impossible. Such data are particularly crucial in view of recent criticisms of the behavior modification of anorexia nervosa (Bruch, 1974; Spector, 1975).

The present case differs from previous reports in several important dimensions. First, the patient was a bulimic anorexic. The patient would overeat and then induce vomiting and take laxatives and/or diuretics. Overeating/vomiting alternated with periods of decreased eating. Second, a behavioral analysis revealed that thoughts which led the patient to feel as though she was a "bad person" usually preceded her maladaptive behavior. The consequences of these bad feelings were either that the patient would not eat, or would overeat, "feel disgusting," and then take overdoses of laxatives and/or diuretics and induce vomiting. These intrusive thoughts which formed an early component in the behavioral and cognitive chain leading to the maladaptive target behaviors described above also required treatment. Finally, data for 6-month outpatient followup period are also reported.

Method

Subject The patient was a 28-year-old registered nurse, referred for admission because she had been losing weight and abusing medications such as diuretics and laxatives for the past 6 months. She had been taking an average of 30 Ex-Lax daily for the 2 months prior to admission. Six months prior to admission the patient had been overweight (79.38 kg and 1.75 m tall), had begun to diet, and had ceased menstruating. Gradually she took more medications to lose weight, ate less, and when she overate, she induced vomiting. Vomiting occurred daily for several weeks prior to hospitalization. Upon admission she was severely emaciated, weighing 49.90 kilograms.

Criteria used in making diagnosis for anorexia nervosa in the present case were those generally accepted (Russell, 1971), namely, (1) behaviors leading to at least 20 percent loss of body weight, (2) cessation of menstruation in the patient above the age of puberty occurring before weight loss was extreme; (3) a fear of becoming obese, with marked resistance to the idea of gaining weight; and (4) no evidence of psychosis, but with other psychopathology usually similar to that described as hysterical personality.

Measures Two measures of eating behavior were employed, caloric intake and weight.

Caloric intake. Immediately after meals, caloric intake was calculated and charted by one of several nurses who had been trained to use a calorie-counting booklet to calculate caloric intake.

Weight. Each morning, at 10:00 A.M., the patient was weighed by a nurse, and her weight was recorded.

Vomiting. The patient was asked to report each time she vomited. Also, staff and other patients observed and reported vomiting, which was recorded by a staff member.

Procedure Procedures involving positive reinforcement and informational feedback which were employed in this study were chosen in light of the data reported by Agras et al. (1974). However, these procedures were modified because of medical complications and the specific psychological complexities of the patient.

The patient was treated on an inpatient unit for 44 days. Three daily meals were served to the patient, who ate on the unit except when she earned the privilege of eating in the cafeteria. Eating in the cafeteria occurred only after baseline. Meals consisted of choices which the patient selected. No food was available other than that served at meals. Meal size was gradually increased by the therapist. The study consisted of six phases, which were completed sequentially: baseline, reinforcement, reinforcement plus feedback, reinforcement, reinforcement plus feedback plus systematic desensitization, and systematic desensitization plus contingency contracting.

1. *Baseline*. Therapeutic instruction communicated that we were interested in the patient, that she should eat as much as possible, that weight gain was expected, that she should vomit only in a specific toilet, and that she should report each time she vomited. The patient was given a minimum of nursing attention and was restricted to the unit.

2. *Reinforcement*. In this phase the patient was told that each 0.5-pound (0.2-kg) increase in weight beyond the previous day's weight would earn her one of the following privileges, which she had selected: dining in the cafeteria for a given day's meals; a half-hour individual therapy session; attending a movie; or an accompanied walk outside. In addition, the patient was asked not to induce vomiting. Other procedures remained as in baseline.

3. *Reinforcement plus feedback*. In this phase the patient was asked by her therapist to calculate her caloric intake after meals and to plot these data as well as her daily weight on a wall graph in her room. These data were checked by a nurse daily. Reinforcement was as in phase 2.

4. *Reinforcement*. This consisted of a return to reinforcement as in the second phase. In addition, since weight gain was occurring due to edema rather than increased caloric intake, reinforcers were made contingent on consumption of a minimum of 2000 calories per day. The patient was told that in order to earn her rewards she would have to consume a minimum of 2000 calories per day in addition to gaining 0.5 pound beyond her previous day's weight.

5. *Reinforcement plus feedback plus systematic desensitization*. Reinforcement conditions of phase 4 plus feedback conditions of phase 3 were reintroduced, and daily sessions of deep muscle relaxation and systematic desensitization were initiated. Desensitization focused on thoughts which led the patient to feel as though she was a "bad person." The rationale for desensitizing the patient to the content of these thoughts was that if the patient could learn to relax in the presence of these thoughts, they would eventually extinguish, since their source of reinforcement (anxiety and its subsequent reduction by suppressing the thoughts) would be absent.

6. *Posthospital systematic desensitization plus contingency contracting*. Sessions of muscle relaxation and desensitization were continued on a weekly outpatient basis. In addition, the patient consented to and signed (on a weekly basis) a behavioral contingency contract stipulating that she would consume between 1800 and 2300 calories per day, that she would not induce vomiting, and that she would not take nonprescribed drugs during a given

day. Thus, the contract could be broken as many as three times daily. The consequence for each time the contract was broken was a $5.00 check to an organization disfavored by the patient (the President Ford Reelection Committee).

Results

Weight decreased over the first 5 days of hospitalization (Figure 8.8). Mean baseline caloric intake was 292 calories. Vomiting occurred once daily during baseline and occurred only twice more during treatment. Following reinforcement, weight increased (0.17 kg/day). However, there was no parallel increase in intake. This discrepancy was clarified after it was discovered that the patient had developed an edema and was retaining an excess of fluid for which Diuril, 500 mg, q.i.d., was prescribed on day 17.

Reinforcement plus feedback began on day 19. Increased caloric intake occurred immediately. Edema had not substantially improved until day 22, when Diuril was reduced to 250 mg, q.i.d. Unfortunately, until day 22 the patient was very concerned that she was gaining too fast. Edema was eliminated by day 23, and Diuril was discontinued until day 27, when some edema reappeared, and Hydrodiuril, 50 mg, q.i.d. was prescribed for the duration of hospitalization. Following the return to reinforcement, caloric intake gradually increased while weight stabilized. When desensitization was added to reinforcement plus feedback, there was a continued gain in caloric intake and weight (0.35 kg/day) followed by stabilization.

During the first week of outpatient treatment, there was a slight increase in both caloric intake and weight. This was followed by a decrease in both these measures and then a stabilization.

Discussion

Results support those of Agras et al. (1974), which suggest feedback plays a most important role in treatment. In the present case, as in two cases reported by Agras et al., the initial reinforcement phase produced little weight gain or caloric intake. The addition of feedback led to gains in caloric intake but not weight. This discrepancy can be explained by noting that the pa-

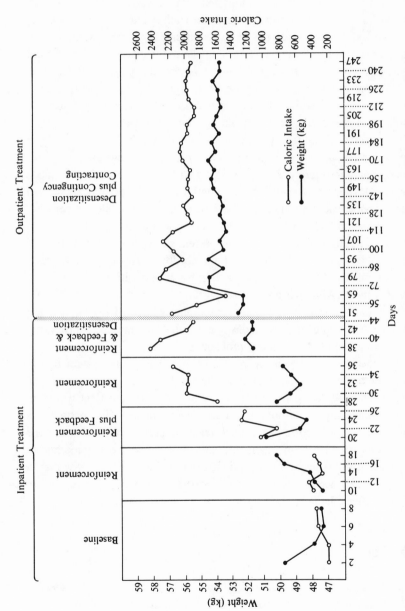

Figure 8.8 Mean weight and caloric intake as a function of treatment phases for inpatient treatment (mean of 2 days) and outpatient treatment (mean of 7 days).

tient's edema and its treatment complicated data on weight. Initially, the patient's weight gain, due to water retention rather than increased caloric intake, was reinforced. When the edema was treated by diuretics, the patient lost this excess water. When her caloric intake did increase, the increase did not immediately result in weight gain. It is possible that the patient was drinking more fluids so as to increase her weight (thus fulfilling reinforcement contingencies). Although when questioned the patient denied this, the importance of reinforcing caloric intake in addition to weight gain is apparent. The method of reinforcing caloric intake and weight gain has not been reported in previous studies of anorexia nervosa. The change from reinforcing weight gain to reinforcing both weight gain and caloric intake was made in phase 4 when reinforcement was contingent on both a 0.2-kilogram weight increase and consumption of a minimum of 2000 calories per day. This combination had a powerful effect on caloric intake.

It is possible, due to the design of the present study, to assess the effect of adding desensitization to reinforcement plus feedback. However, there was a continued gain in caloric intake and weight when desensitization was added to the treatment. Although no data supporting the effectiveness of desensitization to thoughts are reported, some preliminary data (SUDS ratings) and the first author's clinical impressions suggest that this may be a promising approach to a complicated clinical problem.

Followup outpatient treatment involved a continuation of systematic desensitization in conjunction with the behavioral contract regarding eating, vomiting, and pill-taking behaviors. After 3 weeks of outpatient treatment there was a leveling off of both weight and caloric intake. The contract was broken only six times during a 6-month treatment period, suggesting that the contract was effective in maintaining treatment successes. It is important to point out that followup treatment and effective maintenance are essential in treating anorexia nervosa, since many anorexics reportedly redevelop severe symptoms after relatively short-term successes (Bruch, 1974).

References

Agras, W. S., D. H. Barlow, H. N. Chapin, G. G. Abel, and H. Leitenberg 1974. "Behavior Modification of Anorexia Nervosa." *Archives of General Psychiatry,* 30:279–86.

Blinder, B. J., D. M. A. Freeman, and A. J. Stunkard 1970. "Behavior Therapy of Anorexia Nervosa: Effectiveness of Activity as a Reinforcer of Weight Gain." *American Journal of Psychiatry*, 126:1093–98.

Bruch, H. 1974. "Perils of Behavior Modification with Anorexia Nervosa." *Journal of the American Medical Association*, 230:1419–22.

Feinstein, S. C. 1974. "Anorexia Nervosa." Letter to the Editor. *Journal of the American Medical Association*, 228:1230.

Leitenberg, H., W. S. Agras, and L. E. Thompson 1968. "A Sequential Analysis of the Effect of Selective Positive Reinforcement in Modifying Anorexia Nervosa." *Behaviour Research and Therapy*, 6:211–18.

Russell, G. F. M. 1971. "Anorexia Nervosa: Its Identity as an Illness and Its Treatment." In J. H. Price, *Modern Trends in Psychological Medicine*. London: Butterworth.

Spector, S. 1975. "Behavior Therapy in Anorexia Nervosa," Letter to the Editor, *Journal of the American Medical Association*. 233:317.

8.6 Summary

Number of Clients A 28-year-old nurse, having problems with weight loss, vomiting, and drug abuse, served as the subject of this intervention. This study illustrates more of a medical problem and demonstrates the diverse application of the clinical research model.

Specification of Goals The goals in this study were defined "medically" given the nature of the problem. The two primary goals were to stabilize her weight at an appropriate level and to stop her vomiting behavior (which was related to her food intake and weight).

Measurement Strategy The measures were self-determined to a great extent in this instance: caloric intake, weight gain, and frequency of vomiting.

The treatment program was started in an institutional setting. Baseline data were gathered for 8 days prior to intervention. Whereas nurses were originally involved in the monitoring of the target problems, later on in treatment, the client herself had this responsibility (with the nurses merely checking for accuracy). Given the absolute quality of the target problems, that is weight, caloric intake, and vomiting, there was little room for error and hence little need for multiple evaluators.

The authors noted the apparent presence of self-deprecatory thoughts in the client prior to treatment. No attempt was made to measure these nonobservable phenomena, although the authors report clinical impressions suggesting a reduction in such thoughts toward the end of treatment. This would have been an interesting and clinically valuable measure, since the authors relate the occurrence of these thoughts to vomiting behavior.

Design This is an example of a strip/construction design that has been modified in that reversal to baseline procedures was not instituted. In order to understand the design, consider the following:

A = baseline

B = reinforcement

C = reinforcement + feedback

D = reinforcement + feedback + densitization

E = desensitization + contracting

What we have is the following design configuration:

$A–B–(BC)–B–(BCD)–(DE)$

Note that this differs from the "pure" strip/construction design, which would have looked as follows in this instance:

$A–B–A–(BC)–A–(BCD)–A–(DE)$

The main difference is the return to baseline between applications of each treatment.

This is a combination strip/construction design when one considers the different segments. The $B–(BC)–(B)$ illustrates the "strip" portion, and $B–(BC)–B–(BCD)$ illustrates the "construction." To clarify a point already made in the text, note that each of the treatments—B, C, D, and E—signifies unique and different treatment strategies or packages. Each of these treatments could be tested alone and produce some effect.

Data Patterns The data patterns across the several treatment conditions are clearly demonstrated in Figure 8.5. With each treatment there is a clear indication of increasing success. Note also the direct relationship that appears to exist between caloric intake and weight (as would be expected).

The lack of a return to baseline between treatments is a major problem from an analytic perspective of the strip/construction design, in that isolation of treatment effects now becomes harder, since interaction and carryover effects are minimally controlled. In effect, what we have looks more like a "successive-treatment design" with no reversal (that is, an *AB* extension design).

Other Observations In this study, "contingency contracting" was added during the last phase of treatment—an unusual maneuver in a strip/construction design, since the purpose of this design is the comparative analysis of the different interventions. In this instance though, the administration of this previously untested (within this design) final treatment program is clinically justified by the (presumably uncontrolled) changes that take place in the treatment environment—that is, from inpatient to outpatient.

Chapter Nine

DESIGN VARIATIONS

Thus far, we have discussed what can best be described as "clean" or "pure" designs. That is, the design alternatives that have been presented have been fairly easy to categorize into distinctive groups. The *AB baseline intervention designs* have a baseline measurement and a posttreatment measurement; the *ABAB reversal/withdrawal designs* not only have the baseline and posttreatment measures but also have a period of time during which treatment is removed; the *multiple-baseline designs*, on the other hand, are similar to the *AB* designs in that they have baseline and posttreatment measures, but they also have an additional feature—they compare several problems, individuals, or situations simultaneously, which distinguishes this design from all of the former; and finally, the *component analysis designs* are uniquely suited for the comparison of different treatment programs or program components. In general, the component analysis designs may be conceptualized as extensions of the *AB, ABAB,* and multiple-baseline designs. But they are unique in their design goal—namely, the comparison of the components of treatment packages or treatment programs.

In this chapter we look at design variations, that is, those designs that were referred to as design extensions in the earlier chapters and some combinations of these. In essence, the following studies illustrate the possibility of extending and/or combining the so-called clean designs. The clinical research designs in the literature are extremely varied, reflecting diverse interests and practical constraints. We have selected only a handful of these designs to give the reader some idea of the range of possibilities that may be attempted. Before the clinician-researcher does apply a design, however, he or she must have a defined purpose in mind—otherwise this may lead to more confusion than knowledge. While the clinician-researcher may use virtually any combination of the design alternatives, it is well to remember that, the more complex the design, the greater the amount

268

of required planning and analytic complexity. Also, as we noted earlier, some designs will allow for greater confidence than others in drawing conclusions on the effect of an intervention.

Which Design Should One Use?

Thomas (1975) has presented an interesting distinction that should provide the clinician-researcher with additional help in deciding which design to use. He makes the distinction between what he calls a "fixed intervention strategy" of evaluation, and a "criterion-oriented" evaluation. In the fixed-intervention strategy, the focus is on the impact of a given intervention program (independent variable). Here the clinician-researcher has essentially predetermined the clinical research design to be employed and is reasonably assured of the method of treatment. The practitioner in this instance is "interested in the development and evaluation of new techniques" (p. 269). The clinician-researcher in essence, is using this clinical opportunity to test, refine, and affirm the value of given clinical intervention strategies—the procedures themselves having been tested earlier by experience or theory.

In contrast, the focus of the criterion-oriented strategy is quite different. This orientation is "suitable for evaluation of practice outcomes for purposes of providing feedback to clients, the practitioner himself, colleagues, and sponsors. In addition . . . it also provides some information concerning the efficacy of given interventions, albeit less rigorously than would design-oriented evaluation" (p. 262). Here the outcome (expendable variable) takes precedence over the intervention strategy. The primary purpose of the criterion-oriented evaluation would be the client's achievement of the desired goals. Of secondary importance is the definition and specificity of the treatment methods used.

This distinction is a useful one, and the issues raised are most helpful in aiding the clinician-researcher's selection of a design type. For example, after the first *B* treatment phase with less than optimal results, the clinician-researcher may choose between doing an *ABC* design or an *ABAB* design. In other words, the practitioner must ask whether he or she is interested in attaining some other desired criterion level, or following through on the assessment of the B treatment strategy. At the same time, however, the long-term value of the clinical research model precludes such an orientation. Individual clinician-researchers may emphasize the treatment program sometimes and outcomes at other times, but they must all be ultimately concerned with both if they are to develop their own technology for the delivery of services. Thus, in one clinical situation the clinician-researcher may aim for the achievement of a given criterion, while fixed-intervention considerations may be chosen in another. However, it is recommended that the clinician-researcher strive to assess the effect of an intervention strategy, whenever possible, as this increases the opportunity to contribute to a cumulative body of knowledge on clinical practice.

Timeout Duration and Contrast Effects: A Systematic Evaluation of a Successive-Treatment Design

PHILIP C. KENDALL, W. ROBERT NAY, AND JOHN JEFFERS,
Virginia Commonwealth University

Since Wolf, Risley and Mees' (1964) successful reduction of tantrums and self-destructive behavior in a psychotic boy by placing him in his room behind a closed door, a number of investigators have evaluated the utility of timeout procedures (Tyler and Brown, 1967; Bostow and Bailey, 1969; Ramp et al., 1971).

Pendergrass (1971) found that timeout durations of 5 and 20 minutes did not differ, whereas consistent application of one duration produced more response suppression than an intermittent schedule. White et al. (1972) reported that 1 minute of timeout was inferior to 15 and 30 minutes' durations,

Reprinted from *Behavior Therapy*, 6 (1975):609–15. Used by permission of Academic Press.

while these two longer durations were similar in effectiveness. Burchard and Barrera (1972) conducted an illustrative comparison of timeout durations (5 and 30 minutes) and response costs in which swearing, personal assaults, or property damage were followed by periods of isolation behind a partition (timeout area). They concluded that longer timeout durations resulted in greater suppression of targeted behaviors.

Studies that have presented different intervals of timeout to the same subjects have noted the possibility of a sequence effect that might alter the suppressive effects of the various timeout durations. Burchard and Barrera (1972) found that when 5 minutes of timeout was contrasted with the 30-minute condition (shorter duration following the longer), the lower value became functionally less suppressive. They report the same effect for response cost conditions. White et al. (1972) found that, when 1 minute followed longer durations (15, 30), its suppressive effects became less reliable. It was the purpose of the present experiment to evaluate potential contrast effects by comparing the suppressing effects of a short (5-minute) timeout duration with the suppression obtained with a 5-minute timeout which follows a longer 30-minute timeout, across four different undesirable behaviors within a population of adolescent delinquents.

Method

Setting A cottage for delinquent adolescents in Richmond, Virginia. A significant portion of indoor waking hours were spent in a recreation room, including its adjacent room, and these areas were the specific setting for this study.

Subjects Thirty male residents ranging in age from 9 to 14 years with a mean age of 12.1 years. Reasons for commitment included incorrigibility, truancy, and breaking and entering.

The staff were composed of seven males and two females ranging in age from 21 to 36 years. All but one had completed 12 years of education. Prior to intervention, staff members used an array of techniques for disciplining the children (e.g., threats, push-ups, yelling, privilege loss, physical restraint), and few were employed systematically or consistently.

Behavioral Observations Following preliminary observations, four behaviors considered to be the most disruptive were selected for intervention.

1. *Verbal aggression.* Defined as any talking, name calling, or cursing which is of a hostile or aggressive nature.
2. *Physical aggression.* Defined as any hitting, pushing, or physical contact with another in a hostile, aggressive context.
3. *Noncompliance.* Defined as any failure to comply to a staff request.
4. *Out of area.* Defined as any unauthorized attempt to leave a restricted area.

Observations of these behaviors were made by five undergraduate psychology majors. Subjects were pre-exposed to the presence of the coders prior to the collection of baseline data, and all coders had been trained before the planning of this experiment. Each coder's observations were cued by a cassette recording which provided an 8-second observation interval (no tone). Any incident of one of the targeted behaviors during the observation interval was recorded.

Treatment Instrument Timeout consisted of two areas enclosed by a semicircular curtain rod extending from the wall. An opaque curtain hung floor length enclosing a single chair within the area. Both timeout areas were located within the recreation room.

The procedure for placing a child in timeout followed a three-step contingency (Hanf, 1969; Nay, 1974). Staff first *labeled* the behavior, followed by a *warning* if necessary; and if the warning was ineffective, placing the child in timeout without arguing, pleading, yelling, or in any way interacting with the child other than saying, "Because you——, you go to timeout for—— minutes."

Procedures There were six experimental phases: initial baseline, rule posting, 5-minute timeout, 30-minute timeout, second 5-minute timeout, and final baseline, each in effect for 2 weeks. Coders recorded the incidence of target behaviors during each of the phases. During the nontimeout phases, staff were instructed to deal with target behavior in their usual way. During timeout phases, staff placed the misbehaving child in timeout and recorded the incident.

Results

Reliability Reliability of each coder's observations during experimentation was consistently above 85 percent (as percentage of agreement) on four random checks. In all cases reliability was checked to the same expert coder.

Target Behaviors A repeated-measures analysis evaluated the significance of differences across experimental phases (see Figures 9.1 through 9.4) for each target behavior following an arcsin transformation of the proportional data to achieve normality. Verbal aggression ($F(5,27) = 55.42$, $p < .01$), physical aggression ($F(5,27) = 30.62$, $p < .01$), and out-of-area behavior ($F(5,27) = 4.83$, $p < .01$) yielded overall significance, while noncompliance ($F(5,27) = 20$) was not significant. Duncan multiple-range tests of the three significant behaviors revealed that there were no significant differences between specific treatment conditions, suggesting that each contributed relatively equally to the overall variance. A visual inspection of the transformed data (Figures 9.1 through 9.4) provides a clearer description of the results.

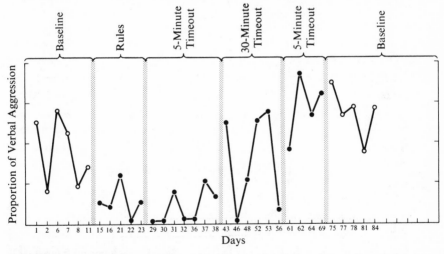

Figure 9.1 Proportion of verbal aggressive behavior for observation sessions during all the experimental phases.

The actual number of placements in timeout (across all target behaviors) was 40 during the first 5-minute timeout phase, 31 during the 30-minute

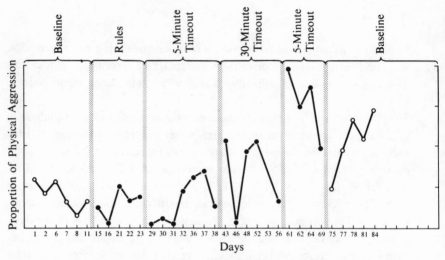

Figure 9.2 Proportion of physical aggressive behavior for observation sessions during all the experimental phases.

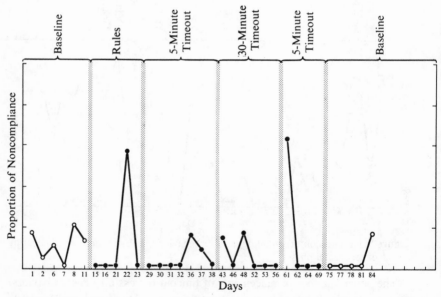

Figure 9.3 Proportion of noncompliant behavior for observation sessions during all the experimental phases.

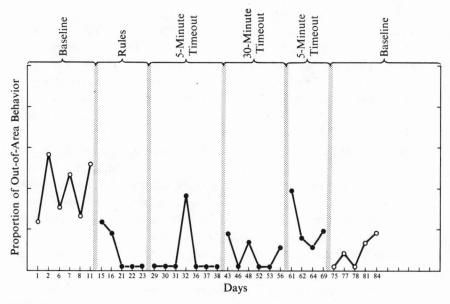

Figure 9.4 Proportion of out-of-area behavior for observation sessions during all the experimental phases.

phase, and 60 during the second 5-minute timeout phase. An overall Chi-Square analysis ($\chi^2 = 7.77$, $p < .05$) was significant. Inspection of the cells shows that, while the initial presentation of 5 minutes of timeout was below the expected value, the second presentation of 5-minute timeout was considerably above the expected value.

Discussion

Because the rate of noncompliance is directly related to the frequency of staff requests and such requests occurred at a low rate, the time-sampling procedure used did not sample sufficient times to produce an adequate sample of responses to staff requests. Because of this limitation, the remaining discussion will not consider noncompliant behavior.

Although rule posting was not the major variable of interest, its effects cannot be overlooked. Contrary to O'Leary et al. (1969) and Ramp et al. (1971), who found rules alone to provoke no significant suppressive effect, rule posting dramatically reduced verbal aggression and out-of-area behavior and provoked a lesser reduction in physical aggressive behavior. Although visual and verbal emphasis placed on the rules was similar to that of O'Leary et al. (1969), the populations differed in that their subjects were second-grade students. Perhaps the effectiveness of rule posting is related to reading and educational levels. The trend toward reduction of verbal aggressive and out-of-area behavior during the first 5-minute timeout phase supports previous evidence that a short duration of timeout may be an effective suppressant (Pendergrass, 1972; Bostow and Bailey, 1969; McReynolds, 1969). The initial suppression then gradual elevation of physical aggression suggests, however, that timeout may be effective in reducing certain behaviors yet ineffective with others. It is suggested that reports of the effectiveness or ineffectiveness of timeout should include a careful specification of the behaviors being considered so that possible treatment behavior effects may be further examined. It should be noted that subjects were not told in advance about the procedures of timeout, thus ruling out ''anticipation effects'' as an explanation for the present findings.

For verbal aggressive, physical aggressive, and out-of-area behavior, a paradoxical increase was seen when 30 minutes of timeout was introduced. Perhaps 30 minutes of timeout, as an increase in punishment, was cognitively viewed as punishing the successful suppression achieved with 5 minutes of timeout, or it provoked increased frustration among subjects, resulting in a subsequent increment in aggressive behaviors. Another alternative explanation is that the effectiveness of timeout, disregarding duration, was weakening over time. In any event, this finding is in contrast to the findings of White et al. (1972) and Burchard and Barrera (1972) that longer durations yield increased suppression.

While the first presentation of 5-minute timeout appeared to reduce certain behaviors, the second presentation resulted in dramatic elevations of verbal aggression, physical aggression, and out-of-area from both the first 5-minute timeout and the 30-minute timeout phases. Furthermore, those three behaviors occurred less during the final baseline when all treatments were removed, suggesting that the discrepancy between the first and second 5-minute presentation could be due to the interpolated 30-minute timeout phase and not other subject or staff variables. The number of placements in timeout (significantly more timeouts during the second 5-minute phase than during the first 5-minute presentation) further illustrates this contrast.

Similar to the findings of Burchard and Barrera (1972) and White et al. (1972), these results may reveal the existence of contrast effects when comparing timeout durations in a successive-treatments time-series design. While this demonstration shows apparent differences in the effectiveness of the first and second presentation of a 5-minute timeout, a more sophisticated design would require two matched groups, each receiving 5 or 30 minutes. Following the initial treatment, subjects in each group would be randomly assigned to a 5- or 30-minute exposure as shown below:

Group 1	*Group 2*
5 min	5 min
30 min 5 min	
30 min	30 min

Used within the animal literature (e.g., Kramarcy et al., 1973) to study contrast effects, this design ensures that both durations are first in a sequence (order effect) and each duration comes both before and after the other duration. Subjects receiving no change in duration serve as controls. Use of such a design in the present study was dismissed for two reasons. Without sufficient explanation, the dissimilar contingencies in such a design would have created an atmosphere of unfairness and mistrust, thus introducing a confounding variable; and second, staff reported that the management coordination required by the use of so many groups was beyond their capability.

The present findings raise an important question: Are successive treatments comparable? Just as a smaller incentive following a larger incentive might appear "less attractive," subjects most likely label the severity of negative feedback in relation to previous feedback received. The successive-treatment design does not take into account such contrast phenomena in viewing each successive presentation of some treatment as "pure," or in the case of repeated treatments as "identical." It would seem that the present findings have implications, not only for successive treatments, but also for any reversal design in which repeated baselines (*A*) follow treatments (*B, C,* etc.).

References

Bostow, D. E. and J. B. Bailey 1969. "Modification of Severe Disruptive and Aggressive Behavior Using Brief Timeout and Reinforcement Procedures." *Journal of Applied Behavior Analysis,* 2:31–7.

Burchard, J. D. and F. Barrera 1972. "An Analysis of Timeout and Response Cost in a Programmed Environment." *Journal of Applied Behavior Analysis*, 5:271–82.

Kramarcy, N., P. Mikulka, and F. Freeman 1973. "The Effect of Dorsal-Hippocampal Lesions in Reinforcement Shifts," *Physiological Psychology* 1:143–47.

McReynolds, L. V. 1969. "Application of Timeout from Positive Reinforcement of Increasing the Efficiency of Speech Training." *Journal of Applied Behavior Analysis* 2:199–205.

Nay, W. R. 1974. "A Systematic Comparison of Instruction Techniques for Parents." *Behavior Therapy* 6:14–21.

O'Leary, K. D., W. C. Becker, M. B. Evans, and R. A. Saudargas 1969. "A Token Reinforcement Program in a Public School: A Replication and Systematic Analysis." *Journal of Applied Behavior Analysis*, 2:3–13.

O'Leary, K. D. and R. Drabman 1971. "Token Reinforcement Programs in the Classroom: A Review." *Psychological Bulletin*, 756:379–98.

Pendergrass, V. E. 1971. "Effects of Length of Timeout from Positive Reinforcement and Schedule of Application in Suppression of Aggressive Behavior." *Psychological Record*, 21:75–80.

Pendergrass, V. E. 1972. "Timeout from Positive Reinforcement Following Persistent, High-Rate Behavior in Retardates," *Journal of Applied Behavior Analysis* 5:85–91.

Ramp, E., R. Ulrich, and S. Dulaney 1971. "Delayed Timeout as a Procedure for Reducing Disruptive Classroom Behavior: A Case Study." *Journal of Applied Behavior Analysis*, 4:235–39.

Tyler, V. O. and G. D. Brown 1967. "The Use of Swift, Brief Isolation as a Group Control Device for Institutionalized Delinquents." *Behaviour Research and Therapy*, 5:1–9.

White, G. D., G. Nielsen, and S. M. Johnson 1972. "Timeout Duration and the Suppression of Deviant Behavior in Children." *Journal of Applied Behavior Analysis*, 5:111–20.

Wolf, M. M., T. Risley, and H. Mees 1964. "Application of Operant Conditioning Procedures to the Behavior Problems of an Autistic Child." *Behavior Research and Therapy*, 1:305–12.

9.2 Summary

Number of Clients Thirty delinquent boys 9–14 years old, were the subjects of this intervention program. All the adolescents were in an institutional setting.

Specification of Goals The target problems to be intervened with were determined after a preliminary analysis of the observational data. The general problem was identified as "disruptive behavior," and its occurrence was signaled by verbal aggression, physical aggression, noncompliance, and out-of-area behavior. In each instance the goal of intervention was to reduce the frequency of occurrence of these target behaviors.

The target behaviors were defined sufficiently well to achieve an 85 percent agreement between observers. Note that the target behaviors are common to the entire delinquent population rather than specific to any one individual—hence this study is directed toward the achievement of institutional goals rather than client-specific goals.

Measurement Strategy The measurement strategy employed in this study is the interval record method within a multiple-evaluator procedure. This is a combination of Type A (in that several different behaviors are being measured by different scales) and Type C (in that five different observers are employed in the measurement process). Since the observers were individuals who were not "naturally found" in the treatment environment, the authors attempted to desensitize the adolescent residents to their presence by not gathering baseline data until after some time after the introduction of the observers. This procedure minimized the possibility of recording "special" behaviors that were "put on" for the benefit of the observers.

While five coders may seem like an unusually large number of observers, it is particularly helpful when the number of target behaviors and individuals to be monitored are large and/or diverse—as in this instance. Such a procedure would help increase the accuracy and reliability of the observational data.

Design The design variation employed in this study is an example of an *AB* extension design (or successive-treatments design). It is, however, modified in that the last phase of intervention is a baseline period (as in an *ABA* design). If signified by letters, this design would read as follows: *A–B–C–D–B–A*.

The posting of rules is the first treatment strategy (*B*), 5-minute timeout the second treatment strategy (*C*), and the third treatment strategy is the 30-minute timeout (*D*). Note the difference between this design and the changing-criterion design discussed in the last chapter. Whereas in this design it is the treatment strategy (independent variable) that is changed, in the changing-criterion design, it is the criterion for the goal behavior (dependent variable) that is systematically altered. This design is also similar to the strip/construction design, the missing elements being the successive addition of treatments and the return to baseline between treatments.

The design allows for the direct comparison of the effects of the three treatment programs, in this instance, the effects of two durations of timeout and rules on the same target behaviors. In this sense, the design takes on the characteristics of the component-analysis designs.

Data Patterns Figures 9.1 through 9.4 present the data. Whereas the authors performed some statistical tests to establish the effectiveness of treatment, simply eyeballing· the data offers a somewhat clear picture as well. Most importantly, there appears to be very little differential impact between the 5-minute and 30-minute periods of timeout. The authors have thus established the efficacy of one important clinical strategy: namely, that a 5-minute timeout period is as effective as a 30-minute timeout period in these cases.

The failure to arrive at any conclusive statement with regard to noncompliance is a good example of the value of adequate and substantial preliminary assessment. If the authors had been aware that requests for compliance were as low as they found them to be later on in treatment, they could either have eliminated these as a problem area or changed the observational methods to suit this less frequent activity.

Other Observations The authors raise an important methodological question with regard to the comparability of the various treatments within this design. To some extent there is an order effect (in that the treatments are offered sequentially with no attempt to counterbalance their application), and as the authors also point out, there may also be a "contrast effect"—that is, a comparison of the various treatments by the recipients, which produces unintended effects. The simultaneous-treatments design with its Latin-square arrangement (discussed in chapter 8) takes into consideration some of these weaknesses.

Setting Generality: Some Specific and General Effects of Child Behavior Therapy

ROBERT G. WAHLER,
The University of Tennessee

Deviant and normal child behavior can be modified if its environmental contingencies are appropriately modified. Within the last few years, this contention has received considerable support. Evidence is available to show that reinforcement contingencies provided by the behavior of parents, teachers, and other children can modify or support a variety of deviant and normal child behaviors (e.g., Patterson et al., 1969; Thomas et al., 1968; Wahler, 1967).

One implication of these findings concerns the specificity of child behavior. If a child's behavior is a principal function of its short-term environmental consequences and antecedents, one could argue that the behavior is situation specific. That is, the child's behavior in various settings should conform to the contingencies present, regardless of between-settings contingency differences. Thus, the child's behavior in his home might be quite different from his behavior in school or neighborhood if the stimulus contin-

Reprinted from *Journal of Applied Psychology*, 2 (1969):239–46. Used by permission of the Society for the Experimental Analysis of Behavior.

gencies in these settings are different. Likewise, while contingency changes in the child's home should affect his behavior in this setting, his behavior in other settings might be unaffected, if the contingencies in these settings remain constant.

This argument holds clear importance for child behavior modifiers. It is often true that a child referred for treatment of problem behaviors occurring in the home may also present behavior problems in the school or elsewhere. In other words, deviant children commonly produce their deviant behaviors in multiple settings.

Most empirical investigations of child behavior therapy have focused on single settings, primarily the school and the home. A few investigators (e.g., Risley, 1968; Patterson et al., 1969) have extended their treatment techniques to both settings. However, we have yet to see an assessment of setting generality; the influence of operations performed in one setting on the child's behavior in other settings. While the previous arguments seem reasonable concerning the low likelihood of setting generality per se, the question is an empirical one.

The present study was a limited attempt to evaluate the setting generality of commonly used child behavior modification techniques. More specifically, deviant child behavior in school settings was evaluated as a function of contingency changes in the children's home settings.

Method

Subjects Two boys (ages 5 and 8 years), referred to an outpatient clinic for psychological problems, were both considered by their teachers to present problems serious enough to warrant psychological help.

Interview information obtained from the subjects' parents revealed that both children also presented problems at home that were quite similar to those reported by the teachers. In addition, both sets of parents pointed out that their children presented equally similar problems in other settings. However, because of the difficulties in monitoring these settings (grandparents' homes and the local supermarket), they were not formally considered in this study.

Recording Techniques and Observer Recordings of subject, parent, and teacher behaviors were obtained through a behavior checklist similar to one described by Hawkins et al. (1966). The method essentially required an observer to make coded checks for the occurrence of a behavior class and its stimulus contingencies within successive 10-second intervals: any occurrence of a class, regardless of its duration during an interval, was scored as a single unit.

All observers used in this study were sophisticated in the use of operant techniques and natural science principles of observation. Two sets of observers were used: one set restricted their observations to the homes and the other to the school. Efforts were made to restrict communication between the sets by telling them that they were working on two separate cases; however, since all observers were graduate students in the same department, this problem was not easy to handle. According to observer reports, the two sets were unaware of their overlap on the same case.

All contingency manipulations were conducted without informing the observers. The author met with the subjects' parents and teachers and provided detailed instructions concerning appropriate changes in their interactions with the subject.

General Procedure Several of the initial home and school sessions were used to adapt the subject, his parents, and teachers to the observers' presence, and to obtain written records of the subject's social interactions. Using these records in conjunction with teacher and parent reports, classes of problem behaviors were formulated. That is, observers made special note of those responses that appeared to represent instances of problem behavior as reported by the teachers and parents. Responses provided by the teachers and parents immediately after these classes were considered as single-stimulus classes, labeled teacher and parent attention.

Response and stimulus classes. Four classes of child behavior were recorded. For subject number one (Steve), two response classes adequately described his deviant behavior and other responses that appeared incompatible with this behavior. These classes were oppositional behavior and cooperative behavior. Both were defined in a functional sense as specific responses following teacher or parental commands. When a request or command was presented to Steve, observers scored his future behavior as either oppositional or cooperative, depending on whether or not the instruction was followed. In order for one unit of cooperative behavior to be scored, the child had to comply with the instruction for a full 10 seconds. Thus, any period of noncompliance during a 10-second interval resulted in that interval's being scored as oppositional. Observers continued to score the child's behavior into these two categories until he completed the requirement or until a new request or command was presented; oppositional or cooperative scoring was then considered in light of the new instructions. Thus, these two categories were inversely related; Steve's behavior was considered either oppositional or cooperative for each 10-second interval.

For subject number two (Louis), two response classes adequately described his deviant and desirable behavior. These classes (disruptive behavior and study behavior) were composed of several discrete behaviors. Study behavior was essentially defined as attention to learning materials. Observers scored this category whenever any of the following behaviors occurred for a duration of 10 seconds: printing or drawing with pencil or crayon, looking at reading material or pictures, looking at teacher or parents when the latter were presenting instructions.

Disruptive behavior included responses that appeared incompatible with study behavior. Observers scored this category whenever any of the following behavior occurred during a 10-second interval: getting out of his seat or chair, looking around the room or out a window, talking to peers or siblings, playing with any object (e.g., pencil or comb). As was true for Steve, these two response classes were inversely related. When observers did not score study behavior during a 10-second interval, they almost always scored disruptive behavior.

Parent and teacher behaviors were considered as two stimulus classes. These classes (parent social attention and teacher social attention) were considered scorable during those 10-second intervals containing any of the previously described response classes. Any verbal or physical behavior that clearly involved the child was scored into these categories. The principal parent and teacher behaviors composing this category included talking to one child and physical contact with him. Eye contact and looking at the child were initially scored into these categories, but observer reliability problems required they be omitted.

A third stimulus class (instructions) was devised for Steve's parents and his teacher. Instructions were scored because of their function in defining Steve's oppositional and cooperative behavior. Any requests or commands were scored into this stimulus category.

Observer reliability and baseline observations. When behavior and stimulus classes were formulated, the 10-second unit checklist was used to obtain frequency counts of the classes. Observations were scheduled once weekly and each observation session was restricted to 30 minutes. In order to simplify the observational scoring and to maximize the likelihood of observing deviant response classes, certain rules were provided for teacher and parents. These rules were in effect for the duration of the study. In Steve's case, the parents and his teacher were told to provide instructions for him at a fairly even pace during the observation sessions. The instructions presented were taken from a list of household and classroom tasks that the parents and his teacher considered aversive to Steve (e.g., folding clothes, stop talking).

Louis's observation sessions were scheduled during times usually devoted to paper work or reading, thus making study behavior the desirable behavior during the sessions. Also, Louis' parents were instructed to schedule his homework during the home observation sessions.

Half of the observation sessions within each baseline and treatment period were evaluated for observer reliability. After reliability check sessions, an agreement or disagreement was tallied for each 10-second interval and the percentage of agreements for the observers was computed for each response and stimulus class. Agreement percentages were always 90 percent or better (range = 90 percent to 97 percent). Baseline observations were continued until unit counts of all behavior and stimulus classes appeared stable across sessions. At that point the experimental procedures were initiated.

Behavior modification procedures, home only. After the baseline sessions, the parents were instructed in the use of a differential attention program; for Steve this program also included a timeout procedure. Both sets of parents were told to use their approval after instances of cooperative behavior (for Steve) and study behavior (for Louis). The definition of "approval" was left to the parents, although they were told that such attention could involve both verbal and physical actions as long as they were of brief duration. Further instructions to the parents concerned the scheduling of their approval. They were told initially to dispense these events "frequently" and then to thin out the schedule. No greater detail was provided.

In addition to the above directions, Louis's parents were told to ignore his disruptive behavior. Examples of study behavior and disruptive behavior were provided and an explanation of reinforcement theory was also given, with particular reference to the concepts of reinforcement and extinction.

Because of prior research indicating that extinction procedures are inefficient in dealing with extremely oppositional children (Wahler, 1968), it was decided to utilize a timeout procedure for Steve. Explanations of reinforcement theory for these parents thus employed the concept of punishment as well as reinforcement and extinction. The parents were told to isolate Steve (in his bedroom) immediately after oppositional behavior occurred. He was to remain isolated for approximately 5 minutes unless he exhibited undesirable behavior such as screaming or crying. If these behaviors occurred, he was to remain in isolation until the behavior terminated.

Parental training in the above techniques was carried out several hours before the regularly scheduled observation sessions. These sessions were designed to provide frequent feedback to the parents following their correct and incorrect responses to the subjects' behavior. The author observed the parents as they attempted to implement the procedures and held brief discussions with them during Louis's "study breaks" or during timeout periods for Steve. The length and number of these training periods depended on parental effectiveness in mastering the procedures. Louis's parents required only two periods, and these varied from 35 to 50 minutes (including study breaks). Steven's parents required three periods, varying from 42 to 70 minutes, including timeouts. Observation sessions differed from the training periods in that the author was not present and the observers provided no feedback to the parents. In addition, study breaks or timeouts were never used. That is, both sets of parents provided a full 30 minutes of differential attention for the two children.

There were two reasons for the decision to eliminate study breaks and timeouts during the observation sessions: (1) to make the session lengths comparable to the baseline sessions, and (2) if Steve's parents had been permitted to use timeout, and to use it correctly, oppositional behavior would have been restricted to one 10-second unit per instruction. Under such conditions, Steve's readiness to follow instructions (as reflected in total number of oppositional units) could not have been evaluated.

Experimental demonstrations of parental reinforcement control. As later data will show, the parents were able to implement the treatment procedures, and implementing these procedures was followed by predictable changes in the subjects' home behavior. At this point, experimental sessions were scheduled to assess the role of the treatment procedures in producing the effects.

Experimental tests were conducted by instructing the parents to resume their baseline contingencies for the subjects' behavior. These instructions were briefly provided by the author several hours before the first session.

After several of these sessions, all parents were instructed to resume the treatment program. These instructions were in effect for the remainder of the study.

Behavior modification procedures, home and school. After the second manipulation of parent–child contingencies, it became evident that the home and school settings were functionally independent with respect to the subjects' problem behaviors. To provide more conclusive evidence of this contention, it would have been desirable at this point to perform contingency operations in the school while holding the home contingencies constant. However, because of parental concern over the prospect of continuing baseline conditions at home for additional weeks, this step was not taken. Instead, the subjects' teachers were instructed in the use of the contingency change procedures used in the home, and the parents resumed their use of the procedures.

Teacher training in the behavior modification procedures was much like the parent training. The author met with the teacher and her class several hours before observation sessions, and brief conferences were held with the teacher to provide the needed corrections or to provide reinforcement for correct teacher behavior. A timeout location for Steve's oppositional behavior presented no problems, owing to the presence of a "quiet room" in the kindergarten. Steve's teacher required three training periods, varying from 30 to 80 minutes (including timeouts). Louis's teacher required only one training period, lasting 60 minutes.

Observation sessions again were characterized by lack of observer feedback to either teacher or parent. Again, study breaks and timeouts were never used.

In summary, the present design did not permit a complete experimental analysis of functional relationships between the subjects' home and school settings. While statements could be made concerning the influence of home operations on the subjects' behavior in school, statements in the other direction were not possible.

Results

Case Number 1: Steve (age 5) was referred to the clinic by his kindergarten teacher for evaluation and treatment of his "stubborn and disruptive behavior." According to Steve's teachers, he was quite oppositional to teacher instruction; for example, he reportedly refused to take naps, talked and yelled during story time, and frequently refused to share toys with other children.

Steve's teacher felt certain that his problem behavior in school was caused by factors within his home. On the basis of her conferences with Steve's parents, it was apparent that Steve displayed his oppositional behavior at home as well as in school. The teacher then inferred that Steve's parents were responsible for maintaining as well as developing his school problems. At this point, no efforts were made to explore the teacher's role in the maintenance of Steve's problem behavior.

Steve's parents were contacted after the interview with the teacher and both agreed to participate in the treatment program. They readily admitted that Steve was "difficult to control," not only at home, but also at his grandparents' home and at the local supermarket.

As described in the procedure section, two response classes were monitored for Steve. One of the classes (cooperative behavior) was considered desirable by Steve's parents and teachers, and the other class (oppositional behavior) was considered undesirable. To simplify the data presentation, only cooperative behavior is presented in the following section. Since oppositional behavior was defined as the reciprocal of cooperative behavior, its frequency can be easily determined from the occurrence of cooperative behavior during the various sessions. It should be remembered that each of the 180 10-second intervals composing an observation session was scored as either oppositional or cooperative.

Figure 9.5 describes 10-second units of Steve's cooperative behavior over all treatment phases at home and at school. As expected, Steve's cooperative behavior at home varied in accordance with parental responses to this behavior; unit counts of cooperative behavior were much higher during treatment sessions than during baseline sessions. Notice, however, that Steve's cooperative behavior in school remained at baseline level over the home treatment periods. Not until contingency changes were performed in the school were stable increments evident in unit counts of cooperative behavior.

Table 9.1 provides information relevant to the data presented in Figure 9.5. Notice first that variations in either parent or teacher instructions could not account for the systematic variation in Steve's oppositional behavior. Whereas instructions did vary over sessions, the variations were not in the direction expected to reduce oppositional behavior. That is, more instructions were given during the treatment sessions than during the baseline sessions. In addition (although not seen in Table 9.1), an examination of the

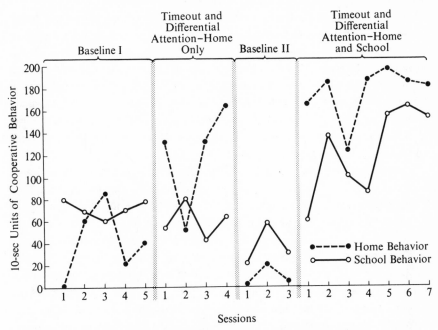

Figure 9.5 Units of Steve's cooperative behavior over all treatment phases.

Table 9.1. NUMBER OF PARENT AND TEACHER INSTRUCTIONS TO STEVE. PERCENT OF PARENT AND TEACHER ATTENTION DURING UNITS OF STEVE'S COOPERATIVE BEHAVIOR. THESE PERCENTAGES WERE COMPUTED FROM TEACHER AND PARENT SOCIAL ATTENTION RECORDED FOR BOTH COOPERATIVE BEHAVIOR AND OPPOSITIONAL BEHAVIOR

Sessions	Baseline 1					Timeout and Differential Attention— Home Only				Baseline 2			Timeout and Differential Attention —Home and School						
	1	2	3	4	5	1	2	3	4	1	2	3	1	2	3	4	5	6	7
Parent instruction	5	7	9	3	8	6	10	13	14	5	7	3	8	4	6	10	6	9	8
Teacher instruction	3	14	8	6	8	12	5	11	9	6	4	10	6	9	8	11	4	10	7
% Parent attention to coop.	7	18	6	8	13	86	92	98	96	8	11	3	97	98	96	100	94	98	100
% Teacher attention to coop.	6	8	2	9	12	6	3	11	4	8	2	10	87	91	90	96	98	100	100

pacing of parent and teacher instructions within sessions showed little variation over all sessions.

Of greatest interest in Table 9.1 are the proportions of parent and teacher attention to cooperative behavior. Substantial increases in parent attention are evident during both treatment periods, indicating their selective attention to Steve's cooperative behavior; however, teacher attention remained roughly at baseline level until the final treatment phase. Therefore, the low frequency of Steve's cooperative behavior at school over the first three periods shown in Figure 9.5 would have been expected on the basis of low proportions of teacher social attention to this behavior. At least there would be no reason to expect increments in cooperative behavior until the final treatment period. Thus, the most likely explanation for the lack of change in the school has to do with the lack of change in teacher behavior.

Case Number 2: Louis (age 8) was referred to the clinic by his second-grade teacher for evaluation and treatment of his "low motivation for school work." According to his teacher, Louis spent much of his class time looking out windows, talking to other children, or wandering about the room. As a result, he accomplished little relevant work in the classroom and his achievement level reflected this.

The teacher also pointed out that her efforts to have Louis do homework were ineffective. She was convinced that Louis's parents "babied" him and seldom required him to assume responsibilities such as homework. Thus, like the teacher in Case Number 1, this teacher assumed that the parents were maintaining Louis's study problems at school.

Louis's parents readily admitted their faults in the development of this problem behavior. They pointed out that they had always been "too easy on Louis" and rarely required him to do things for himself. Both parents saw the homework problem as an example of Louis's inability to assume responsibilities. Unless they worked directly with him, his attention was likely to wander.

Two response classes were formulated for Louis's behavior. One of the classes (study behavior) was considered desirable by Louis's teacher and parents, and the other class (disruptive behavior) was considered undesirable. Although disruptive behavior was not defined to be the reciprocal of study behavior, observer scoring revealed this to be true for almost every session. That is, in most observation sessions, each of the 180 10-second units was scored as either study behavior or disruptive behavior. In only three of the school sessions and two of the home sessions (all in baseline 1) did some of the units remain unscored for either category. Of these sessions, the unscored units never amounted to more than five per session. Thus, as in Case Number 1, the two response classes could be considered to be inversely related to one another. This being the case, only study behavior is presented in the following section, to simplify the data presentation.

Figure 9.6 describes 10-second units of Louis's study behavior over all treatment periods at home and at school. As expected, selective parental attention to study behavior strengthened this response class at home. In addition, further manipulations of parental attention contingencies produced predictable effects on study behavior, demonstrating parental reinforcement control of this class of behavior.

As was true in Case Number 1, parental operations at home were not followed by behavior changes in the school. Figure 9.6 shows no evidence of changes in Louis's study behavior until the final treatment period, which included the modification of teacher contingencies.

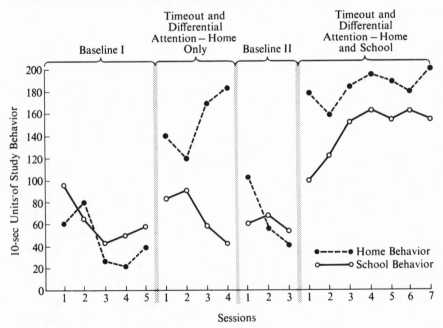

Figure 9.6 Units of Louis's study behavior over all treatment periods.

Table 9.2 provides information relevant to the data reported in Figure 9.6. As these data show, the proportion of parental attention to study behavior varied as a function of the treatment program, and reference to Table 9.2 and Figure 9.6 will reveal that these changes in the proportion of parental attention to study behavior resulted in predictable changes in unit counts of that behavior.

Table 9.2 also provides an explanation for the lack of change in school study behavior over the first three periods shown in Figure 9.6. Notice that the proportion of teacher attention to study behavior consistently remained low over these periods. Not until the teacher was instructed to make her attention selectively contingent upon study behavior did this behavior increase in frequency.

Table 9.2. PERCENT OF PARENT AND TEACHER ATTENTION DURING UNITS OF LOUIS'S STUDY BEHAVIOR. THESE PERCENTAGES WERE COMPUTED FROM TEACHER AND PARENT SOCIAL ATTENTION RECORDED FOR BOTH STUDY BEHAVIOR AND DISRUPTIVE BEHAVIOR

Sessions	1	2	3	4	5	1	2	3	4	1	2	3	1	2	3	4	5	6	7
% Parent attention to study	20	9	11	14	21	82	76	91	93	14	6	8	90	86	94	97	82	87	90
% Teacher attention to study behavior	18	17	11	21	15	15	9	14	13	19	12	9	73	81	92	76	81	79	75

Discussion

The data presented provide no evidence of setting generality, at least as far as home and school environments are concerned. Contingency operations performed in the homes of two children were followed by predictable changes in the children's behavior within these settings. However, the children's behavior in the school setting was unaffected by these operations. Only when similar contingency operations were performed in the school were behavioral changes apparent within this setting. In other words, the settings appeared to be functionally independent, with certain qualifications. That is, while home operations were clearly unrelated to child behavior in the school, design problems did not permit an assessment of the influence of school operations on child behavior in the home. However, there is little reason to believe that functional relationships in the school-home direction should be much different than those in the home-school direction.

In the introductory section it was noted that findings like these should hardly be considered surprising. As expected, the children's deviant and desirable behaviors conformed to the stimulus contingencies presented within the settings. Although the school and home settings supported similar child behaviors during baseline periods, this proved no guaranteee that the settings were members of a common stimulus class.

These findings present some practical problems. Children do tend to produce their deviant behaviors in multiple settings, and some of these settings may not be accessible to the behavior therapist. For example, the delinquent child is apt to produce his law-breaking activities when likely intervention agents are absent. While these aspects of his behavior may be modified in some settings (e.g., a detention home, the school), the generalization of these modifications is dubious. This discussion opens a further question of importance: what behaviors in what settings must be modified in order to effect general changes in setting function?

References

Hawkins, R. P., R. F. Peterson, E. Schweid, and S. W. Bijou 1966. "Behavior Therapy in the Home: Amelioration of Problem Parent-Child Relations with the Parent in a Therapeutic Role." *Journal of Experimental Child Psychology,* 4:99–107.

Patterson, G. R., R. S. Ray, and B. A. Shaw 1969. "Direct Intervention in Families of Deviant Children." *Oregon Research Institute Research Bulletin* 8.

Risley, T. R. 1968. "The Effects and Side Effects of Punishing the Autistic Behaviors of a Deviant Child." *Journal of Applied Behavior Analysis,* 1:21–34.

Thomas, D. R., W. C. Becker, and M. Armstrong 1968. "Production and Elimination of Disruptive Classroom Behavior by Systematically Varying Teachers' Behavior." *Journal of Applied Behavior Analysis,* 1:35–45.

Wahler, R. G. 1967. "Child-Child Interactions in Free Field Settings: Some Experimental Analyses." *Journal of Experimental Child Psychology,* 5:278–93.

Wahler, R. G. 1968. "Behavior Therapy for Oppositional Children: Love Is Not Enough." Paper read at meeting of Eastern Psychological Association, 1968.

9.3 Summary

Number of Clients Two boys (5 and 8 years) in an outpatient clinic served as the subjects in this study. Both parents and teachers noted similar behavior problems being exhibited at home and at school.

Specification of Goals In this study, we see the clinician-researcher focusing on client-specific target problems: oppositional behavior and cooperative behavior in the case of the first child, and disruptive behavior and study behavior in the case of the second child. Note that the behaviors being observed and recorded are in fact incompatible, and therefore, a decrease in one should result in an increase of the other. That is, the problem of oppositional behavior, if reduced should result in increased goal performance, namely, cooperation.

Measurement Strategy Once again an interval record measurement strategy is employed. In this instance, well-trained observers were used in the natural environments of the child. They were obtrusive observers in that they were not naturally found in those environments. The observational procedures were kept simple by limiting them to successive 10-second intervals. Here again, we see the application of Type C procedures in that multiple observers were employed.

Note the selection of measurement environments. While the parents reported that the target problems occurred in the grandparents' house and in the supermarket, the authors elected not to monitor in these environments, owing to measurement difficulties. This is a good example of selective measurement tactics given the goals of intervention. The end result is a concentrated but accurate measurement rather than a diverse and inaccurate one.

Design This study is an example of an *ABAB* extension design, in this instance, an *ABAC* design in combination with a multiple-baseline design across situations. Referring to either Figures 9.5 or 9.6, we see that, during the first intervention phase (*B*), the intervention occurred only at home while baseline measurement was continued in the school. During the second phase of intervention (*C*), the treatment took place both at home and at school—a quantitatively and qualitatively different treatment program.

During the *B* period, it is quite evident that some change was brought about within the home, but not in the school. This clearly illustrates the independence between the situations, which is a requisite of the multiple-baseline design. After establishing the efficacy of the intervention program by applying reversal procedures, the authors extended the same treatment program to the school as well. In effect, the first intervention phase consisted of treatment at home only, while the second treatment phase consisted of treatment both at home and at school—resulting in an *ABAC* design.

Data Patterns Stability aside (note the relative dispersion in scores), this study clearly demonstrates that change in behavior is related to the application of intervention at two points in time. The independence between situations (school and home) is clearly illustrated in Figures 9.5 and 9.6 in that there appears to be very little (if any) carryover effects across situations.

Other Observations Note that the *B* intervention is identical to the *C* intervention in the "content" of treatment. What is different is the addition of a second context. Thus, by calling this study an *ABAC* design, we are in a sense deviating from the classic descriptors, namely, the actual change in the intervention package being offered in *B* being different from the package in *C*. On the other hand, to the extent that home and school environments interact with each other, the intervention during the first intervention phase must be different from the intervention during the second treatment phase.

Chapter Ten

THE FIFTH STAGE: ANALYSIS AND INTERPRETATION OF RESULTS

PREVIOUS CHAPTERS HAVE focused on procedures for the collection of information about client systems and the various clinical research designs. This chapter covers two other major areas, namely, statistical analysis and the issues of external validity or generalization. The reasons for and against the use of statistics are discussed, as well as some elementary methods of statistical analysis. We then move into a consideration of external validity threats or factors that question the clinician-researcher's ability to generalize from one case to another.

10.1 Statistical Analysis

Recent years have seen an impressive array of articles dealing with the statistical analysis of time-series designs (for example, (Gentile et al., 1972; Glass et al., 1973; Gottman, McFall, and Barnett, 1969; Jayaratne, 1978; Kazdin, 1976; Keselman and Leventhal, 1974; Kratochwill et al., 1974; Shine and Bower, 1971; Thoresen and Alashoff, 1974). At the same time, however, numerous authors have questioned the value of these statistical procedures (for example, Michael, 1974; Hartmenn, 1974). Thus, the case for and against statistics in the analysis of time-series designs have been extensively discussed in the literature (for example, Michael, 1974; Risley, 1970; Hersen and Barlow, 1976).

At this point we would like to address some of the major issues in this regard. One significant point in this debate concerns the relative importance given by proponents of both sides to the distinction between clinical significance and statistical significance (originally suggested by Risley, 1970). In cases where the criterion of success is measured by clinical significance the clinician researcher, clients, and/or significant others may define "success" numerically (such as "a reduction of 100% or by 5 points"). The issue of success by clinical significance is something that to a great degree is predetermined by the specification of clinical goals. When the specified goal has been achieved, there has been clinical success.

Consider a heavy smoker who consumes 40 cigarettes per day. The mutually agreed upon goal or criterion of clinical success with this person may be the total elimination of smoking. On the other hand, if the smoking is reduced by 50 percent, we may in fact be able to detect a statistically significant change in the target behavior—but it does not meet with the clinically decided goal. This is a situation that fits Hersen and Barlow's (1976) observation that "applied interventions strive for changes that ordinarily surpass statistical significance" (p. 267).

There is also a potential discrepancy between "visual significance" and "statistical significance." In cases where the criterion of success is determined by visual significance, success may be defined as "some desirable observed ('eyeballed') change on a graph," such as a slowdown of deterioration. Thus in somewhat the opposite direction of the difference noted above, a shift in trend may be detected. (A shift in level—unless dramatic—may be more difficult to detect.) Some statistical procedures (such as time-series analysis) allow for the computation of the differences in trend (as well as level and slope). Under these circumstances we may be able to attain "visual significance" but be unable to obtain statistical significance. Thus, where clinical success is determined by eyeballing, we may reach a conclusion different from that obtained by statistical analysis (Jones et al., 1978).

This discussion was illuminated further by Baer (1977). The argument is rather simple: the statistic-using clinician-researcher may make a greater number of Type I errors (affirm the effectiveness of the treatment when in fact it does not exist), whereas the criterion-level-oriented clinician-researchers may make more Type II errors (deny effectiveness when in fact it does exist). From this perspective, it appears that relying on clinical significance may be a more conservative procedure than establishing the well-known .05 statistical level of significance.

The value of using statistical procedures can therefore be perceived as the determination of success from more than one perspective (clinical, visual, or statistical).

Figure 10.1 presents data from an *ABCB* experimental study conducted by Harris et al. (1964). Eyeballing the data strongly suggests that reinforcing interaction between peers has resulted in clinically significant change. Gottman (1973) performed a Student-t test on shifts in level and slope and concluded that "none of the observed shifts are significant at the .05 level" (p. 96).

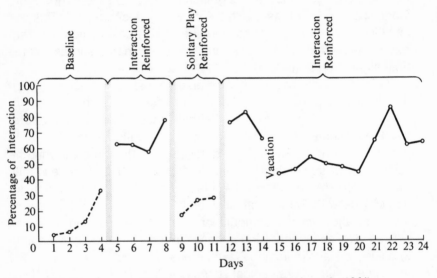

Figure 10.1 Data from an *ABCB* experimental study by Harris et al. (1964).

In addition to determining discrepancies between success levels attained by statistical and eyeballing methods, clinician-researchers may find it desirable to use statistical procedures when they are uncertain or unable to determine clinical success criteria. While this may sound like a "catchall" criterion, it is not. Consider the following example. A clinician-researcher and his or her client may agree upon a goal such as "increased self-esteem." But how much increase indicates success?

Consider the scores on the Generalized Contentment Scale (GCS) (a repeated-measures self-esteem scale developed by Hudson, 1977) (see Figure 10.2). According to the scoring procedures of this scale, a score above 30 may indicate some level of "deviance" or "abnormality." Let us assume that a client scored an average of 66 points after five administrations of the scale at baseline. The goal of treatment, as stated, is increased self-esteem, the normality criterion serving simply as a comparative guideline, not a specifically decided upon goal. Let us also assume that five repeated administrations of the scale after treatment resulted in an average score of 40, and the client reports increased self-esteem and satisfaction with the treatment and general perception of self. Theoretically, then, treatment may be assumed to be successful, although the average score on the GCS does not fall within the so-called normal range. Should the clinician-researcher feel a successful technique has been used?

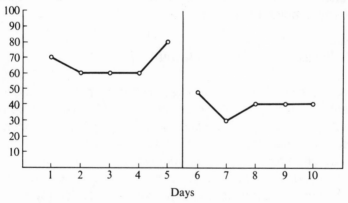

Figure 10.2 Five administrations of the Generalized Contentment Scale before and after treatment.

Thus, three situations, (1) the distinction between clinical significance and statistical significance, (2) the difference between eyeballing data and statistical analysis, and (3) difficulty in choosing a criterion of success, may lead the clinician-researcher to choose statistical procedures. Therefore, for the clinician-researcher it may not be an either/or choice to use statistics. Statistical procedures may often be used in a supportive role. They are usually not appropriate as the singular criterion that serves as the deciding factor in clinical practice. Their role can be ancillary and can provide the clinician-researcher with additional support in his or her clinical decisions. The whole purpose of the clinical research model is to be scientific and empirical; it appears logical to maximize the empirical value of these designs by using statistical procedures.

One danger, however, is in the possibility that the clinician-researcher may spend a considerable amount of time designing procedures that would yield data amenable to statistical analysis. Rather, the emphasis should be on achieving effective control over the measurement situation. Where this occurs, statistical possibilities would more than likely "naturally" follow. After all, as Skinner (1972) so aptly states, "we owe most of our scientific knowledge to methods of inquiry which never have been formally analyzed or expressed in normative rules" (p. 319). This is not, however, license to stagnate, since the pursuit of formative and predictable knowledge is the very lifeblood of science.

10.2 Statistical Rules of Thumb

The two rules-of-thumb procedures presented below are based on inferential statistics. For these procedures to be used appropriately, the data must meet with certain basic assumptions. Unfortunately, clinical data often do not meet the requirements of the analysis of variance and t-test procedures from which these two methods have been derived. After discussing these procedures we shall outline some major shortcomings and concerns of which the reader should be aware.

We would agree with Michael (1974) when he states that "when the assumptions underlying a statistical inference cannot be met, however, the procedure is not necessarily useless" (p. 627). As "rules-of-thumb, rather than statistical absolutes, answers using these methods may provide some information.

The Two Standard Deviation Procedure—Gottman and McFall (1974)

In Figure 10.2 we see five administrations of the GCS at pretreatment followed by five administrations of it posttreatment. The average score at baseline is 66, and at posttreatment it is 40. The question raised is simply this: While there is an apparent increase in self-esteem as recorded by the GCS (lower score meaning higher self-esteem), is the increase enough? Can we establish some sort of statistical verification of this change in score?

As is evident from the title of this procedure, the analytic method is based on the concept of standard deviation. Standard deviation is an index of variability, and it measures the dispersion of scores around the mean. Downey (1975) argues that the "standard deviation is the most important measure in statistics" (p. 98).

According to this model, if the posttreatment mean is more than two standard deviations from the mean at baseline, then we do in fact have a statistically significant change. The major assumption in this process, as already stated, is that the different measures are independent.

Computational Guide

1. Arrange the scores (frequency, magnitude, duration, etc.) in ascending order: Where X_n = the highest value

    X_1 = the lowest value

   In our example: $X_5 = 80$

   $X_4 = 70$

   $X_3 = 60$

   $X_2 = 60$

   $X_1 = 60$

2. Calculate the mean: $\dfrac{\text{Sum of } X}{n}$, where n = the number of scores, $\overline{X}$ = mean

   In our example: $\dfrac{80 + 70 + 60 + 60 + 60}{5} = \dfrac{330}{5} = 66$

3. Calculate the standard deviation: Subtract the mean from each score, which would give you the deviation of that score from the mean.

   $X_5 - \overline{X},\ X_4 - \overline{X},\ X_3 - \overline{X},\ X_2 - \overline{X},\ X_1 - \overline{X}$

   In our example: $80 - 66 = 14$

   $70 - 66 = 4$

   $60 - 66 = -6$ (Note that the sign can be ignored,

   $60 - 66 = -6$ since squaring a minus number al-

   $60 - 66 = -6$ ways results in a positive number.)

4. Square the deviation scores and sum them: Where d = deviation score
   Thus, $(d_1)^2 + (d_2)^2 + (d_3)^2 + (d_4)^2 + (d_5)^2 = D$, where D = sum of squared deviations.
   In our example: $(14)^2 + (4)^2 + (-6)^2 + (-6)^2 + (-6)^2$
   that is, $196 + 16 + 36 + 36 + 36 = 320$
5. Calculate the square root of the sum of squared deviations (D) divided by the number of scores (n). That is $\sqrt{D/n}$ = sd (standard deviation).
   In our example: $\sqrt{320/5} = \sqrt{64} = 8$ the standard deviation
6. Since the standard deviation is 8, then two standard deviations equal 16. (that is, sd $\times$ 2).

The two standard deviation bands are then drawn above and below the mean at baseline. In our example, the higher band (above the mean) should be at $66 + 16$, resulting in (82), and the lower band (below the mean) should be at $66 - 16$, resulting in (50). Figure 10.3 presents the graph depicted in Figure 10.2 with the two standard deviation bands in place.

In this example, the two standard deviation test affirms the verbalizations of the client, in that all but one of the posttreatment scores fall outside (below) the two standard deviation parameters. In essence, we have substantiated the client's self-perceptions that treat-

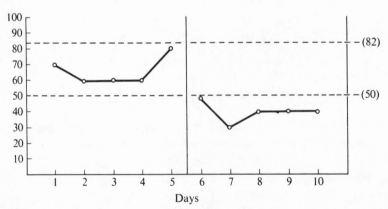

Figure 10.3 The graph of Figure 10.2 with the two standard deviation bands in place.

ment was successful. Note, however, that while the change as reported is significant and presumably satisfactory to the client, it does not fall within the so-called normal range of the GCS. Thus, here we have an example of the clinician-researcher and his or her client's settling on a goal status that is clinically and statistically significant but not objectively significant from the point of view of attaining normality as defined by the measurement index.

We believe this to be one of the simplest procedures available to the clinician-researcher who wishes to substantiate his or her intervention program. Despite the methodological issues raised earlier about the validity of this method, we believe that the procedure has sufficient merit to be employed as a rule of thumb, and we strongly encourage all clinician-researchers to employ this method of analysis.

The Relative Frequency Procedure—Bloom (1975) This method is based on the binomial distribution, which is derived from a situation in which there are a number of trials, each of which has some probability of meeting with success. The trials in this instance refer to the time elements on the abscissa—hours, weeks, months, and the like, during which baseline data gathering and intervention took place. For example, if there were 15 points of measurement, then there were 15 possibilities for a given score to have achieved the goal criterion.

The relative frequency procedure is inherent with some error components, the major one being the assumption of independence. The use of the binomial distribution requires that there be independence between the scores. This will be discussed in more detail later. Despite these limitations, once again we believe the procedure to have merit and encourage clinician-researchers to employ the procedure as a substantiating process.

Figure 10.4 presents the baseline data from 14 days of data collection. In this example, a marital couple reports the "frequency of arguments" per day. According to the data, they had between 3 and 7 arguments per day (the definition of an argument being up to the couple), with a mean rate of 4.7 incidents over the 14-day baseline period.

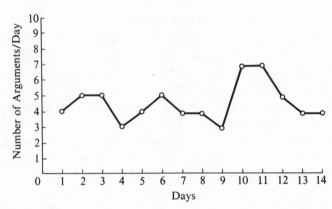

Figure 10.4 Baseline data on frequency of arguments per day between a married couple.

Computation Guide

1. Count the number of time units on the abscissa during baseline: $n =$ number of time units (where time units can be minutes, days, number of treatment sessions, etc.).

    In our example: $n = 14$

2. Identify the typical range. This is the middle two-thirds of a normal curve. (From the point of view of the standard deviation, this is equivalent to one standard deviation on either side of the mean).

    To find the middle two-thirds, divide the number of time units by three and multiply by two: That is, $\frac{n}{3} \times 2$

    In our example: $n = 14$; therefore, $\frac{14}{3} \times 2 = 9.3$ (approximately)

3. The next step is to draw bands enclosing the number of points closest to the middle two-thirds range. Since there will always be a whole number of points or observations, the idea is to obtain the closest whole number. In our example: the closest whole numbers to our middle two-thirds figure of 9.3 would be 9 and 10.

    In drawing the bands, Bloom (1975) points out that "we *must* leave at least one event above and below the typical range in order to calculate the proportions" (p. 182).

    In our example: The two extreme values recorded are 3 and 7. In this instance, we have two sevens and two threes. Since we cannot leave one out and one inside the bands, we end up with four points outside of the middle two-thirds range. Since the goal of intervention is to reduce arguments, the value of seven is considered to be in the "extremely undesired behavior zone" and the value of three in the "desired behavior zone." The area within the bands represent the "typical range" of the target problem.

Figure 10.5 shows the two bands enclosing the middle two-thirds. Note that, to exclude the two highest values and the two lowest values (as required by the procedure), we had to exclude four observations. As such we end up with 10 points being enclosed by the two bands. In effect, we have now established that only on two occasions did the arguments between the two spouses fall within the desired range. This desired range is statistically derived rather than clinically agreed upon (although it could be both).

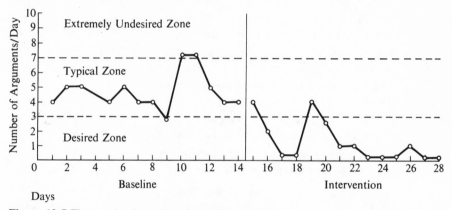

Figure 10.5 The two bands enclose the middle two-thirds.

4. In this step, we calculate the porportion of time the target problem occurred in the desired behavior zone.

In our example: the desired range had 2 points within it, and there were 14 points of measurement.

Thus, the proportion $\frac{2}{14} = .15$

That is, the target problem occurs only 15 percent of the time in the desired range.

It is at this point that we look in Table 10.1 (from Bloom, 1975) and test for significance. Figure 10.5 presents the complete data on this case. As is evident, there were 14 days of baseline followed by 14 days of intervention.

5. The next step is to locate in Table 10.1 the proportion of times that the target problem occurred in the desired zone on the vertical column labeled proportion. Where the exact proportion is not available, the closest proportion is used.

In our example: the proportion was calculated as being .15 in step 4. Looking down the proportion column, we see the third entry is .15. The number of days during which treatment took place (in this instance 14) is then located on the horizontal line. The intersection of the two numbers .15 and 14 gives the minimun number of incidents that must occur within the desired behavior zone for the treatment to be considered statistically significant at the .05 level. According to Table 10.1, there must be at least five points registered in the desired zone. According to the graph in Figure 10.5, we see 12 entries in the desired behavior zone. Thus, this procedure has indicated that intervention with this couple has reduced their incidents of arguments substantially and that this reduction is statistically significant at the < .05 level—that is, these findings would be true 95 percent of the time.

As stated earlier, this model requires that there be at least one point of measurement in the desirable and undesirable zones in order to compute the probability. Since this may not always happen, Bloom (1975) and Bloom and Block (1977) suggest that one assume one incident in these zones. While this procedure has inherent methodological problems referred to below, it is perhaps a conservative argument. Like the two standard deviation procedure, this is a relatively easy computation, and we urge all clinician-researchers to employ it whenever possible.

Note that the procedures delineated here are related *only* to the multiple-point measurement approach in the clinical research model. There are no such methods of analysis currently available for use with single-point measures. It is here that the availability of standard measures and their deployment become valuable. Where normative comparison bases are available, the clinician-researcher has some reference point, whether or not it is used. For example, the clinician-researcher and his or her client may agree that a given improvement in self-esteem has reached their mutually accepted clinical goal, although it does not fall within the "normal" range of the standardized GCS. Where such a normative base is unavailable, the decision of success or failure becomes one of pure judgment or eyeballing. It is in view of such weaknesses and others noted earlier that we strongly encourage the clinician-researcher to pursue a multiple-point measurement strategy.

Having said this, however, we feel we must address ourselves to the criticisms that have been leveled against these two procedures:

1. *Independence of measures*—this is perhaps the most telling criticism of all against the two standard deviation procedure and the relative frequency procedure. The analysis of variance and t-tests on which these two rules of thumb are based, assume independence between the different measures. The fact, however, as Gottman and McFall (1972) point out, is that most time-series data are statistically dependent. That is, the measurement of a target problem at time one is and must be related to the measurement of the same target problem by the same measurement process in times two, three, four, and so on. Where data are nonindependent (autocorrelated), then what happens in time one can be used as a predictor of what happens in time two. That is, by knowing the past performance on a measure, we should be able to better predict performance at a later date—the higher the correlation the greater the predictability. Regardless of the complexity of the clinical research design that we use in attempting to control for this autocorrelation, "such is certainly the case in virtually all clinical situations to which this analysis may be applied" (Loftus and Levy, 1977, p. 3).

Whereas Loftus and Levy's discussion was within the context of Bloom's (1975) relative frequency procedure, the same criticism would hold true in the two standard deviation procedure as well. Although computational methods are available that would allow the clinician-researcher to calculate whether or not the data are in fact autocorrelated and then to perform a statistical analysis on the transformed noncorrelated data, the procedures are rather cumbersome. (The interested reader is referred to Gottman and McFall, 1972, and Gottman et al., 1969.) That autocorrelation is indeed a viable criticism is indicated by Jones et al., (1977), who found significant autocorrelations in 83 percent of the time-series studies they analyzed.

2. *Estimation of baseline values*—Loftus and Levy (1977) argue that "a group" of instances taken during baseline period is only a sample of the possible instances (however good that sample may be) if the baseline period were indefinite or very long (the ideal state). Therefore, the baseline probability (in the case of the relative frequency model) and the standard deviation (in the case of the two standard deviation model) are merely estimates. Thus, the true probability and the true standard deviation are not known. To the extent that this estimate differs from the true values, we will increase the error. The error component will, of course, be inversely related to the number of baseline measures. This error is particularly important in the relative frequency model in view of the probability tables that have to be used (Table 10.1). "Since the accuracy of estimation

Table 10.1. THE NUMBER OF OBSERVATIONS OR A SPECIFIED TYPE DURING THE INTERVENTION PERIOD NECESSARY TO REPRESENT A SIGNIFICANT INCREASE AT THE .05 LEVEL OVER THE PROPORTION DURING THE PREINTERVENTION PERIOD[a]

Proportion	Number									
	4	*6*	*8*	*10*	*12*	*14*	*16*	*18*	*20*	. . .
.05	2	2	3	3	3	3	3	4	4	
.10	3	3	3	4	4	4	5	5	5	
.15	3	3	4	4	5	5	6	6	7	
.20	3	4	5	5	6	6	7	8	8	

[a] Tables of the Cumulative Binomial Probability Distribution by the staff of the Harvard Computational Laboratory, Harvard University Press, 1955. Table constructed under the direction of Dr. James Norton, Jr., Indiana University-Purdue University at Indianapolis, 1973. Complete table available in Bloom, 1975.

depends on the number of baseline instances, there must accordingly be separate tables for various values of number of baseline instances as well as for various values of number of post intervention days" (Loftus and Levy, 1977, p. 4). Such a detailed procedure would require a cumbersome and voluminous set of tables and thus further eliminate their probable use by clinicians.

3. A final issue concerns the relative frequency model. This model assumes that the target problem occurs in the undesirable range at

least once during the baseline period, and where it does not occur, Bloom and Block (1977) argue that the worker is justified "in assuming one instance . . . (since) this reflects the reconstructed history of the client, during which some of these rare events did occur" (p. 134).

If this is in fact the case, then the selection of just one such point is arbitrary (though conservative). Loftus and Levy (1977) argue that "making up probability out of thin air is worse than nothing—it gives the therapist totally groundless premises on which to make his or her evaluation decision" (p. 5). While we cannot agree more from a methodological perspective, we would like to reiterate that, where the procedures are employed in a supportive rather than a deterministic manner, they can be useful.

We have addressed ourselves primarily to the two rules of thumb we will be discussing in this text. The same criticisms would, however, hold true in many of the more sophisticated analytic procedures such as analysis of variance and t-test. It is also true that the interested reader can pursue a statistical course of action that would minimize these errors, such as calculating the autocorrelation or employing the recently developed time-series analysis (Glass et al. 1973; Gottman et al., 1969; Box and Jenkins, 1976). Alternately, the reader may also be able to use a variation of the one-way fixed-effects model of analysis of variance suggested by Holtzman (1963) and Hartmann (1974), or a more "sophisticated" analysis of variance model suggested by Shine and Bower (1971) and Shine (1973).

10.3 External Validity

External validity is a question of "generalizability." "To what populations, settings, treatment variables, and measurement variables can this effect be generalized" (Browning and Stover, 1971, p. 5). Within the clinical research model, "the data do not warrant generalization to ostensibly similar cases" argue Browning and Stover (1971, p. 78). Others argue to the contrary, pointing out that such generalization is indeed feasible (Sidman, 1960; Thoresen, 1972).

However this debate is resolved, external validity can be confirmed only through replication. In order for replication to occur, however, careful descriptions must be provided on the process of treatment, design, and measurement method. This is particularly true where the clinician-researcher is interested in transmitting the "findings" to other professionals. It is possible for a given study to have internal validity but little external validity. That is, the intervention may have high credibility and success with a given client system, but the conclusions cannot be generalized to another similar situation with any degree of confidence.

What follows is a list of the major threats to external validity, and it is based primarily on the works of Campbell and Stanley (1963) and Goldstein et al. (1966).

Pretest sensitizing—the administration of a pretest may cause changes in the client system that may in turn interact with the treatment program and posttesting. This problem would have its greatest impact where the measurement process is obtrusive. This is similar to the internal validity threat of change produced by measurement. The implication here, however, is one of generalization, which means that the same pretesting procedures may need to be administered during replication to produce the same results.

Selection-treatment interaction—if generalization is to take place, clients should not be selected on the basis of availability but on their representativeness. This is always, however, the case in the clinical arena, since the clinician-researcher rarely gets to choose whom he or she will treat. Or, at the other extreme, the clinician-researcher may work only with a particular "type" of client. As such, this is an inherent error in all clinical research designs.

Multiple-treatment effects—while being a threat to internal validity, this is also a threat to external validity. It was argued earlier, that multimodal therapies may produce a given result as a function of the relationship that exists between its components rather than a given treatment component per se. Under these circumstances, generalization would be limited unless the same stepwise procedures are followed in all applications (due to possible order and/or contrast effects).

Treatment environment—this is another threat that is common to both internal and external validity. The artificiality of the clinical research approach may make the treatment environment atypical of the regular environment (Hawthorne Effects—that is, the client may change his or her behavior just to please—or displease—the clinician-researcher), and thus make generalization into the natural environment somewhat confusing. Where such change is irreversible, the same results could never be obtained again—a major problem for the reversal/withdrawal designs.

Instrumentation error—this is the same issue as in internal validity, namely, that irrelevant components of the measures may produce uncontrolled artifacts. Thus, unless the same measures are used in the same manner in replication studies, the same error components will not be present, and hence, one may end up with different results—not because the intervention was different, but because the measures were different.

Irrelevant replicability of treatments—since most treatment programs are complex combinations of strategies, replication may inadvertently exclude some relevant components of the total treatment configuration. This may, for example, lead to the accidental omission of the one strategy or technique actually responsible for the treatment effects. This would be a particularly real problem where the clinician-researcher is administering a treatment package with a number of components.

Assessment variability—this is another source of invalidity that is both internal and external. It is external to the degree that evaluators differ in various environments and possibly with different clients (in the same environment), and along with these different individuals go a conglomeration of personal characteristics. This observation is particularly telling for the clinical research model given its idiosyncratic orientation.

Experience/knowledge accrual—this possible source of error is particularly important when the clinician-researcher is dealing with a homogeneous sample of clients and is replicating treatments. Similar client problem characteristics and configurations could lead to "on-the-job training" (experience), which could result in a disparity in the "quality" of the treatment (a relatively intangible phenomenon) rendered clients over time.

Working with one client system there is often little the clinician can do to control factors that reduce the external validity of this approach. On the other hand, the clinical research approach is a constantly developing empirical model of intervention. As such, replication is not an issue for consideration, it is a requirement. For any science to advance, however, it must proceed from replication to generate some rules and orders for prediction. The clinical research model is still a long way from this goal. This will be discussed further in the next chapter.

These threats to external validity are presented more as a reference list to sensitize the reader to the various error components that may exist in his or her work. Obviously, the clinician-researcher should attempt to select designs strong in both internal and external validity. But given the minimal generalizability of all the clinical research designs, we feel the clinician should address maximum effort to establishing internal validity.

10.4 Conclusion

Our objective in this chapter has been to introduce the reader to some of the methods of analyzing clinical research data. We believe that most clinicians feel uncomfortable in dealing with statistical procedures and research methods. At the same time, however, such procedures will do more to enhance clinical practice and professional expertise than years of nonempirical intervention.

All clinicians make observations (however random they may be) and draw conclusions from these observations during their clinical practice. The procedures we have presented would allow for the systematic analysis of these observations, and consideration of possible weaknesses in the assessment processes. Tripodi (1974) notes that clinical observations are usually judgmental and research data are quantified. The clinical research model suggests the systematic quantification of clinical information (whenever possible). To the extent the reader follows the clinical research approach, and gathers this quantified information, he or she should attempt to use the suggested analytic procedures to further substantiate his or her personal observations and judgments.

Chapter Eleven

OVERVIEW AND CONCLUSION

Like most therapists we have been up and down the same emotional coaster. After some sessions we have come out "high" on our selves as therapists, exhilarated by the experience and feeling confident about our abilities. At other times (perhaps the next session with the same client) we have some feelings like we did not know what we were doing, down in the dumps about our own incompetence. We may have been unable to think of what to say the whole hour. We have each said to ourselves (and meant it) after such sessions, "Well, maybe I am in the wrong field." If you find yourself in this roller coaster you ought to ask yourself that question too, but you ought to recognize that people who are now considered capable were on the same roller coaster once. All we can say is that it does get better; experience does help. We believe the best help comes from having systematic procedures for learning from our failures as well as our successes (Gottman and Leiblum, 1974, p. 8).

THIS QUOTE BETTER than anything else describes our own fears and expectations with regard to the clinical research model. To some, the methods, definitions, and operations presented in this book may be new. To these people we say, "Learn the operations and apply them conscientiously." To others, the material in this book may appear to be a conglomeration of old and new ideas. To these we say, "Yes, it is." In essence we have attempted to unify the pragmatics of clinical practice with the demands of empiricism.

The clinical research model is not a panacea, and the clinician-researcher does not have all the answers. We are very much aware, as we hope our readers are, of both the methodological and practical limitations of the approach. We certainly recognize that what Mahoney (1978) said of experiments is all the more true for clinical-research practice: "Let us therefore dismiss the notion of an ideal experiment and instead devote our attention to the continuum of fallible effort along which all experiments must fall" (p. 660). We believe, however, that such practice contains the elements of a model that can lead to significant change in practice and the more accountable delivery of services. It is, in our biased opinion, the most pragmatic approach to clinical accountability that we have given the current state of clinical practice and research knowledge.

To recap briefly, Gottman et al. (1969) state several characteristics of the time-series or single-subject designs that deserve considerable attention. First, these designs provide descriptive data, the type of data that is of extreme value for clinical purposes in that they provide continuous information throughout treatment. Second, the approach is truly heuristic. The data gathered by the model are of practical value and allow for constructive change in procedures at appropriate clinical choice points. And finally, most clinicians are not in a position to conduct "true" experiments (nor may they want to) using randomized groups of clients. As such, the time-series model allows for a reasonably strong causal statement, although one can never be absolutely certain that treatment in fact produced the observed change. We would like to remind the reader that we are talking about "relationships" or "correlations" between treatment and the target problems and/or goals rather than cause-effect per se—using the principle of unlikely successive coincidences.

Lazarus and Davison (1971) add a few other characteristics of import that have more theoretical relevance than practical value. First, a single study may cast doubt upon a general theory, since one negative finding can question a hypothesis. Second, the model will allow for the study of rare but important phenomena. Third, techniques that have been derived from general theory can be modified to suit specific clinical situations and thus provide valuable generalization data on broad-spectrum theories. And finally, one study employing the clinical research approach can add more data to existing substantive materials and may even generate new theoretical formulations.

There are, however, two major questions with the clinical research model. The first concerns the generalization of data from one case to another. Whereas some methodologists argue that repeatedly testing procedures with individuals provides stronger demonstration than testing across groups of individuals (Sidman, 1960), we have very little evidence about the reliability of time-series replication procedures. Hersen and Barlow (1976) in a careful analysis of the replication issue point out that, "until the time that the process of systematic replication reveals the precise limitations of a procedure, clinicians and other behavior change agents should proceed with caution, but also with hope and confidence that this powerful process will ultimately establish the conditions under which a given treatment is effective or ineffective" (p. 353).

In practice, all clinicians will generalize and replicate successful procedures. If the methods deliberated in this book should be constantly and systematically employed, by virtue of replication the individual clinician-researcher may find that a given treatment strategy or package is ineffective or effective and, therefore, proceed to modify or use it during another application.

If a cumulative body of knowledge is to be established, however, there is a need for some systematic procedures or rules for generalization. Whereas the clinical research model is based on the uniqueness of each client and, hence, the need for individualized feedback, clinician-researchers will still be making judgments about the potential effectiveness of a given technique of intervention across clients. These judgments will, in part, be based on their experiences with previous clients (as well as experiences of others). How should these judgments be made? For example, do six, seven, or eight out of ten successes provide a reasonable basis for assuming the probability of a future desired effect? Under what circumstances? With which clients? These issues need to be addressed, just as we have developed statistical procedures that provide rules for making such decisions in group designs.

The second question concerns the compromises that are often made in the application of this model. Although we have presented and accepted single-point measurement as a viable alternative within the clinical research model, it is perceived as having far less validity and reliability than the ideal time-series or single-subject designs with the preferred multiple-point measurement strategy. Barlow and Hersen (1973) state that at least three data points are needed to determine a trend. These guidelines also have implications for the type of measurement method selected, which is one important determinant of stability and the frequency at which measurements can be taken. Kazdin (1978) points out other important problems in implementing single-case designs in clinical settings. Our concern is that in practice, when changes from recommended procedures are made (for example, a reduction in the number of data points in a given phase of intervention), certain questions arise: How far from the recommended ideal of certain data patterns and particular measurement methods may clinician-researchers move and still be using a clinical research model? What of the crisis worker who can obtain, at best, only a retrospective baseline? Or what about the clinician-researcher who never achieves a stable baseline or uses a method that cannot be repeatedly administered? Although we do not have hard and fast answers to these very important questions, we have attempted to provide some clarifications. But our most important goal is to encourage clinicians to develop and increase their empirical orientation to practice. If compromises from the ideal are made, we hope the clinician-researcher will at least recognize these actions as compromises and continuously strive toward the ideal.

A final comment with regard to accountability is worthy of note. It is probably in this area that the clinical research model can demonstrate the greatest potential for professional responsibility. The model embodies the tenets of evaluation and assessment and thus inherently and constantly improves the delivery of services. Unlike the more traditional treatment programs, which use a nonempirical model of intervention, the data are readily available both for client and colleague scrutiny. An informed clientele will, then, be in a position to judge the efficacy of their respective treatment programs and their respective clinician-researchers.

11.1 Ethical Considerations

"Therapy (of any type) as now practiced is already covertly manipulative, even though it may not be recognized as such by the practitioners. Thus, therapists should learn more about therapeutic influence and consider the ethical responsibilities associated with clinical practice" (Goldstein et al., 1966, p. 150). Combining the research model with clinical practice offers such an opportunity. Whereas it is conceivable that the clinician-researcher might get "carried away" with the research component of his or her clinical activity, "the experimental-clinical method places an ethical check on the investigator, in that the treatment of the patient requires constant monitoring of behavioral change, hypothesis formation, and some degree of experimental design to inform the therapist whether his predictions were correct" (Browning and Stover, 1971, p. 409). To the extent that the clinical research model is explicitly followed, the issue of ethical responsibility is more or less built into the design configuration.

Undoubtedly, the inclusion of experimental procedure in any clinical setting could raise some questions—Is the client a guinea pig? Are we trying to advance knowledge at the expense of the client? We vehemently say no to both questions. We would argue that, to the extent that an unsubstantiated technique is applied with a client system, then *that* client system is in fact a "guinea pig." While the effect of any intervention is always in question, an empirical approach at least strives for constant feedback on effect.

The "clinical" part of the model (if artificially dichotomized) consists of those activities related to helping the client overcome his or her problems. The "research" component merely adds the framework within which these activities are conducted. Together, they form a model that is uniquely beneficial to the client in question, as well as to future clients and to the therapist in the long run. The end result, then, is in contradistinction to the college sophomore who participates in an experiment but is not the direct beneficiary.

Whatever the environment of intervention (that is, institutional or natural), conducting therapy in general requires the consent of the client system. Usually the content, as well as the process, of intervention is discussed (and if necessary, negotiated) with the client system and significant others in treatment (Maluccio and Marlow, 1974; Stuart and Lott, 1972; Tharp and Wetzel, 1969). The primary responsibility for conducting an ethical clinical research intervention lies squarely on the shoulders of the individual clinician-researcher. It is from this viewpoint that the following "ethical choice points" are discussed. These factors were delineated by Stuart (1973). While

Stuart's comments are in regard to research in behavior therapy, they are equally important and applicable in the clinical research model in any mode of therapy.

1. Selection of clinical research goals. Since this is one of the major preliminary steps in the application of any clinical research design, it must meet stringent ethical requirements. Obviously, since the personal values of particular clinician-researchers come into play here, attention must be paid to ensure the righteousness of the goals selected. The goals may have primary clinical focus and secondary research value, although in practice, this dichotomy should not be evident. Have the goals been mutually agreed upon? Are the goals realistic? Do the goals differ from accepted social ethics? How would one know when the goals have been reached?

2. Selection of intervention methods. Usually, the selection of the treatment technique is client specific and problem specific. The cooperation and willingness of the client to undergo the specific form of treatment offered must be obtained. Has the technique being used been successfully implemented in the past with a similar problem situation? What are the possible side effects? Has the client accepted the technology? Have alternative and perhaps better approaches to dealing with the particular problem been investigated? In our opinion the clinical research model is of critical importance in answering these questions, since the formative structure of the model is directly related to continuous evaluation of treatment method and effectiveness.

3. Subject selection. Here, Stuart was concerned with the use of involuntary clients in "pure" clinical research. Are the subjects aware of the research implications? Can a subject not participate? Have the subjects signed a consent form?

Most of these questions really do not apply in the clinical research model. The process of research and evaluation is an integral component in the process of clinical practice. Thus, all activities that take place during intervention must benefit the client. If such benefit does not accrue, then the activity should not take place.

4. Research design. The implications here are numerous, and most of them have already been discussed within the context of the specific designs (although not in ethical terms per se). The method-

ology used is of critical importance, especially when one is reminded of abuses involved in such studies as those involving Chicano women and contraceptive drugs (Associated Press, March 17, 1972) and black men left untreated in a syphilis study (Associated Press, July 26, 1972). In this respect, the nonreversal designs offer some "ethical advantage" over the reversal/withdrawal designs, for it is not known what effect reversal procedures would have on their client. Have possible iatrogenic effects of reversal (or other procedures) been considered? Is there a nonreversal alternative? What is the best possible design for this situation?

5. Reporting of data. This concerns the question of which data should be reported. It is the ethical responsibility of the clinician-researcher to report both positive and negative findings. As Stuart (1973) indicates, undifferentiated reporting "places our procedures in a more credible context and provides a stimulus for the development of means of resolving unsolved problems" (p. 10). Have findings been reported factually? Have alternative hypotheses or explanations been considered in the interpretation? In the clinical research model, reporting is of major value to the client system and therapist, since the data are a central part of the intervention process.

6. Dissemination of research data. Stuart proposes the public scrutiny of research findings. In the long run, such an approach would undoubtedly make clinician-researchers more accountable to themselves and their consumers. Who is doing the reporting and disseminating? Has there been any editing of the report? Who are the direct consumers of the data? In the clinical arena such dissemination is of critical importance, ensuring that both the positive and negative findings of a study are being accurately portrayed.

"A dissemination of precise and reliable information to other contemporary therapists and to future generations of therapists is a prerequisite for therapy to be cumulative" (Risley, 1970, p. 107). In order for this statement to be of any practical value, the process and outcome must be presented in a logical, comprehensive, and detailed manner. Not only must the target problems and the changes sought be presented, but the magnitude of change and the specific intervention procedures that brought about the change must be delineated. In other words, the data disseminated should provide sufficient information, so that a practitioner reading it may be able to use some aspects of the technology in his or her own repertoire with some knowledge of possible outcomes.

As Roen (1971) points out, "the analysis of data goes hand-in-hand with that kind of information about the program one wants to impart to others" (p. 805). The dissemination procedures generally employed by investigators consist of publications in professional journals, presentations at various professional conferences, and personal communications. Conferences and personal communications are used primarily by those individuals who have a personal or academic interest in the topic. Whereas this may lead to further scrutiny and critical appraisal of studies, the likelihood of its practical use is somewhat small. Although the vast majority of the scientific investigations are printed in professional journals, the consensus seems to be that very few "line professionals" read them. The implication is, of course, that those who could benefit from the information the most are simply not exposed to it. The clinical research model is clearly aligned with self-improvement. The model provides feedback and information of unique relevance to the worker in practice situations. In essence, the responsibility of accountable treatment lies with the practitioner, not the administrator. The issue of sharing the knowledge or disseminating information is more a function of professionalism and professional ethics.

It is the responsibility of each and every clinician-researcher to consider these points and to make decisions within the context of societal and personal values and ethics. The client either benefits from or suffers the consequences, and the clinician-researcher must live with his or her conscience. The obligations of the clinician-researcher start from the very inception of any clinical program, and little post-hoc manipulation can undo any damage already done. Clearly, there are no simple answers. As Strupp (1971) so aptly points out, even when the intervention involves a relatively minor problem, it involves another person's life—which should never be undertaken lightly.

In conclusion, we believe the clinical research model can provide a common practice basis for clinicians with diverse theoretical orientations. Most practitioners would agree with Reid and Epstein (1972) in their recognition of the need for evaluation and account-ability. They point out that the traditional models of treatment are dif-ficult to research (and, therefore, systematically evaluate), owing to poorly formulated goals and complex processes. They state:

If one assumes that empirical research is our most powerful means for improving treatment, priority should be given to constructing treatment models that can be improved through research. Such models would need to be addressed to specific goals from which precise, measurable outcome cri-teria could be derived. These techniques would need to be explicitly stated and capable of being defined at operational levels [p. 146].

We believe the clinical research model offers such an opportunity.

References

Associated Press, March 17, 1972.

—— July 26, 1972.

Ayllon, Teodoro, and Nathan Azrin 1968. *The Token Economy*. New York: Appleton-Century-Crofts.

Baer, Donald M. 1977. "Perhaps It Would Be Better Not To Know Everything." *Journal of Applied Behavior Analysis*, 10 (Spring):167–72.

Baer, Donald M., Montrose M. Wolf, and Todd R. Risley 1968. "Some Current Dimensions of Applied Behavior Analysis." *Journal of Applied Behavior Analysis*, 1 (Spring):91–97.

Barlow, David H., and Michael Hersen 1973. "Single-Case Experimental Designs: Uses in Applied Clinical Research." *Archives of General Psychiatry*, 29 (March):319–25.

Barrett-Lennard, Godfrey T. 1974. "The Client-Centered System." In Francis J. Turner, ed. *Social Work Treatment*. New York: Free Press.

Battle, Carolyn C., Stanley D. Imber, Rudolph Hoehn-Saric, Anthony Stone, Earl R. Nash, and Jerome D. Frank 1966. "Target Complaints as Criteria for Improvement." *American Journal of Psychotherapy*, 20 (January):184–92.

Becker, Wesley, Charles H. Madsen, Robert Arnold, and Don R. Thomas 1967. "The Continuous Use of Teacher Attention and Praise in Reducing Classroom Behavior Problems." *Journal of Special Education*, 1 (Winter):287–307.

Benjamin, Alfred 1974. *The Helping Interview*, 2nd. ed. Boston: Houghton-Mifflin.

Benjamin, Lorna S. 1965. "A Special Latin Square for the Use of Each Subject as His Own Control." *Psychometrika* 30 (December):499–513.

Bernstein, Douglas A. 1969. "Modification of Smoking Behavior: An Evaluative Review." *Psychological Bulletin*, 71 (June):418–40.

Bergin, Allen E. 1971. "The Evaluation of Therapeutic Outcomes." In Bergin and Sol L. Garfield, eds. *Handbook of Psychotherapy and Behavior Change*. New York: Wiley.

322

Blalock, Hubert M. 1968. "Theory Building and Causal Inferences." In Hubert M. Blalock and Ann B. Blalock, eds. *Methodology in Social Research.* New York: McGraw-Hill.

Bloom, Martin 1975. *The Paradox of Helping: Introduction of the Philosophy of Scientific Practice.* New York: Wiley.

Bloom, Martin, and Stephen R. Block 1977. "Evaluating One's Own Effectiveness and Efficiency." *Social Work,* 22 (March):130–36.

Bordin, Edward S. 1966. "Curiosity, Compassion, and Doubt: The Dilemma of the Psychologist." *American Psychologist,* 21 (February):116–21.

Bordin, Edward S. 1974. *Research Strategies in Psychotherapy.* New York: Wiley.

Box, George E. P. and Gwilym M. Jenkins 1976. *Time-Series Analysis: Forecasting and Control.* San Francisco: Holden-Day.

Breedlove, James L. and Merton S. Krause 1966. "Evaluative Research Design: A Social Casework Illustration." In Louis A. Gottschalk and Arthur H. Auerbach, eds., *Methods of Research in Psychotherapy.* New York: Appleton-Century-Crofts.

Briar, Scott 1973. "Effective Social Work Intervention in Direct Practice: Implications for Education." In *Facing the Challenge.* Plenary Session Papers from the Nineteenth Annual Program Meeting, Council On Social Work Education.

Browning, Robert M. 1967. "A Same-Subject Design for Simultaneous Comparison of Three Reinforcement Contingencies." *Behavior Research and Therapy,* 5 (August):237–43.

Browning, Robert M. and Donald O. Stover 1971. *Behavior Modification in Child Treatment.* Chicago: Aldine-Atherton.

Buros, Oscar K., ed. 1965. *The Sixth Mental Measurements Yearbook.* Highland Park, New York: Gryphon Press.

Butterfield, William H. 1974. "Instrumentation in Behavior Therapy." In Edwin J. Thomas, ed., *Behavior Modification Procedure: A Sourcebook.* Chicago: Aldine-Atherton.

Campbell, Donald T. 1969a. "Reforms as Experiments." *American Psychologist,* 24 (April):409–28.

—— 1969b. "Prospective: Artifact and Control." In Robert Rosenthal, ed. *Artifact in Behavioral Research.* New York: Academic Press.

Campbell, Donald T., and Julian C. Stanley 1963. *Experimental and Quasi-Experimental Designs for Research.* Chicago: Rand McNally.

Carkuff, Robert 1969. *Helping and Human Relations*. New York: Holt, Rinehart, and Winston.

Carter, Robert D. 1975. "Internal Validity in Intensive Experimentation." Unpublished manuscript, University of Michigan, Ann Arbor.

—— 1976. "Designs and Data Patterns in Intensive Experimentation." Unpublished monograph, School of Social Work, University of Michigan, Ann Arbor.

Carter, Robert D., and Rona L. Levy 1972. "Interim Report on Interaction Research." In Richard B. Stuart and Tony Tripodi, *Contingency Contracting in Treatment of Delinquents*. 1972–73 Continuation Grant Proposal, Behavior Change Laboratories, Ann Arbor, Michigan.

Cautela, Joseph R., and Robert Kastenbaum 1967. "A Reinforcement Survey Schedule for Use in Therapy, Training, and Research." *Psychological Reports*, 20 (June):115–30.

Chun, Ki-taek, Sidney Cobb, and John French 1975. *Measures for Psychological Assessment*. Ann Arbor: Institute for Social Research, University of Michigan.

Ciminero, Anthony R., Karen S. Calhoun and Henry E. Adams 1977. *Handbook of Behavioral Assessment*. New York: Wiley.

Cobb, Joseph A., and Roberta S. Ray 1976. "The Classroom Behavior Observation Code." In Eric J. Mash and Leif G. Terdal, eds. *Behavior Therapy Assessment*. New York: Springer.

Cone, John D. 1977. "The Relevance of Reliability and Validity for Behavioral Assessment." *Behavior Therapy*, 8 (June):411–426.

Cone, John D., and Robert B. Hawkins. 1977. *Behavioral Assessment: New Directions in Clinical Psychology*. New York: Brunner/Mazel.

Cook, Stuart W., and Claire Selltiz. 1964. "A Multiple Indicator Approach to Attitude Measurement." *Psychological Bulletin*, 62 (July):36–55.

Craighead, W. Edward, Alan E. Kazdin, and Michael J. Mahoney 1976. *Behavior Modification: Principles, Issues, and Applications*. Boston: Houghton-Mifflin.

Downey, Kenneth J. 1975. *Elementary Social Statistics*. New York: Random House.

Edgar, Eugene, and Felix Billingsley 1974. "Believability When $N = 1$." *Psychological Record*, 24 (Spring):147–60.

Edwards, Allen E., and Lee Cronbach 1952. "Experimental Designs for

Research in Psychotherapy." *Journal of Clinical Psychology,* 8 (January):51–59.

Eysenck, Hans J. 1952. "The Effects of Psychotheraphy: An Evaluation." *Journal of Consulting Psychology,* 16 (October):319–24.

—— 1965. "The Effects of Psychotherapy." *International Journal of Psychiatry,* 1 (November):99–142.

—— 1975. "Theory Unproven." A Letter. *American Psychological Association Monitor,* 6 (June):3.

Finch, A., P. Deadorff, and L. Montgomery 1974. "Individually Tailored Behavior Rating Scales: A Possible Alternative." *Journal of Abnormal Child Psychology,* 3:209–16.

Fiske, Donald W., Howard F. Hunt, Lester Luborsky, Martin T. Orne, Morris B. Parloff, Morton F. Reiser, and A. Hussain Tuma 1970. "Planning of Research on Effectiveness of Psychotherapy." *American Psychologist,* 25 (August):727–37.

Gambrill, Eileen 1977. *Behavior Modification: Handbook of Assessment, Intervention and Evaluation.* San Francisco: Jossey Bass.

Gambrill, Eileen, Edwin J. Thomas, and Robert D. Carter 1971. "Procedures for Sociobehavioral Practice in Open Settings." *Social Work,* 16 (January):51–63.

Gelfand, Donna M., and Donald P. Hartmann 1968. "Behavior Therapy with Children: A Review and Evaluation of Research Methodology." *Psychological Bulletin,* 69 (March):204–15.

Gentile, J. Ronald, Aubrey H. Roden, and Roger D. Klein 1972. "An Analysis-of-Variance Model for the Intrasubject Replication Design," *Journal of Applied Behavior Analysis,* 5 (Summer):193–98.

Glass, Gene V., Vernon L. Wilson, and John M. Gottman 1973. *Time Series Analysis in the Behavioral Sciences.* Boulder: Laboratory of Educational Research, University of Colorado Press.

Glasser, Paul, Rosemary Sarri, and Robert D. Vinter, eds. 1974. *Individual Change Through Small Groups.* New York: Free Press.

Goldfried, Marvin R., and David M. Pomeranz 1968. "Role of Assessment in Behavior Modification," *Psychological Reports,* 23 (August):75–87.

Goldstein, Arnold P., Kenneth Heller, and Lee B. Sechrest 1966. *Psychotherapy and the Psychology of Behavior Change.* New York: Wiley.

Gordon, Thomas, Donald L. Grummon, Carl R. Rogers, and Julius Seeman

1954. "Developing a Program of Psychotherapy." In Carl Rogers and Rosalind F. Dymond, eds. *Psychotherapy and Personality Change*. Chicago: University of Chicago Press.

Gottman, John M. 1973. "N-of-One and N-of-Two Research in Psychotherapy." *Psychological Bulletin*, 80 (August):93–105.

Gottman, John M., and Sandra R Leiblum 1974. *How To Do Psychotherapy and How To Evaluate It*. New York: Holt, Rinehart, and Winston.

Gottman, John M., and Richard M. McFall 1972. "Self-Monitoring Effects in a Program for Potential High School Dropouts: A Time Series Analysis." *Journal of Consulting and Clinical Psychology*, 39 (October):273–81.

Gottman, John M., Richard M. McFall, and Jean T. Barnett 1969. "Design and Analyses of Research Using Time Series." *Psychological Bulletin*, 72 (October):299–306.

Hackney, Harold, and Sherilyn Nye 1973. *Counseling Strategies and Objectives*. Englewood Cliffs, N. J.: Prentice-Hall.

Haley, Jay 1969. *The Power Tactics of Jesus Christ*. New York: Viking.

Hall, R. Vance 1971. *Managing Behavior: Behavior Modification in School and Home*. Lawrence, Kansas: H & H Enterprises.

Harris, Frederick R., Montrose M. Wolf, and Donald M. Baer 1964. "Effects of Adult Social Reinforcement on Child Behavior." *Young Children*, 20 (October):8–17.

Hartmann, Donald P. 1974. "Forcing Square Pegs into Round Holes: Some Comments on an Analysis-of-Variance Model for Intrasubject Replication Designs." *Journal of Applied Behavior Analysis*, 7 (Winter):635–38.

Hartmann, Donald P., and R. Vance Hall 1976. "The Changing Criterion Design." *Journal of Applied Behavior Analysis*, 9 (Winter):527–32.

Hersen, Michael, and David H. Barlow 1976. *Single-Case Experimental Designs*. New York: Pergamon Press.

Hersen, Michel and Alan S. Bellack 1976. *Behavioral Assessment*. New York: Pergamon Press.

Holland, Cornelius J. 1970. "An Interview Guide for Behavioral Counseling with Parents." *Behavior Therapy*, 1 (January):70–79.

Hollis, Florence 1966. *Casework: A Psychosocial Approach*. New York: Random House.

—— 1968. *A Typology of Casework Treatment*. New York: Family Service Association of America.

—— 1972. *Casework: A Psychosocial Therapy.* 2nd. ed. New York: Random House.

Holtzman, Wayne H. 1963. "Statistical Models for the Study of Change in the Single Case." In Chester W. Harris, ed. *Problems in Measuring Change.* Madison: University of Wisconsin Press.

Howe, Michael 1974. "Casework Self-Evaluation: A Single-Subject Approach." *Social Service Review,* 48 (March):1–23.

Hudson, Walter W. 1977. "A Measurement Package for Clinical Social Workers." Mimeo, School of Social Work, University of Hawaii.

Jayaratne, Srinika 1977. "Single-Subject and Group Designs in Treatment Evaluation." *Social Work Research and Abstracts,* 13(4):35–42.

—— "Analytic Procedures for Single-Subject Designs." *Social Work Research and Abstracts,* 14(4):30–40.

Jayaratne, Srinika, Richard B. Stuart, and Tony Tripodi 1974. "Methodological Issues and Problems in Evaluating Treatment Outcomes in the Family and School Consultation Project." In Park O. Davidson, Frank W. Clark, and Leo A. Hamerlynck, eds. *Evaluation of Behavioral Programs in Community, Residential, and School Settings.* Champaign, Illinois: Research Press.

Johnson, Stephen M., and Geofrey White 1971. "Self-Observation As an Agent of Behavioral Change." *Behavior Therapy,* 2 (October):488–97.

Johnson, Stephen M. and Orin D. Bolstad 1975. "Reactivity to Home Observation: A Comparison of Audio-Recorded Behaviors with Observers Present or Absent." *Journal of Applied Behavior Analysis,* 8 (Summer):181–85.

Jones, Richard R., Mark R. Weinrott, and Russell S. Vought 1978. "Effects of Serial Dependency on the Agreement Between Visual and Statistical Inference." *Journal of Applied Behavior Analysis,* 11 (Summer):277–83.

Jones, Richard R., Russell S. Vaught, and Mark Weinrott 1977. "Time Series Analysis in Operant Research." *Journal of Applied Behavior Analysis,* 10 (Spring):151–56.

Kadushin, Alfred 1972. *The Social Work Interview.* New York: Columbia University Press.

Kanfer, Frederick H., and George Saslow 1969. "Behavioral Diagnosis." In Cyril M. Franks, ed. *Behavior Therapy: Appraisal and Status.* New York: McGraw-Hill.

Kazdin, Alan E. 1975. *Behavior Modification in Applied Settings*. Homewood, Ill.: Dorsey Press.

—— 1976. "Statistical Analyses for Single-Case Experimental Designs." In Michael Hersen and David H. Barlow. *Single Case Experimental Designs*. New York: Pergamon Press.

—— 1978. "Methodological and Interpretative Problems of Single Case Experimental Designs." *Journal of Consulting and Clinical Psychology*, 46(4):629–42.

Kazdin, Alan E. and G. Terence Wilson 1978. *Evaluation of Behavior Therapy: Issues, Evidence and Research Strategies*. Cambridge, Ma: Ballinger.

Keefe, Frances J., Steven A. Kopel and Steven B. Gordon 1978. *A Practical Guide to Behavioral Assessment*. New York: Springer.

Keller, Fred S., and William N. Schoenfeld 1950. *Principles of Psychology*. New York: Appleton-Century-Crofts.

Kent, Ronald N., J. Kanowitz, Daniel K. O'Leary, and Michael Cheiken 1977. "Observer Reliability as a Function of Circumstances of Assessment." *Journal of Applied Behavior Analysis*, 10 (Summer):317–24.

Keselman, H. J., and L. Leventhal 1974. "Concerning the Statistical Procedures Enumerated by Gentile et al.: Another Perspective." *Journal of Applied Behavior Analysis*, 7 (Winter):643–45.

Kiesler, Donald J. 1966. "Some Myths of Psychotherapy Research and the Search for a Paradigm." *Psychological Bulletin*, 65 (February): 110–36.

—— 1971. "Experimental Design in Psychotherapy Research." In Alan E. Bergin and Sol L. Garfield, eds. *Handbook of Psychotherapy and Behavior Change*. New York: Wiley.

Kiresuk, Thomas J. 1973. "Goal Attainment Scaling at a County Mental Health Service." *Evaluation*, 1 (Special Monograph):12–18.

Kiresuk, Thomas J., and Robert E. Sherman 1968. "Goal Attainment Scaling: A General Method for Evaluating Comprehensive Community Mental Health Programs. *Community Mental Health Journal*, 4:443–53.

Kratochwill, Thomas R., ed. 1978. *Single Subject Research*. New York: Academic Press.

Kratochwill, T. R., K. Alden, D. Demuth, D. Dawson, C. Panicucci, P. Arnston, N. McMurray, J. Hempstead, and J. Levin 1974. "A Further Consideration in the Application of an Analysis-of-Variance Model for the Intrasubject Replication Design." *Journal of Applied Behavior Analysis*, 7 (Winter):629–33.

Lake, Dale G., Matthew Miles, and Ralph Earle, eds. 1973. *Measuring Human Behavior: Tools for the Assessment of Social Functioning*. New York: Teachers College Press.

Lang, Peter J. 1969. "The Mechanics of Desensitization and the Laboratory Study of Human Fear." In Cyril M. Franks, ed. *Behavior Therapy: Appraisal and Status*. New York: McGraw-Hill.

Lazarus, Arnold A. 1971. *Behavior Therapy and Beyond*. New York: McGraw-Hill.

Lazarus, Arnold A., and Gerald C. Davison 1971. "Clinical Innovation in Research and Practice." In Allen E. Bergin and Sol L. Garfield, eds. *Handbook of Psychotherapy and Behavior Change*. New York: Wiley.

Leitenberg, Harold 1973. "The Use of Single Case Methodology in Psychotherapy Research." *Journal of Abnormal Psychology*, 82 (August): 87–101.

Levy, Rona L. 1977. "Relationship of an Overt Committment to Task Compliance in Behavior Therapy." *Journal of Behavior Therapy and Experimental Psychiatry*, 8 (March):25–30.

Levy, Rona L., Dennis Yamashita and Gillian Paw. In press. "Relationship of an Overt Commitment to the Frequency and Speed of Symptom Reporting."

Levy, Rona L., and Robert D. Carter 1976. "Compliance with Practitioner Instigations." *Social Work*, 21 (May):188–93.

Linsk, N., Michael W. Howe, and Elsie M. Pinkston 1975. "Behavioral Group Work in a Home for the Aged.' *Social Work*, 20 (November):454–63.

Loftus, Geoffrey, and Rona L. Levy 1977. *"Statistical Evaluation of Clinical Effectiveness." Social Work*, 22 (November):504–6.

London, Perry 1964. *The Modes and Morals of Psychotherapy*. New York: Holt, Rinehart, and Winston.

McNamara, J. Regis, and Toni S. MacDonough 1972. "Some Methodological Considerations in the Design and Implementation of Behavior Therapy Research." *Behavior Therapy*, 3 (July):361–78.

Mahoney, Michael J. 1978. "Experimental Methods and Outcome Evaluation." *Journal of Consulting and Clinical Psychology*, 46(4):660–72.

Mahoney, Michael J., Bert S. Moore, Terry C. Wade, and Marici G. M. Moura 1973. "The Effects of Continuous and Intermittent Self-Monitoring on Academic Behavior." *Journal of Consulting and Clinical Psychology*, 41 (August):65–69.

Maluccio, Anthony N., and Wilma T. Marlow 1974. "The Case for the Contract." *Social Work,* 19 (January):28–37.

Mash, Eric J., and Leif G. Terdal, eds. 1976. *Behavior Therapy Assessment.* New York: Springer.

Michael, Jack 1974. "Statistical Inference for Individual Organism Research: Mixed Blessing or Curse?" *Journal of Applied Behavior Analysis,* 7 (Winter):647–53.

Mischel, Walter 1968. *Personality and Assessment.* New York: Wiley.

Nelson, Rosemary O., David P. Lipinski, and Ronald A. Boykin 1978. "The Effects of Self-Recorders' Training and the Obtrusiveness of the Self-Recording Device on the Accuracy and Reactivity of Self-Monitoring." *Behavior Therapy,* 9 (March):200–208.

Nunnaly, Jum C. 1975. "The Study of Change in Evaluation Research: Principles Concerning Measurement, Experimental Design, and Analysis." In Elmer L. Struenning and Marcia Guttentag, eds. *Handbook of Evaluation Research.* California: Sage Publications.

O'Leary, Kent D., and Ronald Kent 1973. "Behavior Modification for Social Action: Research Tactics and Problems." In Leo A. Hamerlynck, Lee C. Handy, and Eric J. Mash, eds. *Behavior Change: Methodology, Concepts, and Practice.* Champaign, Illinois: Research Press.

Parsonson, Barry S. and Donald M. Baer 1978. "The Analysis and Presentation of Graphic Data." In Thomas R. Kratochwill, ed. *Single Subject Research.* New York: Academic Press.

Patterson, Gerald R. 1971. "Behavioral Intervention Procedures in the Classroom and in the Home." In Allen E. Bergin and Sol L. Garfield, eds. *Handbook of Psychotherapy and Behavior Change.* New York: Wiley.

Patterson, Gerald R., and John B. Reid 1970. "Reciprocity and Coercion: Two Facets of Social Systems." In Charles Neuringer and Jack Michael, eds. *Behavior Modification in Clinical Psychology.* New York: Appleton-Century-Crofts.

Paul, Gordon L. 1969. "Behavior Modification Research: Design and Tactics." In Cyril M. Franks, ed. *Behavior Therapy: Appraisal and Status.* New York: McGraw-Hill.

Perlman, Helen H. 1957. *Social Casework.* Chicago: University of Chicago Press.

Peterson, Donald R. 1968. *The Clinical Study of Social Behavior.* New York: Appleton-Century-Crofts.

Pincus, Allen, and Anne Minahan 1973. *Social Work Practice: Model and Method.* Itasca, Illinois: F. E. Peacock.

Powell, J., B. Martindale, S. Kulp, A. Martindale, and R. Bauman 1977. "Taking a Closer Look: Time Sampling and Measurement Error." *Journal of Applied Behavior Analysis,* 10 (Summer):325–32.

Reid, John 1970. "Reliability Assessment of Observation Data: A Possible Methodological Problem." *Child Development,* 41 (December):1143–50.

Reid, William B., and Laura Epstein, 1972. *Task-Centered Casework.* New York: Columbia University Press.

Risley, Todd 1970. "Behavior Modification: An Experimental Therapeutic Endeavor." In Leo A. Hamerlynck, Park O. Davidson, and Loren E. Acker, eds. *Behavior Modification and Ideal Health Services.* Calgary: University of Calgary Press.

Robinson, John P., and Phillip R. Shaver 1973. *Measures of Social Psychological Attitudes.* Ann Arbor, Michigan: Institute for Social Research.

Roen, Sheldon D. 1971. "Evaluative Research and Community Mental Health." In Allen E. Bergin and Sol L. Garfield, eds. *Handbook of Psychotherapy and Behavior Change.* New York: Wiley.

Rogers, Carl R. and Rosalynd F. Dymond, eds. 1954. *Psychotherapy and Personality Change.* Chicago: University of Chicago Press.

Rosenthal, Robert 1966. *Experimenter Effects in Behavioral Research.* New York: Appleton-Century-Crofts.

Runkel, Philip J., and Joseph E. McGrath 1972. *Research on Human Behavior: A Systematic Guide to Method.* New York: Holt, Rinehart, and Winston.

Selltiz, Claire, Marie Jahoda, Morton Deutsch, and Stuart W. Cook 1959. *Research Methods in Social Relations.* New York: Holt, Rinehart, and Winston.

Shine, Lester C. 1973. "A Multi-Way Analysis of Variance for Single-Subject Designs." *Educational and Psychological Measurement,* 33 (Autumn):633–36.

Shine, Lester C., and Samuel M. Bower 1971. "A One-Way Analysis of Variance for Single-Subject Designs." *Educational and Psychological Measurement, 31* (Spring):105–13.

Shyne, Anne W. 1967. "Use of Available Material." In Norman Polansky, ed. *Social Work Research.* Chicago: University of Chicago Press.

Sidman, Murray. 1960. *Tactics of Scientific Research.* New York: Basic Books.

Simon, J. L. 1969. *Basic Research Methods in Social Science*. New York: Random House.

Skindrud, Karl 1973. "Field Evaluation of Observer Bias under Overt and Covert Monitoring. In Leo A. Hamerlynck, Lee C. Handry, and Eric J. Mash, eds. *Behavior Change: Methodology, Concepts, and Practice*. Champaign, Illinois: Research Press.

Skinner, B. F. 1972. *Cumulative Record*. New York: Appleton-Century-Crofts.

Strupp, Hans H. 1971. *Psychotherapy and the Modification of Abnormal Behavior*. New York: McGraw-Hill.

Strupp, Hans H., and Allen E. Bergin 1972. "Some Empirical and Conceptual Bases for Coordinated Research in Psychotherapy." In Bergin and Strupp, eds. *Changing Frontiers in the Science of Psychotherapy*. Chicago: Aldine-Atherton.

Stuart, Richard B. 1970. "A Cueing Device for the Acceleration of the Rate of Positive Interaction." *Journal of Applied Behavior Analysis*, 3 (Winter):257–60.

—— 1972. "Behavioral Remedies for Marital Ills: A Guide to the Use of Operant-Interpersonal Techniques." Paper presented at the International Symposium of Behavior Modification. Minneapolis, October 5.

—— 1973 "Notes on the Ethics of Behavior Research and Intervention." In Leo A. Hamerlynck, Lee C. Handy, and Eric J. Mash, eds. *Behavior Change: Methodology, Concepts, and Practice*. Champaign, Illinois. Research Press.

—— 1974. "Behavior Modification for the Educational Technologist." In Roger Ulrich, Thomas Stachnik, and John Mabry, *Control of Human Behavior*, vol. 3. New York: Scott Foresman.

Stuart, Richard B., and Leroy A. Lott Jr. 1972. "Behavioral Contracting with Delinquents." *Journal of Behavior Therapy and Experimental Psychiatry*, 3 (August):161–69.

Stuart, Richard B., and Tony Tripodi 1972. *Contingency Contracting in Treatment of Delinquents*. 1972–73 Continuation Grant Proposal, Behavior Change Laboratories, Ann Arbor, Michigan.

—— 1973. "Experimental Evaluation of Three Time-Constrained Behavioral Treatments for Predelinquents and Delinquents." In Richard D. Rubin, John P. Brady, and John D. Henderson, eds. *Advances in Behavior Therapy*, vol. 4. New York: Academic Press.

Stuart, Richard B., Tony Tripodi, and Srinika Jayaratne 1972. "The Family and School Treatment Model of Services for Predelinquents." Paper presented at the American Psychological Association Meeting, Honolulu.

Sulzer-Azaroff, Beth, and G. Roy Mayer 1977. *Applying Behavior-Analysis Procedures with Children and Youth.* New York: Holt, Rinehart, and Winston.

Sundel, Martin, and Sandra S. Sundel 1975. *Behavior Modification in the Human Services.* New York: Wiley.

Taylor, Janet A. 1953. "A Personality Scale of Manifest Anxiety." *Journal of Abnormal and Social Psychology,* 48 (April):285–90.

Tharp, Roland G., and Ralph J. Wetzel 1969. *Behavior Modification in the Natural Environment.* New York: Academic Press.

Thomas, Edwin J. 1973. "Bias and Therapist Influence in Behavioral Assessment." *Journal of Behavior Therapy and Experimental Psychiatry,* 4 (June):107–11.

—— 1975. "Uses of Research Methods in Interpersonal Practice." In Norman A. Polansky, ed. *Social Work Research.* Chicago: University of Chicago Press.

Thomas, Edwin J., Robert D. Carter, Eileen K. Gambrill, and William H. Butterfield 1970. "Signal System for the Assessment of Behavior (SAM)." *Behavior Therapy,* 1 (April):252–59.

Thoresen, Carl E. 1972, "The Intensive Design: An Intimate Approach to Counseling Research." Paper presented at the meeting of the American Educational Research Association, Chicago, April.

Thoresen, Carl E. and Janet D. Alashoff 1974. "An Analysis-of-Variance Model of the Intrasubject Replication Design: Some Additional Comments." *Journal of Applied Behavior Analysis,* 4 (Winter): 639–42.

Tripodi, Tony 1974. *Uses and Abuses of Social Research in Social Work.* New York: Columbia University Press.

Thoresen, Carl E. and Michael J. Mahoney 1974. *Behavioral Self-Control.* New York: Holt, Rinehart, and Winston.

Tripodi, Tony, Phillip Fellin, and Henry J. Meyer 1969. *The Assessment of Social Research.* Itasca, Illinois: F. E. Peacock.

Truax, Charles B. 1966. "Reinforcement and Non-reinforcement in Rogerian Psychotherapy." *Journal of Abnormal and Social Psychology,* 71 (February):1–9.

Underwood, Benton J. 1957. *Psychological Research*. New York: Appleton-Century-Crofts.

Vinter, Robert D., Rosemary C. Sarri, David J. Vorwaller, and Walter Schaefer 1966. *Pupil Behavior Inventory*. Ann Arbor, Michigan: Campus Publishers.

Wahler, Robert G., and William H. Cormier, 1970. "The Ecological Interview: A First Step in Outpatient Child Behavior Therapy." *Journal of Behavior Therapy and Experimental Psychiatry*, 1 (December): 279–89.

Watson, Robert I. 1952. "Research Design and Methodology in Evaluating the Results of Psychotherapy." *Journal of Clinical Psychology*, 8 (January): 29–33.

Webb, Eugene J., Donald T. Campbell, Richard D. Schwartz, and Lee B. Sechrest 1972. *Unobtrusive Measures: Nonreactive Research in the Social Sciences*. Chicago: Rand McNally.

Webster's Seventh New Collegiate Dictionary 1970. Springfield, Massachusetts: G & C Merriam Company.

Weiss, Leslie, and R. Vance Hall 1971. "Modification of Cigarette Smoking Through Avoidance of Punishment." In Hall, ed. Managing Behavior: *Behavior Modification Applications in School and Home*. Lawrence, Kansas: H & H Enterprises.

Werner, Harold D. 1974. "Cognitive Theory." In Francis J. Turner, ed. *Social Work Treatment*. New York: Free Press.

White, Geoffry D. 1978. "The Effects of Observer Presence on the Activity Levels of Families." *Journal of Applied Behavior Analysis*, 10 (Winter):734.

Whittaker, James K. 1974. *Social Treatment*. Chicago: Aldine-Atherton.

Wolf, Montrose M., and Todd R. Risley 1971. "Reinforcement: Applied Research." In Robin Glaser, ed. *The Nature of Reinforcement*. New York: Academic Press.

Wolpe, Joseph, and Peter S. Lang 1964. "A Fear Survey Schedule for Use in Behavior Therapy." *Behavior Research and Therapy*, 2 (May):27–30.

Index of Names

335

Index of Subjects